SHEENA DUNCAN

Sheena Duncan

Annemarie Hendrikz

2015

This edition published 2015 by

Duncan Sisters
Chemin de la Fauvette 71A
CH-1012 Lausanne
SWITZERLAND

First published in South Africa in 2015
by Tiber Tree Press
Cape Town, SOUTH AFRICA
www.tibertree.co.za

Copyright © 2015 Annemarie Hendrikz

ISBN (paperback): 978-2-8399-1653-0
ISBN (epub): 978-2-8399-1654-7

This work is copyright under the Berne Convention. In terms of the Copyright Act 98 of 1978 no part of this work may be reproduced or transmitted in any form or by any means, electronic or mechanical, including photocopying, recording or by any information storage and retrieval system, without permission in writing from the Publisher. The moral right of the author has been asserted.

Cover photograph by gille de vlieg

Photographs are from family albums except:
— Pages 7, 27, 30, 35, 86, 95, 96, 113, 118, 119, 124, 125, 132, 159, 162 by gille de vlieg ©
— Page 55 (bottom right) by Caryl Blanckenberg
— Pages 73 and 81 (right) by Harriet Gavshon (stills from her film *Burden of Privilege*)
— Page 167 by Stewart Ting Chong

Cartoon on back cover by Zapiro, © 1987 Zapiro — reprinted with permission — for more Zapiro cartoons visit www.zapiro.com

Typesetting by GJ du Toit

Cover design by Alessandra Leonardi-Lollis & Ian Preston of ALLART STUDIOS (www.allartstudios.com)

Author's Notes and Acknowledgments

According to Virginia Woolf, *It is no use trying to sum people up. One must follow hints, not exactly what is said, nor yet entirely what is done.*[1] As the author of this particular story of a most remarkable South African, I was much heartened by these words, and by Sheena's own when she commented in a letter to a friend, 'It is most satisfactory to read biographers who do not pretend to understand the whole.'[2] It is my hope that the hints I followed and the fragments I chose will honour Sheena and, with her, some of the other brave women and men of her time who touched her life.

Many of these hints and fragments came from the women and men I interviewed and who wrote to me. In the Data Sources section at the end of the book you will find a brief description of the relationship Sheena had with each person with whom I engaged. The names are listed alphabetically, by first name. I gave some thought to how to use people's names. In the text, instead of using a more formal convention of surname only after first full introductions, I considered first names preferable. Although using first names only is often a way of minimising the importance of people — especially women and working class people — that is not my intention. First names represent a less formal narrative, which this is and, in the case of women, a first name is usually the only name we have that does not link us directly to a man. When the people I interviewed gave me more than one such name, I have tried consistently to use the one they indicated as first choice. If I have erred, it is with regret and not for lack of regard for their wishes. I have omitted all titles. My intentions are not to offend any of the bishops — Arch or otherwise — or the chancellors, vice chancellors, presidents, councillors, dames, doctors, imams, mayors, ministers, misters, mistresses, professors, rabbanim or reverends — many of them with more than one title and strings of credentials. Sheena did not appreciate titles. The women and the men on these pages stand independently, responsibly, generously and free of any trappings except fragments of their own views (*in italics when quoted*) and of their relationships with Sheena.[3]

There are many other people who I would have liked to interview, who knew Sheena well and could have offered meaningful insights to this story. I regret that it was not possible to connect with all of you. My book misses your voices.

I have used the racial categories attributed to people by the apartheid regime where necessary for clarity, but have not accorded them the status of proper nouns or special adjectives.

---

[1] www.online-literature.com/virginia_woolf/jacob-room/3/.

[2] Letter to Anne Hughes, 27 October 1990.

[3] In the index surnames are listed first, for conventionally convenient reference purposes.

The process of writing this book has been nothing short of wonderful and the acknowledgments that follow would be inadequate, no matter how I tried to express them. So, I shall restrain myself to the most basic expression of gratitude — thank you.

Lindsay and Carey, thank you for your initiative and for entrusting me with the privilege of engaging with your beloved mother's life so intimately. Your boundless generosity in time and other resources, your suggestions, your sustained enthusiasm and your belief in the possibilities were an inspiration and, Lindsay, your final polish was awesome.

Thank you, all of you listed at the back of this book, who contributed your memories so generously, granting me the unique opportunity of an interview or taking the time to write to me and allowing me to use your words and treasured resources for these pages, with a special thanks to you, Arch, for so graciously introducing Sheena and the book to readers. Thank you librarians and archivists who welcomed me with patience and friendliness into your magical spaces — in particular Lesley Hart, Liz de Wet, Marj Brown, Michelle Pickover and Zofia Sulej.

Thank you gille de vlieg and Harriet Gavshon for your incredibly generous use of inspiring visual material and Jonathan Shapiro for allowing us to use one of your brilliant Zapiro cartoons.

Thank you Di Oliver and Shauna Westcott for reading the first draft and offering critical insight with affection; thank you 'Just Write' wonderful women and writer 'retreat-ants' at the Grail Centre, who thrilled me with your own creativity, encouraged me and held me safe when the going got tough — in particular my 'table buddies' Carmel Rickard, Chantal Stewart and, most of all and beyond the table, Mary Burton.

Thank you Kylie Thomas for your incisive inroads into my text and for approaching it with such sensitivity and respect. Thank you Nella Freund for your eagle eye and technical support. Thank you Alessandra Leonardi-Lollis and Ian Preston for your creative and patiently crafted cover. Thank you Simon Sephton and your Tiber Tree Press team — Sheena, Lindsay, Carey and I could not have wished for a more appreciative and professional publisher and we are so lucky to have found you.

Thank you Anne Schuster for sharing your genius, your love and the inspiration of your own personal courage and for being beside me every step of the way.

Thank you Sheena Duncan.

ANNEMARIE HENDRIKZ
Kleinmond 2015

Daughters' Acknowledgments

Lindsay and Carey with Sheena

When our mother died after a long illness, we were reminded how much she meant to so many people, not least to the two of us. Suddenly, released from her frailty, she once again became the woman she used to be. Many people encouraged us to make sure that her legacy lives on.

This book is the result of accepting that challenge, and it would not have been possible without the contributions of so many. First and foremost, we thank Annemarie Hendrikz for her dedication and professionalism, whether travelling around the country to interview people, tackling dusty stacks of papers in archives or turning her timetable upside down to write through the night. She really grasped Sheena's essence, sensitively weaving together the many and varied strands of our mother's life. She has vividly captured the humour, integrity, compassion, sadness and depth of Sheena's personality, as well as skilfully setting her story clearly in the context of apartheid South Africa so that even readers who did not know Sheena will be enriched.

We echo Annemarie's thanks to everyone who contributed to the book in any way — generously sharing their insights and memories of Sheena or being more 'hands-on' with reading, editing, typesetting and publishing. We are particularly grateful to Mary Burton for all her support in so many ways. Thanks, too, to gille de vlieg for kindly allowing us to use so many of her photographs, to Harriet Gavshon for use of visual material from her film and to Zapiro for his cartoon.

Without generous donations, we would not have been able to see this work on the bookshelves. It is with deep gratitude that we thank, in alphabetical order, Colette Ball, Iain and Caroline Conn, Rob and Jacquie Conn, Alice and Tim Goodman, Anne Hughes, Neil and Helen McTeague, Karina McTeague and Ewan Malcolm, Oak Foundation, the Oppenheimer Memorial Trust, Liz and George Reid, Rob and Margie Sinclair, and Simon and Barbara Wernli. We are also grateful to the Black Sash for acting as fiscal sponsor to the project, and in particular to our contact, Sonya Ehrenreich.

We hope you enjoy the book.

LINDSAY MCTEAGUE, *Lausanne*
CAREY DUNCAN, *Rabat*

Contents

Introduction

DESMOND TUTU

Welcome to the story of Sheena Duncan — a story that reaches across the period of some of the worst brutality, the most gracious transitions, the greatest achievements and the saddest failures that South Africa has ever known. I am delighted to offer these first words of introduction, in memory of a great woman of courage and I hope you find as much inspiration in reading Sheena's story as I did in knowing her.

I don't really now remember when I first met Sheena but I think it would have been connected with her mom Jean Sinclair, who I knew. Sheena was, like, forever.

Sheena was a member of our church and a prominent person even then. Whenever we bumped into each other I hoped that she was approving of me. She was astute. Not abrasive or anything, but I think she was able to, as it were, see into the heart of things. Instinctively she would be on the side of right. It was just unthinkable for her to be anywhere else. It was unthinkable for her to live in a society where many millions of people could be treated as Leah and I were, even when I was Bishop of Johannesburg. I used to be regularly stopped at a police checkpoint between Westcliff and Soweto. I'd have to get out, maybe with Leah. I'd say to them, 'You can have a police search if you want to and seek to humiliate me at the side of the road here, but if you want to search my wife, you will do it indoors.' Others were not in a position to be so bold.

You will read here some of the story of the Black Sash, which is the human rights organisation through which Sheena exercised much of her extraordinary power as an activist and a leader. These women, initially all white, would relate to us as who we were, as fellow human beings. They were a visual aid to non-racialism.

Here were people who needn't have, but who were doing something that for them was costly. The bulk of white people did actually think that those few who aligned themselves with the struggle against apartheid were traitors, subversives, *kaffir boeties* and scum. Look at what his church did to Beyers Naudé. I don't think we have been good enough to acknowledge the contributions of so many, many others, and books such as this will help future generations to do so.

These whites too could have turned a blind eye. They were in clover.

There was no need for a Sheena to be sitting day after day in an advice office; no need to be confronting authorities about the effects of influx control and pass laws on black family life. Yet, mercifully for us, that's where you will find her in these pages.

Sheena smoked endlessly and I teased her about being a chimney. She had a great sense of humour with her brilliantly sharp mind. She was not afraid to challenge — or laugh. I can still hear her chuckle, or her half hoarse voice, 'Yes, but Desmond ...' It was wonderful having her in our church councils, helped to keep our socks up. We liked each other. I was glad we were on the same side. She was too formidable to have had as an adversary.

I remember as clearly as if it were yesterday the story of Mogopa, which you will find in this book. Mogopa was going to be demolished. All the organisations had done all they could to save Mogopa. The people of Mogopa had done all they could. We had all drawn a blank. We knew — the apartheid government had announced — that Mogopa was going to be demolished on a particular day. On the eve of the announced date we held a vigil, the group consisting of people representing the South African Council of Churches, the Lutherans, the Black Sash and the trade unions.

This was one of those countless days when we were struggling against apartheid, when all you could do was to witness, be present and stand up to be counted there, with the people who would be losing their homesteads, their shops, their churches. I don't remember what Sheena would have said — but I do remember that she was there, a wonderful presence.

Sheena was a practising Christian with a leadership role in a patriarchal church that refused to ordain women to the priesthood until 1992, accepted sexist language at all levels and even sang 'we are all brothers' without — until fairly recently — thinking that was particularly odd. She was without an academic degree but the product of a moderately wealthy family and one of Johannesburg's leading private schools for girls. She was married to a successful architect and enjoyed the security of being financially comfortably supported. Sheena used these privileges and the rights accorded to her racial classification to challenge discrimination against women, against black people, against poor people, against disenfranchised people, against workers, against those who could not work, against all apartheid legislation and injustice.

I think Sheena Duncan made God proud. God was glad that God had created someone like her — God rubbed God's hands, said 'Now this is quite something.'

Sheena had a formidableness about her that made people think twice about having her as an adversary. Her presence, yes, but I think what she stood for could be a threat to people who were more at ease with the status quo. You were aware that you were in the presence of someone who genuinely, with every fibre of her being, thought the apartheid dispensation was abominable.

It was so reassuring in many ways to have had people like Sheena in one's life. She worked tirelessly, thought deeply and then spoke out clearly, intelligently and honestly about all issues of injustice. She was a committed pacifist and this commitment gave extraordinary energy to much of her leadership and work in non-violent protest, campaigns against conscription, militarisation, guns, the death penalty and the structural violence of apartheid capitalism.

In my view, her finest quality as a human being was her regard for other people. You might find other qualities that appeal to you even more, but you will not be unmoved by her profound reverence for this other one, created in the image of God. I think that trumped everything and was what gave her oomph in her work. It wasn't just ordinary work. It was that she was living out what she believed fervently, at every level possible for her. So it was a very deeply religious conviction, but carried lightly. Sheena was not a bible-thumping zealot. Yet she was a zealot in a way. She really couldn't stand another person being denigrated and made to look nullified.

You might be as surprised as I was to learn that Sheena didn't formally study law. Her grasp of the law, and her ability to subvert it in an unwavering quest for justice, was extraordinary. This story goes in search of the core of Sheena's sense of justice. A tough task, but you might come to agree that I am moving in the right direction when I say it is connected to her faith. But maybe she took it in with her mother's milk? Decide for yourself.

God bless you.

ARCH

CHAPTER 1

A Passion for Justice

Sheena lived a life for justice — she went out of her way to make sure that there was justice for the people on the receiving side of a system that was terribly evil. Powerful people want to define justice. Instead, they negate it and rule the world by power that has nothing to do with justice. Sheena would see through all that stuff.

Her whole mind was about rights and justice, and she was firm. Whatever you put on the table for debate or for her consideration, her response would be, 'Is there justice? Are we making justice? Are we falling short of what we are supposed to be achieving?'

FRANK CHIKANE — Interview

Sheena Duncan grew up as a privileged and protected young white person during a time of intense and violent political repression in South Africa, she came to adulthood when apartheid was at its height and she spent her life working to bring about an end to injustice.

Although she herself would not be comfortable to be singled out from among the thousands of South African women who made phenomenal sacrifices in the struggle to liberate their country from the stranglehold of apartheid, Sheena's is indeed a remarkable record of voluntary — all of it unpaid — service to a cause that was hers only in conscience and through the interpersonal allegiances which we in South Africa know as *ubuntu.*[1]

The elder daughter of Jean Sinclair, one of the founders of the influential anti-apartheid women's movement, the Black Sash,[2] Sheena is perhaps best known for her work with the Black Sash. But she also occupied pivotal positions in many other organisations and campaigns working to bring about justice in South Africa, including the sometimes radical and controversial South African Council of Churches (SACC).[3] At the height of apartheid repression, Sheena's life and work offered an inspiring example to those who worked alongside her.

---

[1] In his book *No Future without Forgiveness* (1999), Desmond Tutu gives a working definition as follows: 'A person with Ubuntu is open and available to others, affirming of others, does not feel threatened that others are able and good, based from a proper self-assurance that comes from knowing that he or she belongs in a greater whole and is diminished when others are humiliated or diminished, when others are tortured or oppressed.'

[2] Initially founded as the Women's Defence of the Constitution League by Jean Sinclair, Ruth Foley, Elizabeth McLaren, Tertia Pybus, Jean Bosazza and Helen Newton-Thompson in May 1955. It soon became known as the Black Sash because of the black sashes the women wore as symbols of mourning for the assault on the constitution.

[3] The South African Council of Churches came into being when the Christian Council of South Africa changed its name as well as its structure at its seventeenth biennial meeting on 28 May 1968.

In the Black Sash, as well as being elected by the national membership as their new president when her mother retired, Sheena served in the Johannesburg Black Sash advice office, first as a caseworker and then, although still working on a daily basis with advice seekers, also as the advice office director. She soon added to this extraordinary portfolio[4] of volunteer work the role of national coordinator of all nine regional Black Sash advice offices and their outreach fieldworkers, and rounded off her contribution to the organisation as patron to the Black Sash Trust — and by no means a sleeping patron!

For more than forty years, from 1963 until she could no longer work because of failing health, Sheena based most of her political understanding, leadership strategies and human rights activism on what she learned through her regular face-to-face interaction with the women and men who presented the truth of apartheid to her day after day, month after month, year after year. Her brilliant grasp of the issues affecting her fellow — but disenfranchised — citizens on a daily basis, together with an extraordinary scope of compassion, were perhaps what gave Sheena an edge over many other high-profile leaders.

As Desmond Tutu says in his introduction, this story goes in search of the core of Sheena's sense of justice, and he suggests two possibilities — her maternal heritage or her faith. What he refers to as 'mother's milk' may be more obvious in Sheena's work in the organisation founded by her mother, but her contribution to the SACC is equally impressive and offers an opportunity to understand the humility and spiritual resonance she achieved. At the SACC Sheena was exposed not only to black theology but also to some of the finest black intellectuals and spiritual leaders of the time, all of whom profoundly affected her own prayer and unwavering faith — her ability in the worst of times just to 'do the next right thing'.

Sheena was no stranger to the SACC by the time she was elected to a more formal leadership position. In the 1970s, Sheena had joined the Anglican Church's Challenge Group[5] aimed at ending racism within the church. She was a member of the Church's Provincial Synod and had represented the Anglican Church on the SACC, experiencing general secretaries John Rees, Desmond Tutu and Beyers Naudé before Frank Chikane took over from Beyers in 1987, the same year in which Thudiso Virginia Gcabashe

[4] The full scope of Sheena's volunteer work for the Black Sash was not limited to work in its advice offices, which also encompassed facilitation of many modules of paralegal training. Her service to the membership included serving as editor of *Sash* magazine for eight years (1966 to 1974); chairperson of the Southern Transvaal Black Sash membership group; almost seven years as national president (1975 to 1978 and again from 1982 to 1986); national vice-president for three years between her two terms as president; chairperson of the Black Sash Trust for seven years (1994 to 1999 and again from 2001 to 2002); and, finally, patron of the Black Sash Trust.

[5] Part of what became The Programme to Combat Racism, which *will go down in history as one of the most significant expressions of world Church faith in this century. It ranks alongside the movement for the emancipation of slaves and the missionary movement itself.* Bernard Spong: *Come Celebrate 25 Years of the* SACC: Chapter 5: www.sacc.org.za

and Sheena were elected vice presidents — Thudiso Virginia as senior vice president for their first term and Sheena as senior vice president for their second term. Both women were subsequently elected as honorary life vice presidents, following in the pioneering footsteps of Sally Motlana, who had served the SACC as its first female vice president from 1972 until 1986, after which she, too, had been elected as honorary life vice president. The significance of the contributions of all three of these remarkable women to the liberation of South Africa was recognised with the Order of the Baobab, awarded by South Africa's president.[6]

Sheena's unwavering ethical stance and her command of language and the convoluted workings of the law made her a formidable force in the anti-apartheid struggle for justice. Sheena was not a lawyer but, in the words of Geoff Budlender, one of the young progressive lawyers at that time, *Sheena understood how to read law and how law works — and those are not necessarily the same thing. She was very skilled, absolutely wonderful and incredibly knowledgeable; you could sit down and have a discussion with her about complex legal questions and she could contribute to the debate. Sheena is still a powerful force in the lives of many people even though she is dead. That is the test ... many people would be different, if it hadn't been for her.*

Di Bishop (now Oliver) experienced Sheena as *awe-inspiring, first for me as a young social worker volunteering my time at the advice office and then through all the years we were both members of the Black Sash and the Anglican community. Sheena was so understated and yet so authoritative and bright. She had a wonderful analytical mind and I suppose what I loved about her was that she was a giant in the organisation as a whole, but the advice office was her life. She kicked her shoes off under the desk, she worked in the advice office day after day like Noel [Robb] did, with huge commitment, totally selflessly and totally devoted to monitoring and research. Sheena was not an armchair intellectual, she was hands on. She talked to people she could access by way of resources, to find the possible loopholes in every unjust situation and law.*

Di Bishop, Sheena and Beyers Naudé

[6] Sheena in 2006, Sally in 2007 and Thudiso Virginia in 2009. In 2005 Sheena received the Order of the Baobab on behalf of her mother, when it was posthumously bestowed on Jean Sinclair.

Sheena may have understood and articulated the struggle for justice to be concerned primarily with anti-racism but, as a prominent white female activist in a political and religious context dominated by men, she could not avoid engaging with the complexities of class and gender in her society. During the forty years of the Black Sash's profile as a membership organisation, its leaders were all white women and mostly well resourced; its programme governance was by white women; and the majority of its senior paid staff members were professionally qualified white women. But some of the other organisations to which Sheena devoted her time were generally more diverse, and this was particularly true of the SACC, with its inter-racial, richly textured cultures of Christianity and mixed gender, with mostly black staff members. At leadership levels in these organisations, however, it mattered a lot whether one was a woman or not.

There were several periods during which the membership identity of the Black Sash was questioned, not only as an almost exclusively white organisation (which it continued to be even after the membership had been opened to women of all races) but also, for example, as 'an organisation of women' or 'a women's organisation' — and what was the difference anyway? Sheena endured this questioning with her characteristic acceptance and good humour, but the issues did not seem to be of great interest to her.

Sheena insisted that she was not a feminist, even though women were certainly part of her activist foothold and in many contexts she was also a firm advocate for the rights of women. According to Adèle Kirsten, *Sheena had the capacity, the intellect and the belief, 'let's just go out and do it!' I think she had no sensibility around feminism as a political perspective on the world. Because of her privilege and her confidence, the notion that she was taken less seriously because she was a woman was not a notion Sheena experienced — I don't think Sheena ever felt discriminated against. But at the same time, I think she had a real interest in seeing young women develop and in supporting us and 'growing' us. So in a sense, there was almost an organic practice of feminism — not because she thought we needed more help than men, but because she thought we had something to contribute.*

Aninka Claassens agrees that the *Black Sash wasn't really feminist political. Maybe the issues were overwhelmingly mainstream political because of apartheid but within that, black women lived with double discrimination. I look back now and think my god, how come I did not see the particularly gendered nature of the whole thing.*

For example, Lydia Kompe-Ngwenya (MamLydia) joined us at TRAC[7] *and immediately, just from her own life experience, started organising black women into what became the Rural Women's Movement, which did incredible work and went on to*

[7] Transvaal Rural Action Committee (TRAC), a Black Sash initiative, was established in 1983 to provide advice and support for those facing forced removal in what was then the Transvaal.

become an important force in the constitutional negotiations for the new South Africa. We all really worked mostly with women, because they were the ones that were at home, but forced removals didn't initially present as a gender issue. MamLydia brought out the fact, opened it up and helped us all to see that it was more than a land issue.

Maybe as a black woman MamLydia just had that closer understanding of how these issues were gendered and maybe it needed someone with that personal deep feeling to do it.

Sheena did of course accept that there was much to learn from other women, and how victories in claiming equality were thrilling and inspiring. Aninka tells a story from one of the communities in which she and MamLydia served as fieldworkers: *When Saul Mkhize was shot for refusing to be 'removed' from his land, his wife Beauty became the community leader at Driefontein. Beauty and MamLydia started working with all these other women and they did this incredible case, the KwaNdebele women's vote case. It was all about women's equality and insofar as we were linked closely to the Black Sash — mainly through Sheena, Ethel Walt, gille de vlieg and Josie Adler — there was an immediate welcoming and support for it and a whole lot of funding got diverted to set up the Rural Women's Movement.*

In May 1988 Sheena shared the story in a letter to her friend Anne Hughes:

> The incredibly good news has been the victory of the KwaNdebele women in their application to the Supreme Court to have the KwaNdebele election of 1984 declared invalid because the vote was denied to women. The respondents were the State President, the KwaNdebele legislative assembly, and the 16 members of the government elected in that election. The women won. This means that the elections were invalid, the KwaNdebele government does not exist and that everything they have done since 1984 has no legal force. Imagine. The grounds of the application were that no authority to whom power has been delegated by the State President may use those powers to pass discriminatory legislation which has not been authorized by the South African parliament. Well the SA parliament has authorized almost every kind of discrimination but they forgot about women. Roll on the revolution. It is all in our female hands!

Around about the same time, when George Bizos, for the defence, questioned Sheena about the Black Sash in the Delmas Treason Trial in 1988, he said: *His Lordship has naturally heard something about feminist organisations. Is this a feminist organisation?* Sheena answered without hesitation, 'No, it is not a feminist organisation. It is concerned with women as the victims of apartheid rather than women as the victims of men.'

To this day a hostile patriarchy prevails in our 'racially liberated' and most eloquently constitutionalised South Africa. It is provocative to speculate what might be different had Sheena's answer to Bizos been, 'Yes, the Black Sash is a feminist organisation. It is concerned with the oppression of all women by men, but in present (apartheid) circumstances, it is concerned particularly with the oppression of black women by white men — and white women.' Or what might have been different if the Black Sash leadership had shared Albie Sach's[8] *view that the only truly non-racial system in South Africa is patriarchy.*[9]

It is difficult to look back on what has been, and to question what could have been, says Leah Tutu. *A wonderful thing could have been strong relationships between black and white women in South Africa. Coming from our varying backgrounds, we could have learned so much from and about one another. We were thrown together, for instance — as nowhere else in the world — because so many white women employed black nannies and domestic workers. A lot of South African white women had the opportunity to discuss things, woman to woman, with a nanny or a domestic worker, but did not. Often these two women were in the same age group and might have had much in common intellectually, spiritually and in many other ways, but they were women cast in roles because they were women, and because one was black and the other was white.*

In situations outside the home the differences were also felt. For example, women couldn't travel home together and chat because the enforced separation meant they lived far apart geographically and did not share the same transport. Also, going back home from the office, many white women were going back to a prepared meal. I know they still cooked for their families, but often most of the work was done already. On the other hand, for most black women it was going back to a set-up that was straight away more work. We could have made friends but, usually, we did not.

Perhaps it is true that the legacy of colonialism, and particularly apartheid, is such that we were all part of its power — whether as its designers and perpetrators, its beneficiaries or collaborators, or its victims and survivors — and will remain in its shadow for longer than we can predict.

While it might be tempting in retrospect — given the situation of women and the environment as just two examples twenty years after democracy — to see it as a leadership shortcoming not to have taken the Black Sash forward on a feminist path, the organisation's decision, or lack of decision, did free more energy to be poured into the single and popular struggle against oppression based on race. It also avoided the need for members to agree on a definition of feminism, or eco-feminism, or socialist feminism, or Western feminism, or African feminism. It meant that the politics and legislation of apartheid did not have to be scrutinised in feminist terms. Incoming members did not have to present feminist credentials or

[8] Anti-apartheid activist and, later, Constitutional Court judge.
[9] Christie, Sarah: 'Women's new voices', *Sash*, vol.33, no.2, September 1990.

make feminist commitments — they simply had to be women — and there was no argument about whether or not to allow male feminists to become full members.

An inclusive feminist perspective was not the only challenge in this vibrant organisation. *The Black Sash fascinated me,* remembers Denise Ackermann. *These Black Sash members — of whom I was one — reflected for me basic values that are deeply part of the Christian faith that I shared with Sheena and that I also found in some of the Jewish Black Sash members. They embodied an inner driving sense of justice, a sense of the dignity and the worth of human beings and an understanding that, when justice was not being done and human beings' dignity and worth were being violated, then there is no prevarication.*

This wasn't, however, always a comfortable understanding. Sheena, for example, agonised about violence and non-violence. Hers was the non-violent way: you do not harm, hurt or kill others. But the moment the laws are totally unjust, you have to decide if — and how — you are going to disobey those laws. Civil disobedience and non-violence were at the centre of a tricky debate in the Sash and I have a clear sense of Sheena's stand on that — the way of non-violence was non-negotiable.

What was special about the Black Sash, adds Albie Sachs, *was that they had nothing personal to gain from standing firmly against apartheid. Except, that is, to restore dignity to themselves by fighting alongside those struggling against oppression. They used the privileges that came their way with their skin colour and economic well-being to offer what they had to offer to the oppressed: sisterhood, comradeship, and practical and moral support.*

Marian Shinn was similarly moved by this spirit and remembers how, *as a journalist on the* Rand Daily Mail,[10] *I once spent a day with Sheena in the Black Sash advice office. It was heart-rending and I wondered how these women could do this day after day, year after year. I remember Sheena dealing with one gentleman who wanted to live with his wife in Johannesburg, where he had a temporary job. Sheena spent a long time with him, exploring every option, legal tome and case history in an attempt to find some spark of hope to blow on. There was none. Sheena was thorough, kind*

gille de vlieg ©

Sheena speaking at the Black Sash annual conference

[10] A leading daily newspaper in Johannesburg with an openly anti-apartheid stance, subsequently and controversially closed down by its Board of Directors in 1985.

and, in the end, sympathetic in giving him the bad news. She was fully aware that she was his last hope of living a normal life and that the system she had to deal with was cruel and unfair. She handled his despair with kindness, but gave no room for false hope.

Each day these women got up and went to work in the cruellest environment, knowing that their chance of delivering a happy verdict was negligible. It took a special breed of person to do this job and Sheena held them together and instilled in them the need to carry on. These women — and others like Wendy Orr[11] *— are the great unsung heroes of that time. They broke away from the comfort zones and norms of their class and group to do work that was unpopular, against the status quo, socially alienating and, often, exceptionally lonely.*

Sheena carried with humility what Harriet Gavshon called in her film[12] a 'burden of privilege'. She knew that her burden was nothing like the burdens of poverty and discrimination that she spent her life trying to remove and exposure to which deepened the well of her compassion. The men and women who came for advice were her fellow South Africans, but they were prohibited by law from enjoying the basic rights and privileges that she had, merely because she was classified as 'white' by an illegitimate regime based on 'white supremacy'. As such, she was a woman who could vote; a woman who had the right of residence in her own country; a woman who could live without fear of persecution in a house with her husband and children; a woman who had the freedom and the resources to do whatever she wished educationally, professionally, spiritually and socially.

Sheena came from a family in which generations of women had been impressive role models and she had spent all her school years exclusively in the company of girls and women. In the Black Sash, she drew much from, and gave much to, what was probably as diverse a group of women as one could find in the white community — old and young and middle-aged; fat and thin; robust and frail; rich and poor; unemployed and working; lesbian and heterosexual; married and single; childless and mothering; radical and conservative; fashionable and dowdy; highly educated and poorly educated; Christian and Jewish and a smattering of a few other belief systems here and there; all of them smart, committed and hard-working.

This was also a woman whose background not only graced her with a trailblazing mother but also allowed her to marry the man she loved. The man Sheena loved was Neil Duncan — an able, intelligent and multi-talented man who himself was from a materially privileged background and, by virtue of his race, entitled to attend any school and university he and his parents chose; a man who could study, qualify and practise in his own language, in a profession of his choice to support himself,

[11] Wendy Orr was a medical doctor who worked in the medical examiner's office and exposed the torture and abuse routinely used by the police against detainees in South Africa in the 1980s.

[12] *The Burden of Privilege*: produced and directed by Harriet Gavshon for Television News Productions by Free Film Makers: 1995.

Grandchildren Samir and Kenza

his wife and his children. Neil did this most brilliantly and there can be no doubt that both his status and his somewhat eccentric, unconditional and loving solidarity were a cornerstone of Sheena's greatness. After the tragic death of their firstborn son, Sheena and Neil were blessed with their two most beloved daughters, Lindsay and Carey, and subsequently with their grandson, Samir, and granddaughter, Kenza.

Sheena's story is part of the broader picture of women's activism in South Africa, the history of which remains only partially written. It also chronicles some of the political events of her time, providing insights into a few of the numerous campaigns and institutions in which Sheena played such an important part — not only the Black Sash and the SACC but also initiatives such as the Campaign for the Abolition of the Death Penalty, the End Conscription Campaign and Gun Free South Africa.[13] It is the story of a courageous woman who did all that was expected of her, but at the same time defied the dominant ways of thinking and being of her time. It is the story of the family — in every sense of the word — that formed, held and shaped her life path.

[13] Other organisations and campaigns to which Sheena contributed include the Human Awareness Programme (HAP), Joint Enrichment Project (JEP), Human Rights Institute of South Africa (HURISA), Five Freedoms Forum (FFF), the Speak Out on Poverty hearings and a campaign for a basic income grant.

Sheena won numerous national and international peace awards and three honorary doctorates for her human rights work. In spite of the honours, respect and national and international recognition bestowed on her,[14] by all accounts her zest for life and good humour were irrepressible, she was consistently thoughtful, always approachable, always human.

Sheena's influence was extensive, nationally and internationally. Year after year she spoke on diverse platforms and wrote challenging, politically revealing articles, advice office reports and letters. Her words are not those of an armchair intellectual or critic, they are grounded in real life situations. She — and others in the Black Sash and its advice offices throughout the country — ensured that readers and listeners knew about the harsh realities of apartheid that were being endured, day after day, by individual fellow human beings.

There is no way people could say, 'I didn't know.'

The international community needed verifiable information to support their stance against apartheid. This was not easy to come by in the blur of state propaganda and repression of information that characterised apartheid society. *Certainly,* says Jenny de Tolly, *Sheena's analysis in the form of her writing was seen as seminal internationally and was very influential, particularly in the human rights sector. She had an understanding of human rights that went way beyond the surface. Through the window on the world offered by the advice offices she could look at a thing, analyse it from a legal and a moral perspective and then just lay it out with such clarity, with little peripheral detail and with few extra words. She gave incredible perspective to rights in the context of a world in which white South Africans easily got sucked into all sorts of notions of 'their world and their rights'. Her exposure of violations is so very clear, and for me that was one of her essential gifts to all of us.*

Through her own words[15] and the words of others, through vivid memories and stark facts, Sheena emerges as a whole person, a complex, multidimensional woman — loving, gentle, down-to-earth, flawed, talented, intelligent, strategic, angry, forceful, articulate, hard-working, a product of her ancestry, yet visionary and capable of personal transformation.

Sheena's easy-going manner could not hide what Sean O'Leary experienced as *her rock-solid hatred of injustice in whatever form, her determination to overcome injustices perpetrated on the 'nobodies' of society, and her courage to name and shame those responsible for the injustices. This commitment to justice would never waver.*

---

[14] In the Anglican community, Sheena became the first lay canon of the Diocese of Johannesburg and was also awarded the Order of Simon of Cyrene. The international community recognised her with the Liberal International Prize for Freedom for her contribution to human rights and political freedom, the Maurice Eisendrath Bearer of Light award from the Union of American Hebrew Congregations, and the Order of the Battered Sandshoe from Community Aid Abroad.

[15] Throughout the text and also in a selection of Sheena's own writing presented as an appendix.

It is not surprising, then, that two days after Sheena died, these words appeared in the editorial of the *Sowetan*, a leading black newspaper at the time: *Our sorrows and fears lifted a little whenever her ample figure hove into view. She took up the cudgels and fought tirelessly, without profit or reward, against members of her own race who enslaved us.*[16]

[16] Editorial: 'Woman of Humanity', *Sowetan*, Thursday 6 May 2010 as quoted by Celia W. Dugger: *New York Times*: 7 May 2010.

CHAPTER 2

Heritage and Defiance

I ask White South Africans to cast their minds back thirty years to Hitler's Germany of the 1930s. Hitler came to power with the moral and financial support of the big industrialists. The rank and file soon followed and climbed into Hitler's laager. The German people closed their eyes to injustices, they allowed the Jews and Catholics to be persecuted, they did not protest about the concentration camps; they professed ignorance of the gas chambers; they accepted restrictions of their own liberty; they did not raise their voices, and they did not want to raise their voices, until it was too late …

The Black Sash, I am thankful to say, is still resolved in its determination to continue striving for good government. It will continue to speak out against injustice wherever it may be found. It has the future to gain by pursuing its stand on moral principle; it has the future to lose by failure to do so. We are not concerned with who will be offended, or with expediency, or with how we will benefit, or with what the Government may do, or with what the public may think. We do not fear the Government, we do not fear the public, we are not afraid of the Africans, the Indians or the Coloureds; we are not afraid of justice, we are not afraid of freedom. We are afraid of the fear prevalent in our country.

JEAN SINCLAIR, National President Black Sash —
Opening address Black Sash National Conference: 1963

Not everyone experiences the 'mother's milk' of women like Jean Sinclair.

Jean was already a grandmother at the time she gave the above-quoted address. She was entering her second year as president of the Black Sash, eight years after her role in founding the organisation. This was also the year in which Jean's elder daughter Sheena returned to South Africa from Zimbabwe with her husband Neil and two baby daughters.

Born in Germiston[1] in 1908, the elder daughter of Maggie Smith Campbell and Dr Andrew Hutton Watt, Jean had a thoroughly Scottish ancestry. Her father Andrew was born in Edinburgh, Scotland in 1871, studied medicine and graduated with honours from Edinburgh University in 1897. At the start of the second Boer War — more inclusively known as the South African War — he sailed to South Africa as a medical officer in the British Army and was stationed at Norvalspont in the Northern Cape province. Maggie, meanwhile, had sailed to the Cape in 1901 and worked for six happy years as governess to the young daughter of the Maclean family in Cape Town.

[1] Situated on the East Rand of the Witwatersrand, now part of greater Johannesburg.

The two young adventurers, Maggie on her way back to Scotland at the end of her contract and Andrew on his first trip 'home', met on board ship — and fell in love. They became engaged when they got to London and married three months later, on 12 September 1907, in the Trinity United Free Church of Saltcoats in Scotland. They then returned to settle permanently in South Africa, where Andrew had accepted a post as mine physician and radiologist at the Simmer and Jack Hospital in Germiston. He acquired a sterling reputation, not only for his role in the hospital but also as the man who brought the first X-ray machine into South Africa. This was of great significance in monitoring silicosis and other lung diseases caused by the underground working conditions on the mines. Andrew earned twelve hundred pounds a year and had the free use of two horses, a trap and a furnished house in which the three Watt children, Jean and her siblings — Sheena's Aunt Margaret and Uncle Andrew — were born.

All in all, Jean attended six different schools, some in South Africa and some in Scotland. She eventually matriculated from Johannesburg Girls' High, but failed mathematics, which put a stop to potential university study. Like their father, both her younger siblings studied medicine in Edinburgh and returned to South Africa after the war as qualified medical doctors, Margaret becoming a well-loved physician at Baragwanath (now Chris Hani) Hospital in Soweto and Andrew (Jnr) practising as a respected Johannesburg neurologist.

Although she would really have liked to be a physical training (PT) teacher, Jean had done a three-year teaching diploma at the Witwatersrand College of Domestic Science in Johannesburg and had been teaching for just a few years before her marriage to Robert Sinclair in January 1932.

Sheena's father, Robert Balderston Sinclair, was born in 1897 in Bearsden, now part of Greater Glasgow, and lived there for most of his childhood. He completed his schooling as a boarder in Perthshire, taking several prizes for science — although his ultimate career choice was that of chartered accountant, quite rare and prestigious at the time.

Robert was 17 years old when World War I broke out. His brother James joined up immediately, but Robert hardly ever spoke about the war and family history is not certain about whether he bluffed about his age and became one of the many 'boy soldiers' fighting for the British Army or waited until he was 18 to join the Royal Engineers as a despatch rider. In any event, Robert was shot off his motorbike and, despite major reconstructive surgery, couldn't ever even twiddle the fingers on his right hand again, although he did not lose complete use of the hand.

Following the official end of the war with the signing of the armistice in November 1918, a period of economic stagnation and soaring unemployment prevailed in Britain. Robert was one of many young hopefuls who went to see for himself what was possible in the flourishing economy of Johannesburg, the city of gold. Newly qualified as a chartered accountant, he arrived in 1929, intending to stay for only two years. Happily — although it is not clear exactly where and how — he met the feisty young Jean Watt. They may have met socially at the Johannesburg Country Club or at any one of many gatherings of the growing community of Scottish immigrants in and around Johannesburg. Wherever it was, the romance flourished after a shaky start — family legend has it that Jean slammed the bottom half of the stable door at the Simmer and Jack mine house on him when he first asked her to marry him, in case he came close enough to embrace her!

After their wedding in St George's Presbyterian Church, the young couple moved into their first home in O'Reilly Road, Auckland Park, Johannesburg, just a few kilometres away from the burgeoning multiracial vibrancy of Sophiatown. Situated on the western outskirts of what is possibly the world's largest cluster of city suburbs outside Scotland with Scottish names, from Blairgowrie in the west to Highlands North in the east, the modest home was to be an appropriately welcoming birthplace for the baby girl Sheena, born in the midsummer heat of the seventh day of December 1932.

Baby Sheena with Jean and Robert

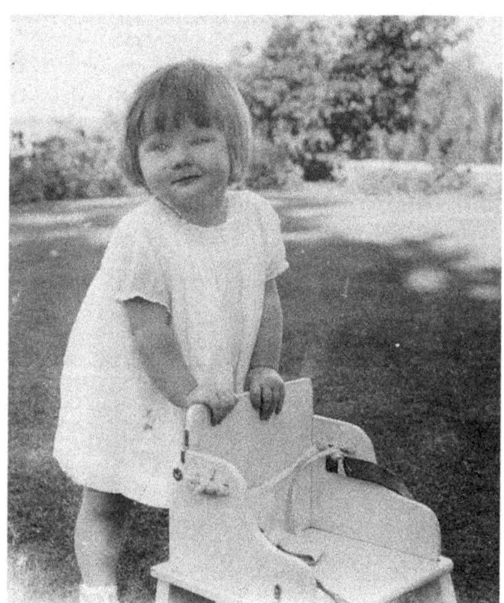

Sheena in The Valley Road garden

Jean's parents, Maggie and Andrew, had by then also settled in Auckland Park, and for a few years, Sheena enjoyed all the indulgent attention that only a firstborn child and grandchild can. After the arrival of their second child, Robert moved his family to a new and larger home at 11 The Valley Road in Westcliff and, in addition to now living some distance away from her own mother, there were growing demands on Jean's time as new babies joined the clan at more or less three-year intervals. Sheena responded to this diminished attention in two significant ways: she developed a lasting need for Jean's approval and she learned to withdraw happily into what was to be a lifelong hobby and skill — reading.

Robert, Sheena's father, encouraged her reading habit — which was a passion he shared — and he also fostered Sheena's sister Liz's appreciation of music by occasionally taking her to concerts. He often took his children for walks around the neighbourhood, rowing at the Zoo Lake, to the Country Club for lunch or a swim, and on rare trips to the Kruger Park without Jean, who did not enjoy 'roughing it'. It was these visits that instilled a lifelong love of game reserves in all his children.

It made a great impression on Sheena that 'Dad used to read quite a lot and was also a man with a solid sense of justice. His family had lived in an area that is part of greater Glasgow now and although I don't think the family had any Highland connections, he considered the Highland clearances a terrible scandal.[2] It was probably his mother who was directly affected, but the memory was an important part of his identity. As a good Scot, he of course also resented what he saw as the domination of his people by England. It always incensed Dad when the issue cropped up here with forced removals, which were the big thing the Black Sash was working on. He identified with that, although he was not politically involved.'

Sheena as a flower girl with her brother Andrew

Because of his war injury and his age, Robert could not enlist for active service in World War II. Instead, he did part-time duty in the 'Dad's army' home guard in Johannesburg, guarding post offices and buildings of that nature, which were vulnerable to local bombing by right wingers. There were many — the advance guard of the notorious National Party — who had not approved of General Smuts's decision to join the Allies against Hitler's army. The war as experienced in South Africa and the war as experienced in Europe did not have comparable traumatic effects at the time. But there can be no doubt that the ideologies that

[2] The Highland clearances were forced removals of farming communities from the lands they had lived and worked on for generations, implemented by landlords seeking to modernise agriculture in Scotland. These clearances, which took place over a hundred-year period, were supported by pseudoscientific theories regarding the imagined racial superiority of the Anglo Saxons over the 'degenerate' Celts.

boiled into widespread destruction in Europe — of people, homes, places of worship, hospitals and many other material manifestations of their civilisation — had a profound, damaging and long-lasting effect on the hearts and minds and — in the case of the majority — the daily lives of people living in South Africa.

As well as the standard violently inflicted 'us' and 'them' principle that is a prerequisite for any war, Hitler's vision of white supremacy and the horrific scope of the Nazi genocide had grabbed the imagination of small clusters of right-wing white 'Christians' in many parts of the world. South Africa was still smarting from its various internal wars and treacheries, as well as the brooding dissatisfactions among most groups following the creation of the 'union' in 1910. There were hearts and minds ready for such extremist views, although the divisions were differently conceptualised. Apartheid, including its deformed economic policy and practice by the all-white National Party, was created both as the system used to oppress all black people and as the mantle of sophistication to hide the truth from those who did not want to see it, to make it look sensible, instead of the ruthless and brutal reality that it was.

Aside from these insidious consequences, the Sinclair children were not much affected by the war. Sheena's sister Liz remembers, *Our war memories are of Mum and Dad listening intently to a crackling reception of every news broadcast on the radio; I remember their concern at times; the occasional blackout with black blinds of the windows in the house at night 'as an exercise', we were told. I remember sitting beside Mum in Thrupps grocery, which was then in the centre of town, for what seemed like hours almost every week, while she dictated lists of food parcels which were to be sent to the relatives in Britain. Relatives later told what a lifeline these food parcels had been for them; food rationing in Britain meant no luxury items, and not enough of anything, though the whole nation miraculously had sufficient food to keep them going. Mum had weekly 'sewing bees' in the house — six or eight women who came to sew flannelette pyjamas under her guidance, for the troops. Her mother — our grandmother Maggie — knitted woollen balaclavas.*

Robert was a quiet person, but he chipped in at the appropriate time to conversations, balanced his role as peacemaker by teasing Jean quite a bit, and seemed constant in his approach and views, his equanimity and good humour. He was someone any member of his family or circle of friends could count on. After he died, Jean heard that he had in fact lost work through her political activities; in the apartheid days, many business people did not want to be associated with activists such as herself. Once the Black Sash was recognised by the authorities as a significant force of opposition to apartheid, the Special Branch twice searched the Sinclair home, taking a whole day to go through the house each time. It was meant as a form of intimidation, but neither Jean nor Robert allowed it to get them down.

Robert, like all white capitalists of the time, was undoubtedly benefiting from apartheid in economic terms, but was not entirely comfortable with the dispensation. He did not, for example, object to any of Jean's anti-apartheid activities, nor did he allow his children to take undue advantage of their privileged relationship with the people in service in their home. *Life was pretty carefree for us,* remembers Liz, *the 'servants' did all the work and during school holidays we seemed to have all the time in the world to please ourselves. Dad realised this wasn't too good for us; he gave us each a room to look after — I had the downstairs cloakroom. I remember him giving one of the boys a row for putting his shoes outside his bedroom door to be cleaned by the 'houseboy' in the morning. Dad said the Africans were there to help our mother, not us, and we must clean our own shoes.*

Sheena's first brother Andrew was born just seventeen months after her. Their sister Elizabeth — Liz — came next, after another three years; then came Robert Campbell — Rob — eight years younger than Sheena and three years older than the youngest brother Kenneth Balderston — Ken — who was born in 1944.

Each sibling remembers Sheena — affectionately known as 'Sheen' in the family — as an ideal big sister, protective, tolerant and caring, but also somewhat detached, so she didn't much interfere with their own growing up antics. The two sisters shared a bedroom and Liz, who says she was frightened of everything as a child, *drove Sheen mad by constantly enquiring whether she was still awake, since I disliked being the only one awake.* Being the eldest, Sheena often filled the expected role of protector, entrusted even by Jean to take all the littler ones, by bus, for milkshakes at Ansteys department store in Jeppe Street, central Johannesburg.

After two years at what was then 'Mrs Trenary's',[3] Sheena spent all of her primary and high school years at Roedean in Parktown, Johannesburg, as did her sister Liz. Each was the senior prefect (head girl) in her time and, in all respects, both were a credit to their parents — and Sheena matriculated with a first class pass and the Myrtle Hamilton Scholarship. Although Roedean was just a few kilometres away from the family home, both girls were boarders once they entered senior school.

All three boys also attended prestigious private schools and were encouraged to study at university — the done thing for middle class boys. Sheena was the only child who was sent 'overseas' straight after school to study in Scotland. In those days, a university degree with some career prospects was just becoming a realistic option for girls, but this was not to be for the Sinclair girls. In addition to prevailing patriarchal attitudes about a woman's 'place' in the home, there were probably several reasons why domestic science was Jean and Robert's choice. For example, they were horrified by what they saw as the number of middle class white women

[3] Founded in 1921 by Maud Trenary with the conviction that every child is special and important. Now Auckland Park Preparatory School.

in Johannesburg who could 'order up' food from their kitchen without knowing the first thing about cooking or good nutrition. Jean herself was a qualified domestic science teacher and seemed to feel it would be a good thing for her daughters. Athol Crescent College of Domestic Science in Edinburgh (also known as the Dough School) had a reputation at the time for being the best college in the British Empire for studying the subject, and was probably seen as something of a 'finishing school for young ladies' too. Perhaps sending Sheena there was some acknowledgement of her potential, and they were justly proud when she came top of the class in physics and chemistry in the entrance exam. Thus it was that Jean chaperoned Sheena, not yet eighteen, on the two-week sea voyage to Britain, introduced her to the relatives in England and Scotland and left her in 'digs', enrolled on the three-year course.

The other four siblings all did their tertiary education in South Africa, possibly for economic reasons, but they suspect it may have been because their parents thought it had been a mistake sending Sheena off on her own at such a young and impressionable age. Sheena tells her own story of the background to what was to follow: 'I had a boyfriend who I had met in Edinburgh. He was a barrister and I thought that tremendously romantic. He was the one my parents subsequently asked my great aunt and uncle to "look into" and they told my parents that he "would never set the Thames on fire" — an expression people still use in derogatory terms — as if anyone could. Anyway, after I qualified at Athol Crescent I went to Glasgow, where he was, to study dietetics. My mother then made what could have been the most colossal mistake: my parents brought me home for the UK summer holidays, and as Mum met me off the plane, she said, "You're never to see that man again". Fortunately for Jean — and Sheena and Neil and all those who benefited from Sheena's role in the struggle against apartheid — 'by that time, I had fallen out of love with this guy.' Much to Sheena's subsequent glee, however, this 'good for nothing' went on to become a sheriff in Fife — a sheriff in Scotland being the most senior judge in a district, responsible for the law and running of the courts in that district or county.

Sheena and her brother Andrew were great friends. Apart from being quite close in age, they shared a wonderful sense of humour, superb intellects, avid reading appetites, a love of literature and, together with Jean, a keen interest in politics. Andrew it seems did not end up studying in the field that really interested him — perhaps something else he and Sheena had in common. A sensitive, sincere and clever boy, he wanted to study journalism and was encouraged by his English teacher, who said Andrew was the best writer he had taught for many years. Alas, his father would not allow that. Robert wanted all the children to be educated in a way that would ensure they could conventionally and safely earn a living — or in the case of the girls, run a home — and he considered journalism a 'shaky' profession.

Robert and Jean in later years

Andrew's acceptance of his father's decision does not mean the young man was a walkover. Liz remembers lively discussions at family meal times, once she was old enough to 'eat with the grownups', and particularly remembers an instance where Jean 'decreed' that Andrew would soon join the Presbyterian Church. *I was amazed at Andrew refusing, and for the first time in my recollection. I thought Andrew was courageous to speak out, and the incident taught me that it's a good idea to think for oneself.*

According to Sheena, her father 'influenced Mum in calming her down. If she hadn't had a solid person beside her she probably would have gone off the face of the planet,' while Sheena's brother Rob recalls that Sheena and their father often collaborated in keeping Jean happy: *Dad was very proud of Sheena and the way she smoothed troubled waters.*

Jean was sometimes moody. *Mum did have bad days, when she was depressed and nothing was right,* says Liz. *These were not happy days in the house. We realised later that she probably had a form of depression, which would last around three days or a week at a time. The days were difficult for Dad and for us all, but we knew it would pass.* Despite her bouts of depression, and even as a young wife and mother and something of a socialite, Jean had kept her eye on current affairs by staying abreast of the news. She had served the United Party (UP) as a city councillor for two and a half years between 1954 and 1957, but, restless in what seemed a repetitive cycle of maternal, social, party-political and charitable indulgences and duties, Jean became bolder and more independent once her youngest son was settled at boarding school and her elder daughter was 'well married'. Through her involvement with the Black Sash, she came to understand how ineffectual the UP really was. She resigned from the UP and stood for election as an Independent City Council Candidate. In her election pamphlet Jean said, *The Johannesburg Local Government is stagnant and unprogressive, driven by party politics, which have no place in local government.* She pledged *to oppose openly and unflinchingly every inroad of Nationalist ideology and invasions of civil liberties which prejudice racial harmony in our City; to work for improved relations between all races;* and *to urge sustained and continuous effort in solving the housing problem of Johannesburg (European, Asiatic, Coloured, Malay, Chinese and African); and the provision of civilised amenities — light, water, sanitation, recreation and transport — for all sections of the community.* Jean did not win that seat, but ultimately took many of the issues forward through the Black Sash, which she was to serve, first as national chair and then as president, from 1961 to 1975.

In setting a slightly broader context for this time and for the issues Jean faced, there is little doubt — through whichever version of history presents itself — that Africa's colonisers had planted seeds of violence and discrimination. Until it was abolished,[4] slavery had epitomised the most brutal aspects of violently imposed race-based oppression. Ideologies of superiority and oppression, as well as various blueprints for genocide — including the infamous exterminations in Namibia[5] — had shaped social 'norms', politics, morality and economies. All but a small percentage of the land had been taken away from black people, with violence, lies and by decree. In a nutshell, this period had systematically and with some stealth, in the dark shadows of two world wars and a period of extraordinary economic depression, stripped black people of almost every basic right to which citizens of the world are entitled. The National Party (NP) claimed governance of the country in 1948 and set out to make sure that the ideal of white supremacy was instilled in as many minds as possible and propped up in every possible way — through legislation and with force. Apartheid modernised the notion that there was something in the

[4] The British Slavery Abolition Act finally came into force in 1834 and the final 'apprenticeships' ended in 1838.

[5] There is compelling evidence that the Nazi genocide and the Holocaust against the Jews is not some inhuman aberration ruthlessly invented and perpetrated by Hitler, but a logical progression of the indoctrination of the German people. Namibia became one of the first major laboratories in which to experiment with theories of racial supremacy. German colonists robbed the Herero and Nama people of land, by treaty, force and cunning. Then, in 1904, General Lothar von Trotha issued an instruction — the Extermination Order — that all Herero men, women and children found within the borders of the colony must be killed. The instruction was ruthlessly carried out. Survivors of direct battles were forced into the desert. The Germans poisoned their water sources. Herero who found their way out of the desert were bayoneted to death or captured and put into concentration camps.

disposition of dark-skinned persons that made them less worthy human beings and perhaps even impossible to 'civilise'.

Yet, despite these nefarious enforcements of ideology, resistance to injustice was remarkably peaceful in the first half of the twentieth century in South Africa.

The African National Congress (ANC),[6] formed in 1912 when Jean was just a 'wee bonnie lassie' of four, is understood to have offered the most inspiring rallying call to resistance for black people.

The Communist Party of South Africa (CPSA) was established in 1921 and was of great significance in labour politics in South Africa. Until its formation, organised labour had almost exclusively represented white workers.

In May 1950 the CPSA had called for a May Day strike to protest against the Unlawful Organisation Bill. The strike resulted in police violence and the death of eighteen people. The CPSA was forced to dissolve the following month due to the Suppression of Communism Act, and the ANC stepped in to take over the planning for a 'Day of Mourning' for those who died in the May Day strike.

Working underground, the communists reorganised themselves as the South African Communist Party (SACP) within just a few years.

One of the earliest major organising strategies was the Defiance against Unjust Laws Campaign launched in 1952. It was the first campaign pursued jointly by all racial groups, under the leadership of the ANC and the South African Indian Congress (SAIC). Through a range of non-violent acts of civil disobedience, people deliberately broke apartheid laws. The regime responded with more than 8 000 arrests and the campaign deteriorated into frustration and riots in a number of cities, resulting in forty deaths and considerable property damage.

Concurrently, in the early 1950s, there were a few other groups, in most cases representing whites who, although not fully persuaded by the means of struggle for liberation as represented by the ANC, were prepared to engage — also at some risk of arrest — in anti-apartheid resistance. This minority-within-the-minority generally represented well-resourced, principled and articulate groups of white liberals who found homes in the South African Institute of Race Relations (SAIRR), the Civil Rights League, the Torch Commando, the Liberal Party and the Women's Defence of the Constitution League/Black Sash. In many cases and with some overlap, they all protested over the various stages of the National Party's actions to legitimise a voters' roll that would be, finally, exclusively white.

Although the SAIRR was the most 'senior' of these so-called liberal organisations (having been in existence for almost twenty years when the National Party claimed

[6] Originally founded as the South African Native National Congress, it changed its name to the African National Congress in 1923.

power) and was less protest oriented and generally more conservative, it was nevertheless valued as a collaborative research-focused ally.

The Civil Rights League was founded in 1948 almost immediately after the National Party was elected. It took a stand against the principle of race-based inequalities and the apartheid regime's intention to remove coloured people from the voters' role. Its overall aim included the creation of a rights-based society with all citizens fully aware of their equal rights in relation to the state and other citizens.

The Torch Commando was founded in 1951 and represented World War II service veterans who were opposed to apartheid generally and, more specifically, to the government's intention to tamper with the voters' role. It was based on principles of its more radical predecessor, the Springbok Legion, and provided a space within which liberal whites who identified with the oppression of black people and their grievances could formulate protest tactics — most of which were torchlight marches. At the height of its brief existence, the Torch Commando had about a quarter of a million members, many of them influential in the legal and economic 'establishment'. Its largest march attracted 75 000 participants but, despite its numbers and dramatic mobilising capacity, the Torch Commando was unable to resolve internal ideological differences and collapsed after the National Party consolidated power in the 1953 elections.

The Liberal Party was founded on 9 May 1953, its members disillusioned with the United Party's lack of liberal influence and progress. It also tried to address the divisions in the Torch Commando on matters of multiracial membership. Its initial conservatism and notions of a qualified franchise shifted with time to acceptance of a policy of universal franchise. There were probably two main reasons for this shift. One was the detention of several of its members and the other was the quality of understanding and respect that developed among its members. This second factor came about largely due to the Liberal Party's practice of including translation facilities at meetings, thereby creating an environment in which all views — and of particular relevance, black rural people's views — could be heard. However, the NP created the Prohibition of Improper Interference Act, which banned any organisation or political party from having multiracial membership, and in 1968 the Liberal Party had to either go underground or disband. It chose to disband.

The Federation of South African Women (FEDSAW) was founded in April 1954 in an attempt, by women, to fight against racism and the oppression of women, as well as to make African women understand that they had rights both as human beings and as women. In the same year, FEDSAW drew up and adopted a Women's Charter and then further amended it in 1955 in preparation for the Congress of the People. Despite its strong ANC links, FEDSAW made an effort to be an inclusive home for all women.

The Black Sash was also formed[7] to protest against the NP's determined and unconstitutional efforts, both through the courts and through Parliament, to remove coloured people from the voters' role. Early in May 1955, six women — among them Jean Sinclair — sat down to consider what they could do and decided to launch a petition. On 25 May 1955, just a week later, and as a direct result of their concerted nationwide networking exercise to add signatures to their petition, a gathering of 18 000 people in front of the Johannesburg City Hall ratified their resolution — for which the women had already mustered thousands of signatures. The demand was that the government 'withdraw the Senate Act', the piece of legislation required to enable the NP to disenfranchise the coloured people. A month later a few hundred women marched to the Union Buildings in Pretoria to deliver the petition, now with over 100 000 signatures. Their midwinter overnight vigil set one of the trends of resilient protest that was to characterise the Black Sash women's resistance to apartheid in years to come.

In the meanwhile, the next major non-racial ANC initiative, the Congress of the People campaign, had been active throughout the country inviting all South Africans to record their demands, to be incorporated into a common document. The document, known as the Freedom Charter, was indeed finally approved and accepted at a gathering of more than 3 000 men and women representing all the people, on 26 June 1955. The campaign had revived hope on an unprecedented scale, and it had united and consolidated an alliance of most of the liberation forces in South Africa — the ANC, the South African Indian Congress, the South African Coloured People's Congress, FEDSAW, the South African Congress of Democrats and the South African Congress of Trade Unions. This initiative, however, also led to the arrest of 156 anti-apartheid leaders and the 'Treason Trial', which lasted until 1961.

In August 1956, just over a year after the Black Sash women marched to the Union Buildings, another and much larger and more diverse group of women marched to the same destination. Led by Lilian Ngoyi, Helen Joseph, Sophie Williams and Radima Moosa, 20 000 women of all races, from cities, towns, villages and 'homelands', also took a petition addressed to Prime Minister J.G. Strijdom to the Union Buildings in Pretoria. He was not in. The petition demanded the abolition of the pass laws and, although it was not the first time black women had objected to these laws, it was a significant multiracial and national development of previous acts of resistance, first in 1913 and then again in 1918 and 1919. In the words of Helen Joseph, *I shall never forget what I saw on 9 August 1956 — thousands of women standing in silence for a full thirty minutes, arm raised high in the clenched fist of the Congress salute.*[8]

[7] Initially as the Women's Defence of the Constitution League.

[8] Joseph, Helen: *Side by Side*, Zed Books, London, 1986.

The Black Sash was perhaps still too young and issue-specific to have affiliated itself to FEDSAW or to have participated in the Freedom Charter campaign as an organisation, but the same reasons would not apply to its absence from the women's march of August 1956. It seems more likely that multiracial activities, even if not yet all illegal, were definitely too provocative for this group of women to tackle — most of them, that is.

Possibly one of the more significant aspects of her influence on Sheena was Jean's position on the issue of race. After the approval of the Senate Act — enabled by the young Queen Elizabeth II[9] through her representative the Governor-General and ultimately passed by the 'rigged' political authority of the National Party — the Black Sash had to decide on its future role. Mindful of what had happened to the Torch Commando, members decided not to disband but to widen their movement to become a permanent, non-party political organisation dedicated to principles of constitutionality and moral governance. This intention was to be served by hosting a national convention of all South African citizens who shared their outrage, and they hoped particularly to include Afrikaans-speaking citizens. Contrary to the general trend in the organisation, Jean argued that if black people were not represented at such a convention, it would have negative repercussions for the Black Sash in years to come.

Although, according to Cherry Michelman, Jean candidly *admitted that this stand for the inclusion of non-Europeans was based on strategy more than on principle*,[10] Jean stood firm, despite significant disagreement of the majority of other members — members who believed that the colour issue was too delicate and that tackling it would undermine the organisation. The Black Sash, it seemed, wanted to identify itself as a group for middle- to upper-class women voters — by definition therefore, only white women — firmly opposed to the ideals and influence of communism and, at that stage, even to any notions of unqualified universal franchise. But by 1963, Jean's more radical views were taking hold; the organisation realised the inherent moral contradiction in this position and opened the membership doors of the Black Sash to women of all races.

It was probably too late: less than a handful of disenfranchised women joined, and the process of reaching this decision was a likely reason for the loss of several key members, including founding leader Ruth Foley. Yet slowly but surely, the Black Sash continued to grow in awareness and eventually adopted a position supporting universal franchise — 'one man, one vote' they called it, not recognising the implications of their use of words until some years later. This decision, too, caused upsets, especially among the women who were fervent supporters of the Progressive

[9] At the time, queen regnant of seven independent Commonwealth countries, of which South Africa was one.

[10] Michelman, Cherry: *The Black Sash of South Africa*, Oxford University Press, London, 1975.

Party and its 'qualified franchise' stance. The respectable middle class character of the organisation was shifting in subtle ways, particularly as more radical and often younger women joined and found their views respected, if not adopted or nurtured. Even the influences of socialism crept in and began to have an effect on Black Sash policies.

All was not lost through the initial conservatism, however. The Black Sash was not harassed by the regime to the same extent as multiracial or 'left' leaning organisations were, nor was it ever banned. With a few exceptions — mostly women who were also actively involved in non-racial and/or underground resistance movements — Black Sash members were not detained or banned or tortured. Perhaps the authorities perceived them as annoyingly well informed, intelligent, morally challenging and influential nuisances, but they were operating within the basic racial boundaries and laws put in place in the name of apartheid, and were, after all, just women — thus not much of a threat in a notoriously patriarchal society.

Black people's resistance adapted and diversified with the changing circumstances of their oppression and their needs. Although there were common threads unifying the various responses, there was not one overarching organising strategy that could meet all the aspirations. In 1958 Robert Sobukwe left the ANC and, the following year, founded the Pan Africanist Congress (PAC) with more militant and less racially integrated policies. By 1959 it seemed unlikely that the PAC and the ANC would cooperate in any manner. The ANC planned a campaign of demonstration against the pass laws to start at the beginning of April 1960. The PAC rushed ahead and announced a similar demonstration, to start ten days earlier, effectively hijacking the ANC campaign. On 16 March 1960 Sobukwe wrote to the commissioner of police, stating that the PAC would be holding a five-day, non-violent, disciplined and sustained protest campaign against pass laws, starting on 21 March. At a press conference three days before the campaign started, he further stated: *I have appealed to the African people to make sure that this campaign is conducted in a spirit of absolute non-violence, and I am quite certain they will heed my call. If the other side so desires, we will provide them with an opportunity to demonstrate to the world how brutal they can be.* And indeed, on 21 March 1960, the world was horrified by the murderous response of the National Party regime against hundreds of township residents protesting in the townships of Sharpeville and Langa. Possibly as many as 300 black Africans were injured and 69 were killed in Sharpeville when South African police opened fire on the demonstrators. Later that day in Langa, police baton-charged and fired tear gas at the gathered protesters, shooting dead three and injuring several others.

The government declared a state of emergency and arrested many members of the PAC and the ANC. The Sharpeville Massacre signalled the start of armed resistance in South Africa, and in April 1960 the PAC and ANC were banned. Working underground in South Africa and from various key locations in Africa and other countries, the ANC organised Umkhonto we Sizwe (isiZulu for 'Spear of the Nation'), also known as MK, to include armed struggle against the regime but focused on symbolic government-related targets rather than engaging in terrorism against civilians.

In July 1963, protected by newly legislated broad powers of arrest without warrant, police raided MK's secret headquarters in Rivonia and arrested most of its leadership. Nelson Rolihlahla Mandela, who was already in prison, was put on trial with the other leaders. All received life sentences. South Africa entered a decade of enforced calm — on the surface. Not so underground, on student campuses, in neighbouring countries, in the prison cells of political detainees, and in the homes and places of work of great numbers of ordinary courageous South Africans. *As history shows us,* wrote Jean, *you cannot hold a people down, even by force, indefinitely. We in the Black Sash do not believe that the White races are superior to the Black races; we believe that discrimination on grounds of colour is an evil thing and we believe that the sharing of our privilege is the best insurance for peace and happiness for all.*[11]

When Sheena returned in October 1963 after eight years in Zimbabwe, she found her homeland in a state of emergency and her mother in full stride as leader of a vibrant women's human rights organisation. South Africa continued in crisis, but apathy prevailed among the majority of whites.

How, one may ask, has our present government, in a few short years managed to prostitute the morality of an entire people, who, by and large, had a traditional and well-recognised respect for the rule of law? queried Jean in her 1964 presidential address to the Black Sash conference. *How have they managed to seduce an honest people into the political thuggery of sectionalism?*

When the Black Sash was originally formed in 1955 to protest against the debauching of our Constitution by the Senate Act — and I say debauching deliberately because the assertion of legality arising from the manipulation of an unfortunate loophole in the Constitution, does violence to our intelligence — we little thought that in so short a time we would be called upon to defend the fundamental human rights and dignities which have been the prerogative of civilised peoples since the middle ages.

Today to our shame, South Africa has sunk to the level of 90-day detention, without charge and without trial and in solitary confinement. It is a measure which offends all the tenets of Christian teaching, justice, civilised values and decency.

Over time, the Black Sash became renowned for its ability to provide accurate and verifiable facts to support its campaigns and in this same report Jean gave pages of statistics of various banning and detention infringements of human rights in the

[11] Sinclair, Jean: Extract from opening address, Black Sash national conference, 1963.

past year. Jean also saw fit to remind members of the words of Abraham Lincoln: *There is a special place in hell for those who remain neutral in a moral crisis.*

Jean's analysis of the situation was that the principal reasons for the apathy of white people were the relative prosperity of the white population in a buoyant economy, and fear. She named fear in several dozen forms, including its character as *the deadly enemy of a free society* and as the inhibitor of independence of thought. She pointed out that the Black Sash, particularly through the work of its advice offices and its resistance and issue campaigns, was becoming increasingly aware that *the liberty of all South Africans is sacrificed on the altar of apartheid; but it is our non-white people who suffer the most. They have suffered endless assaults on their dignity and the constant humiliation they endure by decree is shameful.* She called on white South Africans to get off the fence and take sides, because freedom was precious. With a tone that was to characterise her leadership and inspire the women who followed in her footsteps, she concluded that it *may not be comfortable to think differently from friends or business associates, so silence is prudent. On the other hand, outspoken criticism could bring to light a surprising amount of sympathy and support. Courage to speak out gives courage to others to do likewise.*

gille de vlieg ©

Jean Sinclair demonstrating

Sheena had in the meantime also become active in the Black Sash. 'When my children started going to school I started working in the Advice Office one morning a week. I have been there ever since, although in those days it was different. We would take our knitting or writing material to catch up on our correspondence. Repression was at an all time high, people were scared to ask for advice and the tradition of serving the community, now established in the Black Sash, had not yet emerged. People asked me why I joined the Black Sash. The answer is that there wasn't anything else to join.'[12]

Indeed, the South African Congress of Democrats had been banned in 1962. But Sheena would have known about the Liberal Party and that it represented non-racism. With her own views on universal franchise, she would have been attracted

[12] Villa-Vicencio, Charles: *The Spirit of Freedom*, chapter 'Sheena Duncan: Surprised by Joy'.

by its 'one man, one vote' franchise policy. So her choice of the Black Sash must have been deliberate. This may have been due to her mother Jean's involvement, or it could be that she did not want to join a political party.

Perhaps initially Sheena was caught up in a narrower understanding of what was going on in South Africa, powerfully and intimately influenced by the policies as well as the activities of the Black Sash — which at that time were conservative although brave — and by the even more conservative nature of nearby parishes of the Anglican Church.

Whatever her reasons, there is no doubt that her future human rights activism was profoundly influenced by her work in the Black Sash advice offices and as an active member in the organisation itself, as well as by her work with black theologians of note in the South African Council of Churches.

Despite some encouraging trends in the political atmosphere after the first year of John Vorster's leadership of the NP, the Black Sash was not in the least taken in by government propaganda, and Jean wrote in her 1969 conference address: *It is fair to say that the lives of all South Africans are controlled by the state. They have little liberty left. All that they have are their thoughts, which as I have suggested, are conditioned by the skilful use of propaganda. The sequel to thought conditioning is a willingness to conform and a susceptibility to react to an emotional rallying cry.*

In South Africa's present predicament of being unhonoured and unloved by most countries of the world, and with the threat of terrorism on her borders, the call to patriotism serves to divert public attention from the fact of South African life.

Patriotism is a call to submit. The white population is prepared to submit, in fact to do more than submit. It is prepared to go along actively defending government policy as long as their economic health and their privilege are maintained.

Patriotism does not mean loyalty to an ideology or to a political philosophy. Nor does loyalty to a political party imply patriotism. Patriotism is not sectional and it does not exclude the right to criticise and question.

Authority in South Africa places the narrowest construction on the meaning of patriotism. It has come to mean, in fact, the compulsion to accept policy without question. One who criticises the policy is considered to be an enemy of South Africa; to protest, however lawfully, is construed as subversion, to expose any abuse or scandal is almost traitorous and to hold liberal opinions is un-South African and dangerous.

Patriotism has become the public's refuge and its apology for its apathy, silence and acquiescence. There has been a moral corrosion of the public mind. It has made it easy for authority to depart from the accepted principles of Parliamentary government and even from accepted standards of humanity and decency and justice. Patriotism is not a valid moral basis for government. Neither is the acquisition of absolute power compatible with action based on moral principles. Authority requires a yardstick by which to measure its use of power. If power is exercised in such a way that individual rights are violated, Parliamentary government gives way to tyranny, and tyranny has little respect for moral principles.

In her final presidential address in 1975, which is also a reflection on the first twenty years of the Black Sash, Jean noted with amazement that the Black Sash had changed so radically, yet was still alive and active. She acknowledged the conservative and naive character of the group in the early years, but said further that *our lack of political knowledge was certainly compensated for by enthusiasm.*

Jean's frankness was remarkable, as was her extraordinary commitment to learning and to change. Regarding the initial mobilising issue, for example, she notes that *many members were less concerned about coloured voting rights than they were about the violation of the Constitution.* Yet she goes on to concede that it was the very matter of constitutionality that the United Party (of which she and most other women of the Black Sash were members at the time) had, a decade earlier, used through a *perfectly constitutional* amendment to remove the entrenched protection of the voting rights of African people of the Cape. *The fact that this point was not recognised by us in 1955 was an indication of the thoughtless disregard and ignorance of the needs and feelings of the majority of South African people.*

Jean remembered how, following the failure of their mobilising campaign against the Senate Act, the Black Sash had gathered to decide whether to disband or not. Under the leadership of Ruth Foley and Jean, they agreed unanimously to carry on and decided that the work of the organisation would be driven by their conviction that *there was one standard and one standard only of morality. The thing is either morally right or it is morally wrong. It matters not what section of our population is threatened with discriminations, injustice or lack of liberty. We shall protest on moral grounds.*

This resolution — an example of how strong and influential Jean and others were — was, however, too radical to be accepted by the bulk of the membership of the Black Sash and by the white public in general. The membership melted away from about 10 000 to approximately 2 000 women.

Jean continued to serve the Black Sash as a dedicated member for more than thirty years, most persuasively during the years in which she was the national president — also the time in which South Africa experienced some of the worst effects of the discriminating legislation that was put in place step by step by the NP. The women with their black sashes protested at every step. They stood silently with placards, proclaiming each new infringement of the rights of the majority of South Africans. Through the work they did in the Black Sash advice offices and in rural communities, they developed a thorough knowledge of the effects of enforced removals from black spots, from white farms, from one rural area to another, and from urban areas. They supported coloured and Indian people in their resistance to forced removals; they formed the Citizens' Action Committee, which launched a national campaign to protest against the wholesale uprooting of thousands of Africans from their homes and also the government's intention to house 60 000 African men in hostels in Alexandra township; they encouraged a handful of lawyers to assist people in court challenges to unjust laws; they highlighted the infamous 'volunteer' Farm Labour Scheme in which teenaged Africans who were arrested under the apartheid laws were induced to 'volunteer' for farm labour instead of appearing in court — and in some cases died due to the atrocious working conditions; they monitored the steady erosion of civil liberties and, in effect, they tried to make white South Africans gain some understanding of what it would be like to be black.

In her concluding words as national president, Jean did much to clear a track for Sheena: *South Africa does not belong to any one group to the exclusion of all others. Its citizens are Black, Brown and White and none of us has any moral claim to privilege or property at the expense of others. We are called upon to share political and economic power and with no further procrastination. If we do not, our future will be too ghastly to contemplate.*

It is little wonder that now eminent, then idealistic young lawyers like Geoff Budlender remember Jean as *formidable, with an acute mind and bright penetrating eyes; quite fearless and quite eccentric.* Jean is also remembered with appreciation for the fact that even though she was as old as their grandmothers, she treated these young activists with respect and dignity.

When Jean retired as president of the Black Sash in 1975, Sheena was the obvious choice for the organisation to elect in her place. It was a sound decision for Jean to step aside, even though she needed some gentle but firm encouragement from her husband Robert to let go of the power she had in the influential organisation she had helped to found.

The 'mother's milk' had done its job. The daughter had taken it in, transformed it to a deeply personal integrity and, when the time came, was well prepared and ready to accept the baton passed to her by her mother.

gille de vlieg ©

Jean and Sheena outside St Mary's Cathedral, Johannesburg

CHAPTER 3

Leadership

Sheena had high expectations not only of herself but also of other people. She brought out the best in people, but also accepted people for who they were and valued the very different kinds of contributions that different people made. It was wonderful to hear Sheena's deep laugh erupting from the backseat position she preferred to take in meetings, and always reassuring to see her approaching, swaying slightly from side to side. I felt she was our anchor and our backstop. Her powerful intelligence, compassion and indefatigable hard work were buttressed by a deep faith that enabled her to radiate reassurance in a chaotic world where the rest of us could otherwise have faltered.

ANINKA CLAASSENS — Interview

At the core of great leadership rests a capacity to inspire and encourage — both of which can be exercised through creating an environment of fear, or of love. Sheena had an abundant capacity to inspire and encourage and her chosen field of influence was through an authentic recognition that love accomplishes a particular quality of action. She was able to show a new way and then walk alongside others towards it, offering herself as example when example was needed and encouraging when courage was needed. Although it is not possible to single out any one aspect of Sheena's anti-apartheid activism as more important than others, it is important to acknowledge her presence as a bold, intelligent and thoughtful leader. Her leader 'persona' gave her a firm foothold from which to take steps into the unknown, consider new steps within the familiar — and open the way for others to join her or challenge them to stand up to her and claim responsibility for their own views and actions.

Sheena was an unequivocal leader, says Jenny de Tolly. *She just simply took leadership. I was a bit in awe of her and sometimes felt a bit like an argumentative schoolgirl in her presence, as though I had done something wrong. But Sheena was not patronising, so I didn't get a feeling of being 'tolerated'. We differed in leadership style but I never had any differences of ethical perspective. Sheena motivated from a sense of outrage and justice, not through guilt or from an angry or dark place. She would say, 'There is a light beyond there, let's try and go there out of this darkness.' I learned enormously from her.*

Sheena's leadership qualities, practised in many respected organisations and anti-apartheid campaigns, were not unique in a society graced with numerous intelligent, dedicated, hard-working, generous women of all races, who believed in and worked

Sheena getting her daily 'news fix' on the stoep

for the possibility of South Africa as a non-racial democracy. What was perhaps unusual was Sheena's ability to balance her single-minded focus with the diversity of her experience, and her brilliant intellect with her unconditional compassion.

These qualities played a defining role in the functioning of the Black Sash under Sheena's leadership. To outsiders the Black Sash may have seemed to be a fairly homogeneous group of white women, relatively politically conscious and well resourced, with liberal views and some time to spare. However, this was not so, and sustaining harmony among members was a complex matter. Kathy Satchwell remembers that *there we would all be at meetings: the oldies and the newies, the young and the old, the workers and the non-workers, the radicals and the conservatives. Things would sometimes be said and we would have mutterings and mumblings but on the whole it got held together quite happily. The Black Sash was inclusive and gentle. We would get het up; everybody would interrupt, but it wasn't competitive. I don't think anybody ever felt Sheena was competing to be our lord and master or that she saw herself always as the person that was right. She wasn't the first speaker on every issue. She would listen. She had a contribution and other people would also talk. She didn't hog it. But hers was always a profound intervention — a significant one. I think because of her clarity.*

I don't remember Sheena ever being rude or nasty or denigratory. Some women may have seen others as stupid, or think less of them because they didn't work outside the home or have experience, even though their hearts were good and they were there. Certainly in the white left, whatever meetings we had, there was always the 'in' group and the 'out' group; the talkatives and the non-talkatives; the stupids and the non-stupids; the connected and the unconnected. You didn't have that in the Black Sash and Sheena was one of the women who helped that evolve, who ensured it stayed.

As a leader, Sheena knew the value of being well informed and her sources of information were expansive. Throughout all the years of her activism, her morning ritual was one of extensive tea drinking in bed — at least a pot or two — while she read the papers. Sheena would not get up until she had read from cover to cover whichever relatively credible morning newspaper was in print at the time. Yet, she could still get to a city office for 8.30 meetings when needed, sometimes by bus — still reading. While these publications remained in print, her morning, evening and weekend reading covered the *Rand Daily Mail*, *The Star*, *The Sowetan*, *The Weekly Mail* (later the *Mail and Guardian*), *The Economist*, the Saturday *Financial Times* and latterly *The Citizen.*[1] Sheena listened to the radio news across several stations, and with the advent of television in South Africa in 1976, she also watched the evening news and, occasionally, current affairs programmes. She absorbed what she needed from the media, but her information gathering did not rest there.

Many of the people with whom Sheena and Neil socialised were involved in anti-apartheid work in some way and were exceptionally knowledgeable in their fields of work. The sharing of unpublished first-hand accounts of what was happening around the country was often a feature of informal meals, dinner parties and ordinary evenings of bridge. *We were seeing the same events from different angles*, says Allister Sparks, *I as a reporter on the front line, sometimes with bullets flying and that sort of thing; Sue*[2] *and Sheena from the perspective of the different things they were doing, mostly as members of the Black Sash. We would share anecdotes and opinions. Sheena and Neil were charming hosts. People would swarm around that house and we were all able to bring back stories from the 'battle front' as it were.*

Embroidery and gardening were Sheena's favoured creative activities

[1] *The Citizen* was government-funded, but useful for insights and information concerning policy and legislation.

[2] Sue Sparks, Allister's late wife.

To these sources Sheena added long hours of evening and weekend reading: reports, spiritual and philosophical reflections, Government Gazettes and Hansard, balanced with crime novels or thrillers — she knew well the value of detective work and the spotting of clues when wading through mountains of information. From time to time she replenished herself with Jane Austen.

Although several friends and colleagues mentioned that Sheena did not suffer fools gladly, she did have an extraordinary capacity to listen. Sheena listened with an open heart to others, even when she thought she might disagree. Without interference, she would allow others to think out loud to her, to explore possibilities, to make decisions and choices and to do and say things that made sense to them. If it was in the scope of her work, she made sure that they knew they could count on her if they needed support on the way. Listening to their reasoning and observing the way they actualised their ideas allowed her to learn from others. Sheena was willing — and able — to change, if she learned from another that her or his interpretation was better. Because of this quality of respect for others Sheena earned their trust.

Then there is the significance of humility in the character of Sheena's leadership, the insight that leadership is about being part of a team — and does not exist outside of the team. Mary Burton agrees that *sometimes we forget those very strong teams and support systems the leaders in the Black Sash had, but I think there are two things that made Sheena different. One was her 'presence' and leadership in meetings; the other was her awareness all the time of the needs of the whole organisation. She kept all the load of concentrating on the law and the issues and the political decisions, yet she never seemed to lose sight of the fact that there were people all round the country who needed to be kept 'in the fold' — a kind of biblical image of the shepherd. For the smaller regions she was accessible at all hours, regularly on the phone to them, but for all of us, those magnificent letters that she wrote always made one feel, yes that's what we need to talk about; those are the issues; that's what we need to think about. It was fantastic leadership in terms of showing the path ahead. I think she sometimes even used those letters to explore her own thinking — they weren't cut and dried. She was engaging all the time with the different parts of the Black Sash. To compare her with Jean — Jean was in Johannesburg and Johannesburg was the centre. Yes of course there was discussion and voting and so on, but the action stemmed from the Johannesburg committee. Sheena seemed to spread that more widely. I think she was genuinely democratic in that sense. Although she was often way ahead, she brought everyone with her and she was prepared to consider any new issues that anyone raised.*

Joyce Harris spanned the two of them. I think of Jean with her impetuousness and her rage against injustice — she had beside her Joyce's wisdom and brains and exceptional writing ability. Joyce was always there, diffidently but brilliantly. Sheena 'inherited' her in a way and I'm sure relied on Joyce enormously for guidance and teasing out of

Joyce Harris, Sheena and Ethel Walt

the issues — and then she had Ethel Walt, who really loved her and I think brought to Sheena a kind of softness she might otherwise not have had.

Sheena knew how to develop teams, without loss of individuality — hers or anyone else's. *What Sheena did for the next generation of Black Sash women,* says Judith Hawarden, *was that she gave us space — she was immensely generous in giving space. I think some people who are in senior roles find it hard to give space, but Sheena did. Yet she was there for you, being wise counsel if you needed to ask her something. She was a role model: brilliant, fair, always tuned in to what was happening, but also so relaxed; her glasses skew-whiff, held together with a gem clip; dropping ash on her ample bosom. It was her humanness that set her apart from other Black Sash leaders, she was so natural.*

Sheena was always ready to stand back and allow other people to do things, agrees Ashnie Padarath, *but also her approach was very developmental. She had a different way of looking at the world. We were young and we were junior but she never treated us like that. Sheena had a great sense of humour but if we had an opinion she would engage with us seriously. She was fearless and allowed us to see how one can just walk one's path unwaveringly.*

Sheena knew better than to allow her own particular leadership presence to become a fixed 'model' in the minds of others. *Sheena was iconic and often embodied Sash for the members,* says Laura Best. *But I remember her always working against that: 'Don't personify the Sash around me.' What made her different perhaps was that she did more work in the advice offices than other leaders and knew more than most about the real effects of apartheid. She was vocally adamant about her issues but she was firm about being part of a leadership collective.* In her November 1985 presidential letter to members, Sheena added the following post script: 'I do not intend to stand for election as National President at the next conference in March. There is nothing strange or new in this decision. I have always said that I believe in shared leadership and that the Black Sash benefits from regular changes in the National Executive. We have a plentiful supply of leaders and each one contributes new and different emphases. I believe that we are enriched by change at the top.

'Joyce Harris brought new perspectives in her four years as president and I am now ending the fourth year of my second spell, having told the National Conference in March this year that I was absolutely determined not to exceed the four-year limit, which is written into our constitution.

'The Transvaal region is nominating Cape Western as headquarters region for the 1986/87 year. We always used to move headquarters around the country but that stopped as the regions got smaller. Now we are growing again and it is healthy that we are able to resume our original practices.'

Aninka Claassens comments that *there are people one relies on in life and respects forever more. It doesn't necessarily mean that you take them with you, but they are terribly important touchstones. I liked the fact that Sheena was outspoken, that she swore and she drank and she didn't always conform. She wasn't always tidy and it pissed me off that some of those Black Sash women sniggered at her; some of the Transvaal people were very classist. I don't know why she drank so much; maybe that's where she could block out her acute perception of what was wrong. Many other people protected themselves by not seeing things or not doing things, by putting up barriers. Sheena saw things, dealt with things. In a sense she must be allowed the kinds of things that enabled her to do that, whether her big garden, her drinking, her smoking or whether it was being impatient sometimes — how few people have that capacity to unflinchingly be there, in the midst of such shit and bring their whole presence and intelligence and respect to the situation; the quality of her intellect was quite extraordinary and that did set her apart from other people, but she was never arrogant about it.*

In Sheena, women of the 'younger generation' identified leadership characteristics to which they could aspire. As Ashnie put it, *We joked that we wanted to be Sheena when we grew up.* Alison Tilley agrees, *I didn't just admire her; I sought and seek to emulate her. I won't succeed entirely, but when I sort of do, it will be a good day.* Tapping into the memories of just a few more of these younger women — Anita Kromberg, Beva Runciman, Glenda Glover, gille de vlieg, Jillian Nicholson, Janet Cherry, Lauren Nott, Marj Brown and Sue van der Merwe — the words that rise to the surface time and again refer to Sheena's sense of humour, her relaxed yet totally attentive attitude to life, her honesty and, above all, her uncompromising integrity.

Every time I heard Sheena speak was like an intellectual revolution, says Beva. *Her mind and her work never remained static but developed new, sometimes dramatic aspects that were all laid before us to choose to develop if we so wished.*

Sheena's brain was always something that we leaned on, agrees gille. *We respected her evaluations, her analysis. She allowed us to do what we needed to do and she just carried on with what she needed to do. Sheena had a lot of clout, but often kept herself out of debates, just allowing them to happen around her without trying to influence our thinking, although she definitely was a strong and powerful guide for the processes that happened. She had a motherly approach as well. You knew if you were in trouble you could go to Sheena and you knew that whatever you were discussing with her would not go somewhere else. She had no time for gossip — it wasn't part of who she was at all.*

In Glenda's view, *If you needed a lesson in ethical strategy, then you just needed to observe Sheena at work. She could touch your heart describing the back of the neck of a vulnerable young boy in a police station; shine a light of understanding on murky issues; and get you to give your best, simply by expecting you to. Her sense of justice and fairness was tough, unwavering, uncompromising and demanding, yet her leadership was clear and enabling.*

Sheena had such a formidable reputation that I quailed at the thought of meeting her, says Jillian. *But right from the start she was approachable and reassuring, although she never minimised the challenges we faced. She became, as she did for so many others, an inspirational and energising force in my life as well as a mentor and a friend. She was the kind of leader that no one wanted to let down.*

Sheena was the fiercest woman I ever met, says Sue. *Perhaps it was because I was quite a bit younger but it was a quality that was both incredibly useful and also intimidating. The other thing about her was her meticulousness. She was so good at doing everything properly, methodically but simply. She had a brilliant mind but it was not a highfalutin mind, and her logic was completely practical although she could compete with any academic in this country. Sheena was a great leader. With her in the Black Sash one had the certainty that everything was going to be done properly. She had a beautiful handwriting and she had this theory that you had to use every inch of the paper so she wrote from the top, even it didn't have any lines, and it was all compact and she never seemed to have to redo a page either. Incredible. She was utterly devoted to the task at hand. In many ways, I think Sheena taught me to concentrate — maybe not directly — but just how she could sit down and focus. Maybe she taught me logic. What very much stuck in my mind with her was the way in which she constructed her documents and her thought processes and her arguments. It was just her natural practicality, the way her mind worked. When I think of Sheena, there's a saying that immediately comes to mind: 'When all is falling about you, just do the next right thing.' If you need to consider what 'right' means, your entire value system — whether you are religious or not — will guide you. Obviously you have to have the moral integrity and the value system, but for me it's a wonderful phrase that epitomises Sheena. She could identify what needed to be achieved, and even if the next right thing was just a plan, with hurdles to cross to get there, Sheena managed to pull it all together into a form that enabled us to take the next right step. I miss that.*

Somewhere between these young women and Sheena's contemporaries were many others — people like Hillary Morris, who became the second director when the Black Sash disbanded its membership and fully 'professionalised' its advice offices, with Sheena still as the chairperson of the Black Sash Trust for several years. *Sheena never set herself apart from others,* says Hillary. *Her generosity of spirit impacted on people and they were able to warm to her. Sheena never made herself special and so people trusted her and we moved with her flow, without feeling that we were being guided or that Sheena was playing a hidden agenda role. I don't think Sheena knew what a hidden agenda was.*

I remember laughing a lot when Sheena was around. She was able to see the humour in things. If there were any particular organisational tensions, I felt a lot of sympathy from her, but part of her initial response was always to chuckle.

Rosie Smith and Mary Kleinenberg, both leading Black Sash members in the smaller regions, were equally inspired by what Rosie remembers as Sheena's *integrity and wonderful warmth. Sheena was somebody who you knew wasn't going to lie to you; somebody you could really trust; somebody who was thinking out what could be done in very difficult situations. She was a good listener; we would tell her things and she would keep them in her head and then think of — not necessarily a solution, but a way of looking at things. You just looked up to her.* Mary highlights three great leadership qualities that emerged from one late night phone call from Sheena after she had seen a report of action in which Black Sash members were involved: *She wanted to know if we were safe; only when asked did she offer sound advice on how to proceed peacefully; she wanted us to know how proud she felt of all the women, us and others, who had dared to participate.*

Being a member of the Black Sash could be a lonely business, even in big cities. Laura Best, who was one of the younger, more radical members, first experienced Sheena as a mentor to a somewhat isolated pocket of members. *We had quite a young group of Sash members in Pretoria, and Sheena obviously understood that Pretoria was the formal heart of the apartheid government and that having a branch there was significant. We were small but we got very special support from her. She would come over and talk to us, going out of her way to make sure we were still functioning. I remember her as a strong presence, a compass for the issues that Sash was dealing with. That's one of the things I respected about her the most, it was always about the moral correctness of the issue. If it was morally correct we should have the courage to take it on. To me, this is the essence of leadership. I always go back to that lesson to guide me when I am not sure of what to do; I go back to the essence of the issue and then decide — and then act, with what was another marker for me, her boldness. Sheena could also find the golden threads between causes that needed to be drawn together, although she would choose wisely because there was such a call on her time. For her, it was always about social justice. It was remarkable how much she gave of herself.*

Then, there is the matter of charisma, on which Kathy Satchwell provides a useful perspective: *Sheena as personality — whether Black Sash, Human Awareness Programme, or a public speech or anything, anywhere — was remarkable. Sheena in any meeting listened well, read what needed to be read, and when she talked there was this wonderful deep trombone voice that captured everyone's attention. It was lovely. She spoke well. Sheena gripped attention with a combination of intellect and voice and physical participation through her very descriptive hands. She was an enormously clear presenter of ideas. 'There are six issues here terrum, terrum, terrum, terrum ...' and we could all follow.*

I remember her efficiency and professionalism. I think everybody would say that. Professionalism in so many ways: professional about being on time, professional about always writing everything down, professional with having all the documents and reading whatever needs to be read, professional with following up. It wasn't as though, 'Well, I've got a life and I'm kind of helping a little bit with the struggle in between.' This was a serious thing. Whatever Sheena did was deserving of attention, diligence and commitment. She didn't add her name to lots and lots of things and then float in and out. She was selective in what she did and she was respectful of it, and of all the people involved.

Brigalia Bam agrees: *On the whole, Sheena had very strong principles whether you accepted them or not. She was not an easy person on always accepting other people's opinions because she was so strong, but I liked it very much about Sheena that she was so principled. Another of her greatest gifts was to be able to speak. She had such a voice! Even her physique was helpful, so when she stood up on the stage or anywhere, you listened. You couldn't ignore her.*

After Sheena's first term as president of the Black Sash (March 1975 to March 1978), Pat Tucker included the following words in her tribute: *Under her leadership, the organisation has gained members and prestige as a fact-finding organisation whose protest is based on solid, well-compiled information. Whether it was working in the advice office, the day-to-day grind and trauma of helping sort out people's lives; her extraordinary grasp of the intricacies of influx control laws; taking the chair at a national conference; standing in lone protest; accosting a Cabinet minister; giving evidence to a commission; Sheena was as much part of the organisation as her leadership was its guiding light.*[3]

[3] Tucker, Pat: 'Sheena Duncan National President March 1975-1978: a tribute', *Sash*, vol.20, no.1, May 1978.

Eight years later, Joyce Harris wrote: *Sheena Duncan is completing the fourth year of her second term of office as National President. This second term has been a period of increasing uneasiness as the government began to vacillate and black people became ever more angry. It is always easier to operate in a situation with clear-cut parameters, more difficult when they begin to blur and extra factors enter into decision-making and in the maintenance of direction.*

Our organisation could not have wished for a better or more effective leader during these demanding times than Sheena. She has a broad political perspective combined with an extraordinary knowledge of relevant facts. She has a penetrating mind that unerringly gets to the root of the problem and almost immediately finds a solution for it. She has the confidence which is an essential element of strong leadership combined with the readiness to listen and be influenced. She is an outstanding public speaker, much in demand both here and overseas, and she writes as well as she talks. Because of her many remarkable qualities she is involved in a number of organisations and activities outside of Sash, all of which clamour for her presence.

But perhaps the most remarkable thing about her is that, despite her many strengths which might have had the effect of distancing her from ordinary people, she remains lovable, approachable, a joy to talk to and a delight to know.[4]

Sheena inspired by example. The national headquarters' report to the 1984 Black Sash annual national conference, also written by Joyce — who herself was an embodiment of intellectual excellence and many of the other qualities she attributes to Sheena — is a striking record of the exemplary and often practical elements of Sheena's leadership and the sheer volume of work she contributed. The period was March 1983 to March 1984 and Sheena was in the second year of her second term as president of the Black Sash. In the report, Joyce also appreciatively acknowledged the outstanding work done by other members of the national executive committee and national office staff, but Sheena's example, even without considering any of her work in the advice office, even without taking account of the fact that this was all unpaid and voluntary commitment, stood in a class of its own:

Circulars to Regions

There have been 19 circulars to Regions in the current year. [Typically, the national president wrote the circulars.] Apart from giving specific information regarding projects, activities, statements, poster demonstrations and so on, they contain a fascinating running commentary on current events. In them she gives her views of the Freedom Charter, the UDF, removals, the referendum and the Constitution and conscientious objection, among other subjects. This report has already quoted from some of them but they should be recommended reading for all members of the Black Sash, at least, for

[4] Harris, Joyce: 'Awards and accolades 1985/6', *Sash*, vol.29, no.1, May 1986.

they are informative, they clarify many very blurred issues, they give their readers the benefit of Sheena's clarity of thought and expression and, added to all that, they are full of humour.

Correspondence

Sheena has conducted a vast correspondence, not only with regions, but with individuals and organisations locally and from all over the world. People and organisations are constantly writing to the Black Sash requesting all sorts of information, and Sheena goes to endless trouble to supply this information accurately and fully. Some of the topics she has dealt with are the Black Local Authorities Act, the Natal code, advice offices, the Constitution, court monitoring, legal assistance available in rural areas and a host of queries regarding possible sources of further information, publications, etc.

Other organisations

Headquarters has been in touch with or worked closely with many other organisations including the South African Council of Churches, the Institute of Race Relations, the Progressive Federal Party, the Human Awareness Programme, the National Council of Women, Lawyers for Human Rights, the Legal Resources Centre, the Legal Aid Bureau, Quaker Services, the UDF and others. In most of these contacts Sheena herself has been actively involved, attending meetings in many instances.

Talks delivered by the National President

I have tried to be accurate about numbers but cannot vouch for the completeness of this list or the following ones. Sheena addressed 70 meetings during the year, some of them large public meetings, some house meetings, some meetings of organisations, schools, churches, political parties. Amongst the topics she covered were the Pass Laws, mass removals, the Defence Amendment Bill, Pensions, the Black Sash, the poverty survey, conscription, lodgers' permits, the Constitution Bill, Influx Control, the removals vigil, squatting, the Rikhoto court judgement, black housing, group areas, family life and removals, Namibia, and the Koornhof Bills.

Interviews given by the National President

Sheena gave interviews on a number of topics, including many of those mentioned above, to visitors from Germany, the Natal Witness, Capital Radio, Radio 702, the National Women's Register, various individuals, SABC TV, an MP from the UK, UPITN, the NBC, Finnish Broadcasting, the Financial Times, Reuters, the BBC, Fuji telecasting, USALEP, and the New York Tribune, in addition to countless telephone calls and statements made to the local press.

Visitors to the office

Visitors to the office come from as far afield as Munich, Belgium, Denmark, Holland, Germany, Canada, the United States, Israel, Austria, Sweden, Australia, Japan and Britain. There were representatives from the Australian South African Association, the Austrian Embassy, the Swedish Embassy, the Ford Foundation, the United Nations Model Conference, Rhode Island University, the US Consulate, the British Consulate, the Carnegie Corporation, the Austrian Department of Foreign Affairs, the Department of the Director of South African Affairs in Washington, Oxfam, the French Embassy and the Canadian Embassy.

Local visitors included representatives of Africa Today, NUSAS, the University of Cape Town, City Press, the Urban Foundation, the Huhudi Civic Association and the University of the Witwatersrand.

A minimum of 300 visitors have been to the office during the current year, and our national president is probably even better known internationally than she is nationally. In addition to everything else she accomplishes, she does this marvellous public relations job.

Sheena has attended meetings with the SACC, the Legal Resources Centre on Rikhoto and their poverty survey paper, Jeremy Keenan and students on rural research, the SACC relocations committee, the CPSA commission on rural ministry, the diocese of Johannesburg Labour ad hoc committee on the UIF submissions, the Catholic Bishops on their document on removals, Karel Tipp on farm workers, the Anglican Church, the IRR, HAP, the Northern Transvaal Council of Churches in Pietersburg and the Midlands Council of Churches in Pietermaritzburg on removals, the Catholic Church on removals, the Catholic Bishops Conference and IFOR support group.

Visits by the National President

During the year she has visited Queenstown, East London, Port Elizabeth, Grahamstown, Pietersburg, the OFS, Transkei, Durban, Pietermaritzburg, Cape Town, Khayelitsha, Tzaneen, Louis Trichardt, Dennilton, the Western Transvaal, Pretoria and the Reef.

She always reported back on what she had seen, particularly on her visits to rural areas. Of Transkei she said, 'I came home with an overwhelming conviction that nothing can be done beyond ambulance work to rescue homeland people until there is a new political dispensation. Their condition is disastrous.'

It is indeed difficult to credit that all this has been accomplished by one single human being, but it has, and much more besides, and we lesser mortals can only gasp in wonderment and be deeply grateful that Sheena is ours. Sheena, in addition to the magnificent job she has done, has also carried the onerous job of director of the Johannesburg advice office.

Sheena leads with sureness, ability, confidence and charm. We admire and respect her enormously, and we all love her. We hope she knows the depth of our admiration, regard and caring for her.

Sheena inhabited her talent for leadership with apparent ease — at ease with her own power, her faith, her love of others and her own fears. Men too were deeply moved by her presence.

Sheena was recognised for what she was, a leader in her own right, says Frank Chikane. *You wouldn't think of her as a woman — even when she was with men, you would think of her as a leader among leaders. She belonged there.*

Until the last days, remembers Patrick Banda, who stayed with the Duncans for more than a year in hiding from the security police, *she was propagating non-racism and equality across the races, across the sexes, across the religious segmentations. When I look back and think what she taught us, people like myself and many others, I see that she was a true global citizen. She saw the true rainbow nation that Nelson Mandela was talking about, but in practice, not just in terms of words. She would assist people, not only those who stayed in her home; she would campaign for the hopes and aspirations of underprivileged people, even outside her community. For me that will always be an example of what it means to be a true democrat, a true South African who dearly cared about their country.*

Sheena was very much against corruption. The scourge of corruption that is bedevilling our country right now is something that all of us say we are against, but most of us are not brave enough to express our true views on it. Sheena was not shy to express her views. Maybe that's why she wasn't made an ambassador or anything like that. She wanted everybody to live ethically in all sectors of society. She would share this with me: 'Here now Patrick, you are a businessman, do your business in an ethical manner. If you win you win, if you lose you lose. But remember if you get corrupt you are not only enriching your pocket, you are actually stealing from the poor. You are actually defeating the very same cause that all of us fought for.' So I think that helped me in business. Even now. At times business gets very bad: you get approached by politicians who say, 'You know what, we can change things around if you do this or that.'

Sheena would say, 'I would rather starve than steal from the poor.' I will always remember she stood for those values. Not only will I remember her for standing firm, but also for teaching some of us who were younger to follow suit, to espouse these values and to pass them on to our children and our children's children. I think that we need many Sheenas in the current South Africa.

Sheena would listen to any debate, any point of view, openly and calmly, remembers Jonathan Walton. *I admired that so much. Civil society in this day and age lacks her kind of leadership. If there was an issue or a grumble, Sheena would not make that a personal thing. She would open it up for the whole organisational 'family' to participate in finding a solution. She was never offended if you disagreed with her; she would just encourage you to share your view more fully and then respond to that. She would acknowledge if you put a good argument on the table. With Sheena it was not ever, 'a decision is a decision'; it was not only about her ideas, she considered what she could learn from other ideas. Sheena taught those of us working in the advice offices and on advocacy issues to remember that we were serving, not ourselves, but 'the people out there'. Sheena was principled and articulate — and without contradiction.*

I would associate Sheena with a light in a dark tunnel, says Wellington Ntamo. *It was a good feeling, a sigh of relief, that there were white people who were prepared to work with us, to risk standing up even if they got teargassed or imprisoned. It highlighted the bad of the system — to us, and also to other white people. So, for those who didn't want to see because of propaganda or whatever, Sheena was* inhlansi yokukanya *— a spark of light. With her, suddenly you are able to see in the dark — oh, there is something, there is a road. There is a spark of* ubulungisa, *of justice. A spark might ignite others, help others see — even those who are staring at a wall of darkness. It gives hope.*

However leadership is defined, in essence this is what leaders do best — they nurture hope.

CHAPTER 4

The Heart of the Matter

As you have brought them together by your providence, sanctify them by your Spirit, giving them a new frame of heart fit for their new estate, and enrich them with all grace, whereby they may enjoy the comforts, endure the trials, and perform the duties of life together as your children under your heavenly guidance and protection; through Jesus Christ our Lord. Amen.

REVEREND R.H.R LIDDLE: 19 March 1955 — From the invocation, traditional Presbyterian marriage service

The great organ of St George's Presbyterian Church, Noord Street, Johannesburg soared with Felix Mendelssohn's wedding march as the young couple turned to smile at family and friends. Twenty-two years old, her feet tightly wrapped in her great-grandmother Maggie's beaded and sequined pointy-toed cream satin shoes, Sheena Sinclair was now, and forever after, to be Sheena Duncan.

Her groom, Neil Forsyth Duncan, was born in Johannesburg on 21 March 1926, the only child of John Collie Duncan and Marion Laing. John Collie started his working life as a railway clerk, first in Aberdeen, Scotland and then, after he came to South Africa in 1905, for the South African Railways and Harbours. After World War I, in which John Collie served in the artillery, he returned to South Africa and met Neil's mother Marion while staying in a boarding house in Kensington. Marion's parents had moved to South Africa from Aberdeen at the turn of the century. Elegant, cultured and impeccably groomed, Marion taught Latin at St John's College in Houghton for most of her working career, was an excellent bridge player and was known to be an astute investor on the stock exchange. Although it is not known if he had formal training in accountancy, John Collie ended up as head of the Control and Auditor General's department in Johannesburg, handling the railways audit. Marion and John Collie were both keen golfers, which may have been one of the reasons they chose to build their home on Westcliff Drive,[1] where Neil was born — literally around the corner from Valley Road, where Sheena's family decided to settle.

Neil did not disappoint his parents' high expectations. He attended the prestigious school where his mother taught and proved to be an exceptionally bright student, skipping a year and then graduating as an architect from the University of the Witwatersrand at twenty-one. His father died the following year and Neil went

[1] Relatively nearby were Parkview, Houghton and Killarney golf clubs.

on to do postgraduate studies in London, living there from 1948 to 1951 — some of the time with his mother.

In later life Marion — who lived for thirty-two years as a widow, many more years than she had been married — became somewhat of a trial in Sheena and Neil's lives, although Sheena was more patient and gentle with her than Neil was. It is said that at first Marion did not fully support her son's choice of a wife and perhaps this accounted for some of the difficulties Neil experienced in his relationship with his mother. But Marion came to love and respect Sheena enormously, and she adored her two granddaughters. She came to lunch regularly with the Duncans on Sundays.

Neil was urbane, charming, witty, inclined towards the 'bohemian' but with an ingrained allegiance to duty guiding his life. A snappy dresser, he had an excellent eye for design and colour — not only in his clothes, but evidenced in every aspect of his life. Neil was also a perfectionist. According to his daughters, *Everything had to be 'just so'. One slightly negative side effect of this was that our school drawings were never pinned up — not even in our rooms or on the fridge — nor were we allowed to wrap Christmas presents in anything other than the aesthetically designed paper he had chosen for that year.*

Neil loved shopping, especially for food and clothes. He often brought home exotic food items — his most unusual 'foodie' buy was apparently a can of tinned bees — and, in the clothing line, he once came home with a pair of bright red pants that his family considered outrageous. Neil was the kind of shopper who might be drawn to a fancy new shirt on one day and then on his next excursion set out to find the required trousers to match. His daughters recall that *once when they were burgled, all of Dad's clothes were taken — except his rather skimpy underpants — but nothing of Mum's was touched. Mum once made him a kaftan that he wasn't shy about wearing out to friends' houses for dinner, and he had a couple of Moroccan outfits too after Carey married Abdou. When they went on holiday to the UK or Europe, Dad always had the enormous suitcase with an item of clothing for every possible occasion, including matching headwear (to protect his bald patch from the sun — if it shone), whereas Mum had a carry-on size suitcase.*

In terms of appearance Neil and Sheena stood in vivid contrast to each other. Sheena was taller and considerably larger than Neil. He was quite vain about his general looks and his hair, which he would insist on having blow-dried when he had a haircut, even though there wasn't much of it as he matured. Sheena, on the other hand, seemed not to care much at all about how she looked. Neil would have to nag her to buy new clothes, not to be fashionable but because she wore her clothes to a thread, often with holes — although these were sometimes from dropped cigarette ash, not age.

Despite — or maybe because of — their differences, Sheena and Neil turned out to be a remarkably well-matched couple, with friends and family all attesting to an extraordinary, loving and supportive partnership. It had not, however, been a predictable relationship. Although they had seen each other in passing during various stages of their neighbourly youth, Sheena and Neil first met formally, although briefly, while they were both studying in the UK — Neil in London as a post-graduate student, and Sheena newly enrolled at Edinburgh. At the time, Neil was living with his mother in her mews flat and Jean and Sheena were en route to Scotland. Marion and Jean were acquainted through bridge and other social activities in Johannesburg, and Marion had invited Jean and Sheena to tea at her flat. Sheena remembered: 'I was wearing a green tweed suit that my mother had made — I'm sure made beautifully, but I hated it — and a pink blouse and a pale pink hat which was sort of furry felt which "framed my face" my mother told me. Neil was there and told me long after that he had said to his mother when we left, *What a singularly unattractive girl that is!*'

Jean, however, was wily. She had her eye on Neil, who returned to Johannesburg after completing his studies and joined the firm of architects that was to grow into Nurcombe, Summerley, Ringrose and Todd. Jean knew exactly when Sheena would be back for her summer vacation and 'she just had Neil redo the kitchen in Valley Road at the same time — so that she could introduce me to him again. She had decided he would be a suitable person and, after that, invited him to every party they had for me.' Some years later, Neil told Sheena that he had looked across the room and said to himself, *That's the girl I'm going to marry.* For indeed, rather like Mr Darcy in *Pride and Prejudice*, Sheena's favourite Jane Austen novel, *no sooner had he made it clear to himself and his friends that she hardly had a good feature in her face, than he began to find it was rendered uncommonly intelligent by the beautiful expression in her eyes.*

Sheena with Robert and Jean on her wedding day

It turned out Jean was right: even her headstrong daughter could not resist how 'suitable' Neil was. 'I fell in love with him. We got engaged in August. I didn't go back to finish my studies, I stayed. In those days — you got engaged and you started planning your wedding. You didn't get engaged and then shack up and get into a partnership for years and years and years. We probably chose that date for our wedding because the danger of summer storms would be over and it was also Neil's birthday two days later.'

After the wedding Sheena wrote to her parents, quite simply: 'I am terribly happy. I really am on top of the world and thank goodness you brought me home in July.' Neil, immensely proud to be Sheena's groom, had no wish to take control of her destiny but he was indeed to become and remain an intrinsic part of all its dimensions.

Soon after returning to Johannesburg after their honeymoon, the newlyweds moved into a flat in Bellevue, where they lived until early in 1956, when Neil's firm made him a junior partner and sent him to Zimbabwe to open an office in Harare.[2]

Sheena and Neil at their wedding reception

Sheena gave up her job as home economist with the Johannesburg Department of Welfare and they soon settled happily in Zimbabwe, although as Sheena put it, 'Those first months in Harare I'll never forget — we stayed in this little boarding house with a double bed mattress that sagged. Before we found a flat, we used to sit on the bed playing patience or one of those card games that you only need two people to play.'

Sheena and Neil established a warm circle of friends in Zimbabwe, mostly young couples like themselves. As was the convention, the men were professionally active and the women were bearing and raising small children, perhaps working during intervals between children. The closest of their friends were Liz and Dave Hagen and Rozel and Patrick Lawlor — Rozel and Liz to become Sheena's lifelong friends. Patrick provides an informative context for the hopes of these young friends: *In South Africa, the United Party (UP) of General Smuts had been replaced in 1948 by the National Party (NP) of D.F. Malan; the UP believed that the whites should behave decently towards the 'natives', while the NP was determined to secure white Afrikaner supremacy and to make sure that the 'natives' were kept in — or sent to — their 'proper' places. The NP was determined to control the economy, which was mostly in the hands of the English-speaking community of Johannesburg. Nobody was thinking about doing anything substantial for the Africans.*

[2] Known at the time as Southern Rhodesia and Salisbury respectively.

So, although Johannesburg was much the same for the whites as it had always been, there were big changes being made to the whole political spectrum. There were now two official languages, with Afrikaans being promoted; only white Afrikaners could expect to join the lower levels of the civil service or police; and of course the whole awful apparatus of apartheid was being geared up.

Onto this scene floated a hot air balloon with Southern Rhodesia painted on its basket. Southern Rhodesia and its capital Salisbury were the centre of the newly established Central African Federation (CAF) and were expanding at a furious rate. Rhodesia was a British colony with a British past. The language was English, and the English heritage ran through everything — schools ran on English lines and had their public exams set in London, the social structure was English as were the armed forces and the civil service. Of course the main difference was in the race relations in the two countries. Rhodesia had good relations between the Africans and the whites. Not only was there no policy of apartheid, but active steps were being taken to do away with the segregation which existed.

In the early fifties it was attractive for liberals like me (at the start of my career) and Neil (already in practice) to climb into the Southern Rhodesia balloon's basket (with Sheena and Rozel of course) and fly away.

Sheena was a great admirer of Garfield Todd, a New Zealander who was the moving spirit behind the multicultural, liberal movement that we found so attractive. Sir Edgar Whitehead was a thoroughly decent and sensible prime minister, who continued down the path laid out by Garfield Todd; but as is so often shown elsewhere, the liberal wing was supported by academics, many lawyers, doctors, engineers, architects and intellectuals; it was not popular with the majority of white voters, many of whom were influential farmers with right wing tendencies.

Sheena with her firstborn John in Harare

Sheena and Neil were all too soon going to need all the support these friends could offer.

Less than three years after their arrival in Harare, as they sat in a small parish church on a Sunday morning that was certainly not the normal Sunday morning it was for everyone else, Sheena could not believe that the minister, their friend David Jenkins, was saying those

The Sinclair family celebrates John's arrival with Neil and Sheena: Left to right sitting: Neil, Ken, Jean, Sheena with baby John, Liz, Robert. Standing: Andrew and Rob

words about *their* son: *John Robert Forsyth Duncan, born in Salisbury, Rhodesia on 20 January 1957, died in Salisbury on 14 August 1958.* She had heard these same words, and more, at the funeral the previous day, before the little box slid quietly through the curtains. She and Neil had been going home to an empty flat for three nights. Still she did not believe the words.

Why had this happened? What if they or the doctors had seen in time how serious it was and managed to hydrate the toddler, put him on a drip immediately? What if they had not gone back to South Africa for their holiday? What if the rare and virulent virus had not struck their little son?

Even as these thoughts raged through her head, she held on to Neil's hand, as she had the whole day before. Even when David invited her — invited her personally because she was not an Anglican at that time — to come forward to celebrate the Eucharist, she held on to Neil's hand, all the way up the aisle and all the way back.

Neil described John's funeral in a letter to his mother in the following way: *I'll tell you about the funeral first. We wanted him to be cremated and the ceremony was both comforting and harrowing. The crematorium is about five miles out of town — a quiet and peaceful oasis set in the grove of Msasa trees. With a large and simple garden, not quite fully developed yet, but it will be lovely and one could hear the birds singing in the trees. The drive out there was mostly through open country and soothing and peaceful. I know you would want to know this, as you must have had visions of the grimy smoke laden atmosphere of the one in Johannesburg. The building itself was modern but quietly dignified and the little coffin was already on the platform draped in a blue velvet cloth with three wreaths on top, from both sets of grandparents and from us. From you we chose a simple wreath of snowdrops and violets, which we felt both he and you would have liked. David Jenkins gave a very beautiful and moving service and the music was very good — recorded, but of a very good choir instead of the ragged hit and miss singing of an ordinary congregation.*

We both broke down completely as the bier slowly disappeared from view.

In the car, going home to the flat that was so quiet now, still holding Neil's hand, she looked at him and he at her. Suddenly, for no apparent reason, Sheena realised that her heart had warmed up.

'It's a funny feeling when the Holy Spirit grabs hold of you and it lasts forever,' she said years later. 'It's not fleeting — but just that feeling of being grabbed. When I was at school it was more a question of custom and example. School wasn't a sharp sudden event as it was on that day after John died — there was no doubt on that day. I wouldn't have called the Holy Spirit a who or a he. It was a flood of strength, which kept me going through the weeks that followed.'

It also offered a moment of choices. Sheena was still a Presbyterian, raised in a staunchly Presbyterian tradition. The Anglican Reverend David Jenkins responded to Sheena's grief with insight and compassion. David's wife Elizabeth, who at the time had only recently met Sheena, vividly remembers that Sunday at St Luke's Church in Salisbury: *David called her up. He gave her communion, and he blessed them both, Neil and Sheena, together. In those days it wasn't done. Sheena, as a Presbyterian, couldn't go to communion; she had not been confirmed. I'll never forget the moment David did that, ever. Quite utterly beautiful for me when he passed the cup to her and gave her the bread.*

Years later, in conversation with Charles Villa-Vicencio, Sheena reflected on that moment and on the change. She told him how as a student in Edinburgh, 'I used to lie in bed on winter mornings listening to the church bells ringing, thinking I would not attend church that morning, and then invariably rush out into the snow to get to church on time. I have always had what you might call a religious conscience. Holding to the moral values which were taught to me in the church and in my childhood home, the practice of religion was however a rather burdensome thing. There was no real integration between what I intellectually knew Christianity to be and my religious practice, neither in terms of my devotional life and worship on the one hand nor my actual moral engagement in life on the other.'[3]

That Anglican communion after John's death moved the young woman to a new dimension of gratitude and spirituality: 'A strange thing happened, a kind of

[3] Villa-Vicencio, Charles: *The Spirit of Freedom*, chapter 'Sheena Duncan: Surprised by Joy'.

moment of recollection, and my life seemed to come together. I realised that I could no longer sit around as a spectator, taking no more than an academic interest in politics and in what was going on in society around me. My life was about to begin and there was much to be learned.'

Committing herself fully to Anglican practice of faith seemed the right thing to do, and Sheena was confirmed about three and a half months later. She was pregnant again at the time, but miscarried shortly thereafter. 'I was in that wonderful nursing home run by nuns. I can remember one of those nuns saying, *Do you want communion*? and I said, "I've only just been confirmed and I haven't had my first communion." So it was that I had my "first communion" in my hospital bed.'

I don't know why Sheena converted from Presbyterian to Anglican, reflects Denise Ackermann. *Anglicanism is a strange hybrid, standing between the reformed and the Catholic world, born out of a king wanting to marry someone he shouldn't have married. The reformed branch of Christianity, of which Presbyterianism is one in the Calvinist line with pretty solid theology and some good leaders, has far less need for ritual.*

Presbyterians have a great sense of justice. Calvin talks about freedom of conscience; you don't have to accept the rules imposed on you if you feel they are unjust. Sheena's mother Jean was part of that particular Scots stream of Presbyterians who were good Calvinists — not neo-Calvinists like the Afrikaners who embrace what is in many respects a parody of Calvinism.

The Anglicans retain from the Catholic history the need for liturgy. The Book of Common Prayer *is at the centre of being an Anglican. It's what we use when we go to church and it has all the prayers in it. It is a work of genius and, interestingly, the person who wrote it spent a year with Calvin — who helped him to write it.*

There's a feeling among Anglicans that your common sense is really what guides you in your understanding and, as I know Sheena, that would have appealed greatly to her, as would the ritual. I'm speculating here — but if you lose a child there is a great comfort in the funeral rites that are offered by a church like the Anglican; they are quite beautiful.

Perhaps it was the comfort of words; perhaps it was her enormous respect and regard for her headmistress at Roedean school, Ella le Maitre, or the influence on her young mind of people like Trevor Huddleston who Ella invited to share experiences and views with the Roedean girls; perhaps it was that Neil was an Anglican; perhaps it was just the kindness and compassion of their friend David; perhaps it was a combination of all these and many other factors but, as David puts it, *Sheena became one of the most famous Anglicans in the whole Church of the Province of South Africa and I feel very honoured that I was in some way instrumental in bringing her into the Anglican Church.*

It is likely that for Sheena, no explanations were necessary. It was enough to have come home:

Oh God, my heart is ready, my heart is ready:
I will sing and give praise with the best member that I have.[4]

In the months that followed, with Neil back at work for most of the long days, Sheena did what she had done all her life when her inner self needed to be alone: she gardened, she read and read and read, and she prayed. She was intent on conceiving again and so it was to be. Lindsay was born two years after the death of the little brother that she and her sister were never to meet, on 8 September 1960, and Carey Jane three years later on 17 July 1963.

'After Lindsay was born without any problems, I had two more miscarriages and then Carey. I had a Shirodkar suture for Carey — they sew the baby into you, putting stitches in part of the womb. I had another miscarriage after her — Shirodkar suture or not, I miscarried. Nowadays of course, they would know it was smoking. Smoking is one of the first things you have to stop if you get pregnant now. I didn't smoke so much then, but I smoked.'

Sheena kept two photographs of her toddler son in her walk-in cupboard in her bedroom for the rest of her life, but she rarely spoke of him or of the impact of his death, other than to say to her brother Rob once that she felt she could communicate with John through prayer. It seems that Neil was more easily able to share his pain with others. Sheena's friend Liz Hagen observed the difference and that it sometimes generated — although extremely rarely — sparks of conflict between Sheena and Neil in years to come. *Sheena was brought up in a very stoic tradition. She hardly ever talked about her feelings, except for her rage at the architects of apartheid. She never complained about physical ailments either and would go to great lengths to 'carry on'. I do remember one evening when she lost her temper with Neil and accused him of losing his self-control over John's death. I never dared*

Sheena, baby Carey, Neil, Lindsay

[4] The Church of England: *The Book of Common Prayer (1928 revised form)*, Psalm 108 Paratum cor meum. 1.

try to draw her out about the loss of John. In our clumsy way, we all tried to stay in touch and continue our normal activities, but Sheena was not available for confidences; we young (white) South African women were not very open with each other.

By 1962 the liberal government of Whitehead had been replaced by a much more right wing government led by Winston Field, which slowed down movement in the direction of multiculturalism. *The golden dream we all shared when we went to Rhodesia was ending,* says Patrick. *The economic bubble burst and Neil was recalled by his firm; the Salisbury office closed.*

When the Duncans were due to leave Zimbabwe, Sheena's initial desire was to live anywhere that was not in Africa. Ultimately, however, she and Neil accepted that, despite the dreadful things that were happening to people under apartheid, they were too rooted in Africa to leave — and anyway, Neil said he could not bear the thought of all that cold and constant drizzle if they went to the UK, which was the likely alternative, given their family roots.

They returned to Johannesburg and so began Sheena's extraordinarily significant life in her turbulent home country, in the city of her birth, with her beloved Neil as lover, friend, confidante, provider, co-parent, fellow traveller, and intellectual and political sparring partner. From the start, although he did not always agree with her views, Neil was also her unconditional champion — and he was called to be just that soon after they arrived back and she got involved with the Black Sash. *Do you think Sheena should be doing this sort of thing?* asked some of the senior partners, *it could be bad for the firm's image* — to which Neil simply replied, *What Sheena does is none of the firm's business.*

The firm took note and Neil flourished in his career as an architect. Despite the politics, Johannesburg was in a period of great expansion, including the construction of the Carlton Centre in the middle of town and the development of Hillbrow and Rosebank. Neil was involved in some of the bold new commercial building initiatives, including the Johannesburg Stock Exchange. He did a lot of work for several leading schools, including Roedean, St Mary's, St Andrew's and St Peter's, as well as designing homes and home extensions or alterations for their many friends. In a more personal expression of his artistic talents, Neil designed the new family home and garden in Parkhurst, creating a haven of security and comfort for Sheena for the rest of her life. The plot they had bought was an acre and a quarter of long grass which, when set alight and burned to a cinder by some naughty local children, revealed itself as a rubbish dump on a dirty little dribble of a choked-up stream. It was all the Duncans could afford because the only way they had been able to sell their home in Harare was through Deed of Sale, which yielded almost no capital. According to Sheena another reason for buying in Parkhurst was that 'it was one of

The garden in Parkhurst

the very few suburbs in Johannesburg that allowed tin roofs. I've never regretted that decision. It's so lovely when it rains.'

They did not even have enough money to have the heaps of old cars and other scrap removed, so Neil skilfully alchemised all of this debris into a retaining wall just off the stoep. Once the basic structure was up, they did the rest themselves — Neil after work, and Sheena, as her work. With small girls trailing behind her, Sheena painted walls, cleared the stream and planted shrubs and trees to Neil's design. The garden grew into a nourishing paradise for the whole family, and for many friends, colleagues, burned-out activists, international visitors and local homeless people.

Neil working on an ostrich egg

Many of Neil's own sculptures graced the garden and he found further aesthetic expression taking care of the interior decoration. Neil had a superb eye for design, and it is hardly possible to separate his architectural skill and training from the things he loved to do, because everything he did was so integral to his taste. There was evidence of this everywhere, inside and out — numerous sculptures, carpets, furniture, curtains, cushions, tablecloths, crockery, glasses and almost everything else. Neil made interesting pieces of furniture — a dining room table made from brass curtain rods stuffed with broomsticks to make them strong enough to hold the wooden top; a desk for Sheena trimmed in kiaat with multi-coloured drawers — and he also collected interesting furniture including modern and antique pieces. His famed and exquisitely painted ostrich, duck and chicken eggs are to this day highly valued by those who received them as gifts — or bought them at the Black Sash morning market or at the annual fete of the Progressive Party[5] which was his chosen political home. He blew the eggs himself and mounted them on glass stems.

Sheena appreciated his designs and choices and was supremely happy in their home. Perhaps it was just as well that she either didn't have any fixed design ideas of her own or, if she did, surrendered them and turned her attention elsewhere.

Not surprisingly, Sheena and Neil may have been overprotective parents. They certainly adored their two girls and their unconditional love flourished over the years, developing into extraordinary, enduring, affectionate and respectful adult friendships.

Sharing thoughts and memories on behalf of both sisters at Sheena's memorial service at Regina Mundi in Soweto many, many years later, Carey acknowledged the constant refrain from others, *she was like a mother to me*, and told the assembled mourners what it felt like to them to *really* have Sheena as a mother.

She loved us totally and unconditionally, no matter what we were doing, what marks we got at school or what we looked like. This could be rather irritating when we got to the stage of teenage parties and had spent the whole afternoon trying on and discarding outfits to ensure we looked our best. Mum's opinion on all of them was, 'You look beautiful, darling.'

Mum was patient and good tempered with us. She never smacked us (as she didn't believe in physical punishment), but explained why we shouldn't be doing something and that was generally enough to get us to stop.

Until we were old enough to stay at school in the afternoons, we had to have a rest after lunch every day, ostensibly to prevent us from getting overtired and bad tempered. We now suspect that this was because Mum wanted to have some time to read her own book! She was an avid reader and tried to foster a love of reading in us. We remember many happy annual family holidays in the Kruger Park, where we actually spent most

[5] It became the Progressive Federal Party, then the Democratic Party and then the Democratic Alliance.

of the time, apart from a two-hour game drive morning and evening, reading and resting. We used to take our full complement of library books away with us, and a ritual holiday treat was to go to the Children's Bookshop in Rosebank, where we could buy three paperbacks each for 30c apiece!

Sometimes Mum used to read us a story on the divan in our family room after lunch. C.S. Lewis's The Lion, the Witch and the Wardrobe *was one of her favourites. On one occasion, there was suddenly a commotion, and our 'illegal' Zimbabwean gardener came rushing into the room and ran to the door that led to the stoep and garden. He was pressed up against the door, trying to unlock it. He had a look of sheer terror on his face. Hot on his heels came two policemen, in full uniform, which was scary for us. Without a moment's hesitation, Mum turned to them and said, 'What on earth are you doing in my house?' They gestured towards Amos. She continued, 'If you want to visit please go outside and ring the front doorbell like everybody else.' They retreated meekly, by which time Amos had disappeared up the garden and into the adjoining veld.*

Mum loved cooking and was an excellent cook, conjuring up the most delicious and inventive meals even when there appeared to be 'nothing in the fridge'. Our parents' home was open and they enjoyed casual entertaining, happy to invite people for an impromptu lunch or supper (often after a meeting). And here I must emphasise my father's role, because without his love, generosity and support, Mum would not have been able to accomplish all that she did. Dad never complained when the house was full of people or when Mum was travelling all over the country and even overseas. He was sneakingly proud of her and happy to look after us. (He was also a dab hand in the kitchen.)

In our early schooldays Mum was always at home when we got back from school, even if she was doing some work at her desk. However, whenever school holidays came around, she couldn't stop her work in the advice office, so we had no choice but to be dragged in on the bus to the advice office. Now that Mum has gone, we can actually admit that we quite enjoyed bashing around on the manual typewriters, making tea for the advice seekers in the waiting room and turning the handle on the Gestetner machine.

To us as children, our parents were our parents and we thought that everyone lived in a similar way. Both of them used to work in the evenings, after a family supper, so we thought this was normal too. As Mum became more involved in the various organisations she worked with, she stayed up until midnight most nights, analysing laws and advice office statistics, writing booklets and speeches, preparing for the next day's work.

When we grew up and moved away from South Africa, both our parents were totally supportive and there were never any recriminations: 'If only you lived closer ... if only we saw you more often,' etc. They focused on the positive side: 'We're looking forward

Neil and Sheena on the stoep

to seeing you ...; thank you for coming for Christmas,' etc. They were interested in what we were doing, but never interfered.

In sum, as a result of both our parents, we had a secure, stable and loving childhood, and we enjoyed their support and love to the end.

Sheena loved, respected and appreciated Neil, not only for the person he was and for the privilege he afforded her, but with full awareness of the dimensions of his support and the power it enabled her to claim and then exercise. She appreciated how his support was such an integral part of what allowed her to shine. It was not only Neil's professional success and hard work, but also his willingness to share in responsibilities not typically popular with men, that made it possible for Sheena to devote herself to an incredible range of voluntary and unpaid human rights activism for more than forty years. She appreciated the enormity of this privilege. But it did mean that once she gave up work when her children were born, she had absolutely no financial independence for most of the rest of her married life — until Neil gave her a lump sum

Carey, Sheena, Lindsay and Neil at Sabi Sabi

to invest when his mother died and she inherited a further sum when her own mother died. Sheena knew what it meant to come out on the R60 weekly allowance Neil gave her for groceries when they first moved back to Johannesburg and to have to ask for money to buy petrol, and she was delighted to be able treat Neil to some special holidays once she could.

Their daughters were impressed with their father's dedication. *Dad was always very supportive of Mum's work and what she was doing. Although he sometimes complained about meetings and people always at the house or the phone ringing every time we sat down to dinner, I think he was really proud of Mum and secretly enjoyed having people around. He enjoyed a good grumble and could sound like a 'glass half-empty' sort of person, but his actions were always the opposite.*

As well as being her 'financial backer' and taking on many of the responsibilities of the home once Lindsay and Carey were more than toddlers, Neil was also the unfailing backup parent when Sheena had to go on extended trips, either nationally or internationally, or became unavoidably overextended. He also supported her work in person, whenever this was practical. Many Black Sashers, for example, will remember Neil, as well as other husbands of course, as barmen at Black Sash events in Johannesburg. Sometimes they would don black sashes and boater hats; always, they would charm the members. *We were fascinated by Sheena's relationship with Neil,* recalls Ashnie Padarath, in all likelihood reflecting on the views of most of the younger Sash members. *Neil was a real 'ladies' man.' He would come to our functions and Sheena would pretend she'd never seen him before in her life — she really would act as if she had no idea who he was — and he would just spend his time filling up our glasses with wine and telling us these stories about how he and Sheena met. We spent the rest of the time we had with Sheena trying to extract the stories out of her and she would never ever confirm or deny the things he told us, she would just laugh — heartily.*

Over the many years of Sheena's human rights activism, Neil welcomed hundreds — if not thousands — of Sheena's fellow activists into what others might have considered a private space. The outside stoep of their home, with its view of sweeping lawns, trees and stream, became a famed site for easing tensions, forging resistance strategies and generally providing a convivial and creative space for thinking as well as for laughing, drinking, smoking and replenishing hope. Sheena herself delighted in this 'wonderful stoep. If I ever had to move — which I have no intention of doing and I don't want to — but if I am unable to stay, the thing I would miss most would be to be out on the stoep.'

Neil and Sheena's entertaining and generosity were legendary. *One forgets that, added to her human rights work, her amazing insight, her capacity for analysis and her eloquence, Sheena was also a gracious hostess,* says Kathy Satchwell. *I immediately felt at ease in her home, which had a lot to do with Sheena and Neil and their relationship.*

Theirs was quite a liberated family and, at first, I was surprised by Neil. He did a lot of the cooking and saw to a lot of the girls' school stuff. He was obviously not threatened by Sheena's high profile. They just got on with what they liked.

Their guests included local and international luminaries, diplomats, archbishops and various church people, people from other religions (except those with principled positions about alcohol, of which there was always an abundance and variety in the Duncan home), work colleagues, old school friends, human rights lawyers, politicians, neighbours, friends of their children who had become their friends, visiting siblings and cousins, ageing relatives such as their widowed mothers Jean and Marion and Sheena's Aunt Margaret, visiting foreign interns, itinerant house guests, homeless young activists or those hiding from the security police. The house and garden were also a great attraction for the larger social events of various organisations such as the annual party of the Citizens Advice Bureau, to which the mayor was invited and which caused the mayoral chauffeur consternation as he tried to negotiate the deep dip in the drive without ripping off the car's exhaust pipe; the St George's church annual sidesmen's party; Rotary events; and a range of workshops, discussions or staff celebrations organised by the many civil society groups with which Sheena (and Neil) worked. Except when an unexpected drop-in was included, the table guests were combined with as much care and attention as the ingredients and courses of a 'cordon bleu' meal.

Sheena's extraordinary intelligence, understanding and knowledge of what was going on in the country and her opinions about national and world events riveted the attention of their guests, sometimes impaling their opinions, sometimes causing feisty arguments, sometimes intimidating those who might not have had a particular interest in such things, sometimes infuriating those who disagreed. Neil, himself not as intensely interested or involved in the matters that interested Sheena, was a consistent if quiet foil to any excess, dispensing charm, excellent wine and liqueurs or second helpings in generous proportions as needed.

Younger people loved and respected Sheena deeply — perhaps more as a mother than a friend, but one who treated them fully as equals. Patrick Banda remembers that *while I was staying with them Sheena was strict in terms of discipline. I was the one who stayed the longest, but others would come in and out and Sheena made sure that we understood etiquette and that we behaved in a proper manner. It was important as there were Neil's clients and Sheena's guests and if I had acted in a manner that was unbecoming it would raise alarm. She would say to me, 'Patrick, when you wash be careful; the Security Branch is monitoring electricity and water usage and so on.' I would stay indoors most of the time and we made sure that we did not fill up the bath, so that the water levels did not increase too much and cause suspicion. In terms of culture, coming from the townships, we learned how to liaise with people, how to*

Lindsay, Neil, Carey, Abdou, Sheena and Jeremy at Carey and Abdou's garden wedding

fit in with people. Most of all, I found Sheena personified many of the ideals all of us in the struggle were fighting for, in terms of non-racialism, non-sexism — in terms of non-segregating even on a religious basis. I knew Sheena to be a Christian, but I met in her home Muslims, Hindus, Jews, Pentecostals, Catholics and Anglicans and she would treat everyone the same — equally. I met her when I was a child of twenty-five and now I'm fifty-two. Even in my adulthood I would go back to Sheena's home and she treated me like one of the family and I treated her like a mother and a friend.

Lindsay and Carey's husbands, Jeremy and Abdou, basked in Neil and Sheena's warmth and loved them dearly. Abdou notes their uniquely respectful and complementary relationship with each other: *One could almost feel some kind of complicity in their behaviour* — subtly excluding of others perhaps — *but always fun to be with and Sheena made me feel at home. She welcomed me, a 'coloured' arab and muslim stranger, to stay in her place and later on to marry her daughter.*

Both Neil and Sheena had an enormously positive effect on me personally and welcomed me as a son, says Jeremy. *Sheena totally confounded the stereotypical portrayal of 'the mother-in-law'. It would have been impossible not to be enormously proud and honoured to have known and been loved by her. If there is one person in my life that I would not want to disappoint it would be Sheena. Yet strangely, I never felt the need to gain her approval or recognition or be praised by her. Sheena took me as I am, without judgement.*

Reflecting on the social life of their parents, Lindsay and Carey concede that despite the warmth and hospitality that surrounded them, *it can't always have been easy, as some white people definitely didn't approve of Mum or what she was doing. So if they were invited out to dinner it could be tricky, as Mum was not able to keep quiet if she disagreed with what people were saying. With time and lots of practice, she got to think it wasn't worth getting into an argument, especially if she wasn't going to be able to change someone's mind. But sometimes I think they weren't invited in the first place, which wouldn't really have bothered Mum, but Dad liked seeing a variety of people. Ironically, now that the 'bad old days' are over, I think some people have revised what they think they thought and have forgotten their disapproval of Mum!*

Beth Still, Sheena's school friend and contemporary, would agree that Sheena was not always easy to be with, but *Neil was a very dear man, a buffer. He always kept it together, whereas Sheena was absolutely honest and quite acerbic. She didn't suffer fools gladly. She was the most admirable person, but not everybody's cup of tea. She would rub people up, trying to get them conscious of the unfairness that was going on. We had lots of friends who would say, 'That bloody woman — if she's invited, I'm not coming.'*

Alan Maker, the parish minister at St Columba's church — where Robert Sinclair worshipped for many years and to whom Jean became devoted after Robert's death — also found Sheena difficult: *Sheena was forever telling me that I should do more to make changes in the country. I wasn't a bishop or an archbishop and I didn't know what more I could do, but Sheena had that ability to get under your skin. She just went on and on and on. I think what Sheena couldn't understand was that as a parish minister my job was to change you to change the country — my job wasn't to change the country. Sheena had an easy ability to get your temper up. She was in your face. She could get up your nose. If she were a man she would have been a front row forward!*

Neil and Sheena, although they did not always go to church together, shared a similar commitment to nurturing their spirituality in church and through work in the church. For a while, Neil used to worship at St Paul's in Parkhurst with Sheena and this is where their small girls spent early years in Sunday school, but St George's Parktown was where he settled. St George's was the church most closely linked to Roedean and once Lindsay and Carey had moved into the senior school, it became the family church. Over the years, Neil involved himself increasingly in sidesmen's duties, organising all their parties and doing many administrative tasks. Sheena, however, found St George's a bit 'rarefied'. Although she had been a churchgoer since childhood, before her 'conversion' she had not experienced a true integration between her intellectual understanding of Christianity and her practice of it. Her work at the Black Sash advice office expanded this integration; biblical concerns for poor and oppressed people merged with the realities of the people who came there for advice, and she came to understand what it meant to truly and morally engage with life. It is not surprising, then, that Sheena's preferred place of worship was with the more mixed congregation at St Mary's Cathedral in central Johannesburg, even if this meant she went to church alone because Neil did not enjoy the longish journey into the city on a Sunday, let alone what the rest of the family considered an interminable service with too much incense. Once their daughters had left home, however, Neil and Sheena tended to go to St George's together, and even after the diocese made her a lay canon, Sheena only went to the cathedral on 'high days and holy days'.

Other lifestyle preferences Neil and Sheena shared were that they both smoked and drank with huge appetite and loved their garden, working in it or simply being in it — in warm weather often swimming in the trendy black swimming pool that Neil had created, a first in Johannesburg. They also both worked in the evenings — Sheena usually much later into the night than Neil. Day or night, inside the house, Sheena's study — the workroom — was the centre, both in terms of its physical position in the house and the political energy and hospitality that emanated from it.

Providing support in keeping the Parkhurst house and garden reasonably clean and in some sort of order over the years were: a loyal 'maid' Vicky Modikoe, whose grandchildren Dick, Mule and Mamane often stayed with her; Maria Dlamini, who took over when Vicky retired; Alina Dlamini, who took over when her mother Maria died; and Sam Kgalushi, the gardener who worked for Neil and Sheena for thirty-six years. Sam retired the year after Neil died, himself dying shortly afterwards. His son Million sometimes did odd jobs in the garden and helped out at the occasional Black Sash event and Sam's wife Joanna worked around the corner but mostly lived with Sam.

Although it horrified many — not least of all their neighbours — it came as no surprise to anyone who knew Sheena and Neil well that also living on the property, and of no practical assistance to the household, were various partners and relatives of the people who worked for them, as well as several groups of informal squatters in different sheltered spots in the garden.

Sheena's passion for justice was not an intellectual exercise. She recognised every person around her, not only her family, friends and colleagues, for who they were — a fellow human being. *I've never known anyone,* writes their granddaughter Kenza Jane Haouach, *as great as my grandmother, she was attentive, kind, patient, adorable and a little silly — she smoked and drank so much and was too generous with people, she trusted them easily. If I was her I would never have accepted that the gardener, the maid and the painter all lived in my house, but she did and she was happy. I would have loved to be like her but I could never bear to see thousands of persons every day in my house.*

The political activism of her mother certainly played a part in shaping the direction of Sheena's life and work. The loss of her first child and the strength she found in religion also accounted for the path of compassion for others she was to follow. There can be no doubt, however, that without Neil by her side, Sheena would not have been the woman she was.

Saturday, 7 December 2002 marked Sheena's seventieth birthday and enthusiastic celebratory ideas were floated by friends and family — with and without caterers and with choices of venue ranging from home to the Country Club. Sheena's choice was a simple pâté and Pimm's party in their lush midsummer garden and that, more or less, came to pass — another jolly good Duncan party in Parkhurst. 'Thank you for all the recipes,' Sheena wrote to her daughters. 'The problem is that your father has got the bit between his teeth and is planning hot things like bacon rolled around prunes and cocktail sausages. I have tried to tell him that those are not pâtés and that the only extras I was planning were asparagus with horseradish sauce and his marinated mushrooms. Well, he knows what he wants and he will do it, so when you arrive, Lins, expect lots of bad temper in the kitchen as he occupies the whole space and uses every utensil in sight. I warn you now that on my eightieth birthday I am going into retreat in a convent where no parties will be allowed!'

Celebrations were marred by news of her brother Andrew's failing health, and by Sunday night, when all messages from family in the UK indicated that he was dying, Sheena 'lay in bed and just talked to him and willed him to come back.' But Andrew died two days later from a post-operative infection.

Greater sadness lay ahead. Less than a week after Andrew's death, she wrote to Carey, 'Dad got much more lame and exhausted over all the parties. He can barely walk anywhere and has just come back from the shops saying that his shopping days are over. It is wonderful of you to say you will come again next year because I don't think we will be travelling again. Dad has just said to me that he thinks he had better get a walker. I didn't know how to raise the subject with him but now that the suggestion has come from him it will be easy to just go and get one.'

Two weeks on, Neil was again much better and 'has a new stick with four little feet instead of one as well as a walker on three wheels with brakes on the handles and a little basket.' Alina called the walker *Madala's*[6] *pram*. By February, when Sheena took Neil for a routine medication check-up, the doctor said the stiff reactions in his legs had improved, but 'Dad says he does not notice any improvement. It is not me that suffers this affliction, so I am not in a position to comment but he is certainly no worse.'

On 9 March 2003, Neil had a brain haemorrhage. Sheena described the events as follows:

'What happened was that we were at a mild kind of church party on Sunday morning. He was sitting in a chair opposite me and I saw he seemed to be leaning

[6] *Madala* means 'old man' in several African languages.

over to one side. As I asked him why he was leaning so far over, thinking it might perhaps have been bad breath on the part of the person on his left hand, he suddenly went very white and just keeled over. I rushed to hold him but was on the wrong side. Some muscular Christian caught him and managed to lower him gently to the ground. Three nursing sisters were at the party and rushed to help. In no time at all they were all laughing at whatever jokes he was cracking. It was just one of his Transient Ischemic Attacks which he has had on and off for the past ten years. I know about three of them but I think there may have been more that he never told me about. Each is like a minor stroke where instead of a huge burst in the brain there is a whole series of tiny little blood clots.

'Anyway he recovered as if from a faint and once he felt able, I drove him home and he went to sleep as he normally does after these attacks and every afternoon for a zizz. He slept all afternoon and then got up for an hour but complained about a splitting headache. He went back to bed and to sleep but on Monday morning I asked our GP James to come to see him. James found him a bit confused but heart, lungs and blood pressure in good order and his reflexes much better than they were before he was put on medication for the mild Parkinson's he has.

'I spent last night worried out of my mind because he was getting more and more confused. But between spells of agitation he slept soundly. He had in fact slept for about 36 hours, which is not at all normal, so this morning I phoned the GP, who spoke to the neurologist who had treated Neil when he had the first of this kind of attack ten years ago. The result is that Neil is now in the Milpark hospital awaiting a cat-scan and blood tests and whatever else they think is necessary. Last time he had to undergo that ten years ago the electricity failed half way and they had to pull him out and start all over again. Being his old belligerent self at that stage, he insisted that they pay for his parking because he had been there much longer than they had said it would take!

'Your poor old cat, Carey, is distraught. Cleo has been in the habit of coming to sit next to him on the divan as soon as we turn on the TV for the 8 o'clock news. Tonight she just wandered around the house crying for him. I feel a bit like that myself but the acorns are starting to drop off the pin oak and crash on this tin roof which is a comforting noise, better than the rats we have had in the ceiling from time to time.'

Fortunately, Sheena's brother Rob was working in South Africa at the time and, although his place of work was far out in Westonaria, he visited his big sister regularly, often with delicious pizzas, fettucine and other delicacies — including brandy — in hand. Rob was a great source of support and comfort to Sheena as she dealt with her own organisational commitments, all the household and financial management tasks that had been Neil's responsibility, the health challenges he faced, her own emotions — which she kept mostly to herself — and those of others, particularly their two daughters. 'You must not worry,' she wrote. 'It does no good at all. Everyone is doing all they can for Dad. I can do no more and must leave him in the hands of the professionals. If he dies I have to cope with that, as everyone has to do in a lifetime. If it is a stroke and he comes home, we live in a big sophisticated city with lots of support systems and rehabilitation care — speech therapists, physios, etc. Rob is an angel and it is so good to have him here.'

Lindsay and Carey were both able to return to South Africa by mid-March. In some ways Neil's situation stabilised, but a day or two after the start of the 2003 war in Iraq, which troubled Sheena deeply, his own seventy-seventh birthday came and went, with no real possibilities of celebration, except that Lindsay and Carey were there — although soon due to return to their respective homes in Switzerland and Morocco.

Sheena visited Neil regularly in hospital even though he often didn't seem to know who she was, or what was going on. 'When I said goodbye,' she wrote after one of these visits, 'he asked where I was going so I said "home". He said, "But you are at home." So I told him he was in hospital and I was there with him. Then he actually asked why he was in hospital. I told him it was another one of the bleeds in his brain but a bit worse than the other ones. He didn't answer that but you could see he was processing the information. When I kissed him good bye he actually kissed me back!'

In her search for a more congenial place for Neil to stay while he still needed constant professional care, Sheena chose the NGK Witwatersrandse Tuiste vir Bejaardes, quipping that the name was a bit of a mouthful for the family and would probably be easier on their tongues when its registration as the Park Care Centre came into effect in the coming weeks. However, not only was it affordable, the nursing standard was friendly and good, there were hardly any restrictions on visiting hours and the Tuiste's location in Edgecombe Road, Parktown West was convenient for Neil's friends to pop in and visit, either from home or on the way to or from their places of business and recreation. It also was not too far from the Duncan home in Parkhurst.

On 5 April Sheena writes, 'Today has not been such a good day for me. When you were here in March, we saw Dad in bed in hospital and sitting in that reclining chair and we got used to him being in bed. Today when I went to see him he was in a proper chair on the verandah with two pillows on either side, among a whole lot of other old people in various degrees of Alzheimer's or senile dementia, looking quite gaga himself. They had dressed him in someone else's old clothes because I had not realised that they meant to get everyone up and in their clothes every day so he had on a pair of orange trousers just like those awful bright red ones of his. Anyway I have spent the evening packing his own clothes after marking them so that maybe he can be a bit colour co-ordinated as he would like. The sister also asked me to bring a duvet with two covers so I have done that as well.'

On 12 April: 'Someone asked me if I feel safe in this house without Neil which made me laugh. He has always slept very soundly. I remember once when we were in Harare there was a kleptomaniac doing the rounds and I rigged up a bell on a string across our bedroom door into the courtyard. One night the bell clanged as it dropped to the floor and I chased the intruder up the garden in my nightdress without being fast enough to catch him — fortunately because I don't at all know what I would have done with him had I caught him. He was apprehended some months later, poor man, with all the shiny things he had stolen stashed under his bed. Neil heard none of the drama.

'So I feel quite safe but I do miss being able to chat about the day's events and the extraordinary things our friends tend to say at dinner parties.'

Neil died on 13 April 2003. Suddenly, this living, loving man with whom Sheena had spent almost fifty years of her life was no longer there — not even his frail vulnerable self of the past year.

For all that Sheena was a mountain of a woman and Neil was always seen as this little man at her side, recalls Marj Brown, *she was absolutely bereft after he died. I felt in her a deep sense of loss. She coped by keeping herself busy and by drinking, earlier and earlier in the day. I think that she was desperately lonely and yet she was actually surrounded by people who cared, who would phone or visit her all the time. She was so appreciative of everything but hung on to that fierce independence of spirit — never let her guard down. Like if I was there for an hour, she would get at least three phone calls within that hour and it was always this terribly polite but removed, 'I'm fine thank you, it's so nice of you to call.' The real Sheena, beneath the Black Sash Sheena, the SACC Sheena, was not there. There was always that distance, that reserve; something that didn't allow her to ever let the public face down. Yet she wasn't cold.*

Janet Shapiro remembers Sheena at Neil's funeral: *She seemed smaller. She was all in black for the church service. This was unusual for her. She was distracted in a way I'd never seen before.* Emma Mashinini agrees. *Yes, Sheena did wither when Neil passed away, but her concern for others did not. She called me and said, 'Emma, please don't drive and come to the funeral. I know you'd love to be here but it is too risky around Easter time and the roads are very busy.' I saw Sheena several times after Neil died. She was deserted after his passing.*

I saw a side of her that I'd never seen before, remembers Adèle Kirsten. *I never saw her crying yet I think his death was a key to her vulnerability and sadness. In a way, she had seemed so dominant in that relationship and people — even though we were supposed to be progressive — were quite stereotypical and conservative around the nature of that relationship. I think none of us fully appreciated how important he was for her. Until then, from the outside, many would have said, 'This is her domestic realm — in which there is Neil, and in which it is very clear that Neil is important to her and that she loves him — but really her meaning in life is not in the domestic realm.' I think we got that wrong. Her meaning was there, with him. It's what allowed her to bring that meaning into her public social justice work.*

Sheena kept up her human rights work as well as her legislation monitoring. A day in her life could look like this:

'The Gun Free meeting went on all day and was exciting and forward-looking with our partners in a research project in SADC countries. The minestrone soup went down well in large quantities, with cheese and crusty bread. They all left at about 4. Marcella Naidoo arrived at 4.30 to spend the night. Then Martin Hood, who is my opponent on the gun issue but more recently joined the Rotary Club, brought the whole Vocational Services Committee here for a drink at 5.30 after their meeting, to pay their respects. I made sure the Gun Free papers were left lying around for him to see when he poured the whisky! They all left at the same time, after a few drinks and smoked salmon dip. Then Yasmin Sooka and her husband asked if they could come because Yasmin wanted to see both Marcella and me. They are Hindus and vegetarian so we hauled out the cheddar cheese again and made toast and salad which seemed to be enough with Lorciene's delicious carrot cake which I had taken from the freezer the day before for the meeting.

'By the time I had finished loading the dishwasher it was midnight, so I was very glad not to have any pressing things to do early this morning.

'I am trying to juggle time against all the kind people who want to come to see me. I enjoy them all but sometimes it gets a bit much. Like the other day, I had a first year journalism student who is doing a project on me. I was prepared not to be visibly irritated but she had done her homework and certainly it was an easy one and a half hours. I asked her how she knew so much about me before she came. She said she just looked me up on the internet with Google and found a mass of stuff by just searching for Sheena Duncan. I am completely awestruck. I cannot imagine why I would rate such a listing and I don't know who feeds all this stuff in. She said my CV is there and speeches and all sorts of things.'

Sheena confessed to getting emotionally exhausted by all the people who kept asking her how she was. She virtually stopped going to church, to avoid the constant enquiries about her wellbeing. She got sick, went 'to bed with Vicks Vaporub and Infludo' and got better again.

Only now and then did Sheena write about the loss of Neil. 'I think I was lucky to have had that long five weeks without him while he was in hospital because it eased me into independence and loneliness before he died.' She described patches 'since Dad died, when I can't lift my limbs when dozing in the afternoons'. She missed countless dimensions of Neil: most of all, probably, simply his presence. 'I am back into the swing of things — with a lot of stuff swinging around in my brain. The trouble is I no longer have Dad as a sounding board. He quite often would ask a question which made me think again, or else just put on his expressive face indicating that he did not agree at all!

'Life is very different for me but he is not really gone because everything he created is all around me. I really am fine but am experiencing a kind of inertia. I don't feel quite real. Everything takes me twice as long as it should and I am not concentrating properly on anything. I am not getting on with things like writing thank you letters and must apply my mind but sometimes that file just seems too overwhelming.'

The seasons changed. 'Everything in this house and garden reminds me of him as the season changes and that is also a blessing. Nothing can destroy the wonderful things he created and the bonds of friendship which he forged with so many different people. We were richly blessed in our marriage, not least in having given birth to you two.

'Sam is bounding around the garden on his thin legs now that the spring is here. The prunus blossom is over and the leaves are coming out. The Malus is in full bloom and the Jasmine and Yesterday, Today and Tomorrow fill my bedroom with the most delicious smell. It is much warmer and I am full of energy except when it is bedtime!

'Liz phoned yesterday. She says that I must just do one thing I don't want to do every day which I think is very good advice.' Sheena tried just that, and although she was not ever able to write to thank people for their messages of condolence, it was not long before she had picked up on all her other commitments, as usual. Or so it seemed.

As Rilke says, *Even time does not 'console' … It puts things in their place and creates order. We simply do not know what can be destroyed in a heart through suffering, or what suffering can achieve there.*[7]

[7] Baer, Ulrich (ed.): *The Poet's Guide to Life: The Wisdom of Rilke*, The Modern Library, New York, 2005.

CHAPTER 5

South African Council of Churches

I got elected as vice president of SACC on Thursday. When I got home and told the family, all I got was a blast because there were no onions ...

SHEENA DUNCAN — Letter 5 July 1987

'I had tomorrow crossed off with large letters saying "no interruptions" but it will be Frank Chikane's first day in the SACC office as general secretary and I feel I should be there,' Sheena wrote two days later. 'I take my new responsibilities seriously and *The Citizen* and Current Affairs are going to town on the SACC's support for the liberation movements.'

There was to be no shortage of problems for the two new vice presidents, Sheena and Thudiso Virginia Gcabashe. Over and above the enormous challenges they faced in the struggle against a racist regime in the outside world, these two women faced some internal SACC problems. Their predecessor Sally Motlana[1] had smoothed the path only slightly. Apart from being made welcome by John Rees — *that man had a heart of gold, like Sheena, he accepted me as I was* — Sally had a particularly difficult time as the first woman to be an SACC vice president *because I wasn't a priest and I was a woman. I remember one of them said to me, 'How can they elect a black woman to be vice president of the SACC?' I said, 'Times have changed — if you are still living in the dark ages you had better come out of them. I am here to stay and to stay for a long time so you better accept me as I am.'*

Despite Sally's firm words, little had changed: in general, women in the SACC were still not given proper respect in their positions. Thudiso Virginia recalls that *it was as though men always thought 'women are just women'. This attitude was not so much at the highest circle of leadership of the SACC, although I do remember one incident at a conference, which was dedicated to fighting for the rights of women in the church. The conference was called 'Women, a Power for Change' and for once women almost took centre stage. I overheard one of the very senior male members talking to another male saying, 'Well, now they've had their thing, next year we will go back to how it was.'*

Thudiso Virginia valued Sheena immensely as a sister vice president, as a strategist around the role of women in the SACC and, above all, for Sheena's enthusiasm, honesty and engagement with all people as equals. *She did not hesitate to put her foot into something that others might have thought was dangerous. She was brave and she*

[1] The first female SACC vice president, Sally served the SACC in this capacity from 1972 until 1986.

had that aura of making you feel confident that you had in her someone with whom you could share any problem.

Sheena was indeed a very powerful and forceful presence in the SACC and in other church meetings where I saw her in operation, says Paddy Kearney. *She was every bit the equal of any of the most powerful high-ranking clerics in the land. But respectful and strategic in the way she used her power, so that I think they were mostly in awe of her knowledge and competence and sense of what was the right thing to do. She didn't try to bully the bishops — she didn't need to. They would have gone with whatever she said because she would be able to give a rational explanation of where she stood on any issue. They knew very little about the things she was talking about and they would defer to her experience. I vividly remember her courage, her clarity of thought, her wise counsel, her knowledge of the law, her humanity, her infectious confidence, her encyclopaedic knowledge of apartheid oppression and her boldness in speaking out prophetically. She was also friendly and witty.*

In Frank Chikane's view, those years during which he and Sheena served may have been among the worst for the SACC and, indeed, the South African government's campaign against the churches had intensified. It bombed[2] the SACC headquarters at Khotso House in August 1988, and two months later, the Southern African Catholic Bishops' Conference offices were burned down. The following year, thirty-nine staff members of St Barnabas College in Bosmont, Johannesburg, were hospitalised after contact with toxic acid that had been splashed on the chapel walls and floor prior to the opening of the SACC's annual conference. Agents of the apartheid regime also tried to assassinate Frank by poisoning his clothes, and almost succeeded.

The conflict in the country was like low intensity war and as a result I needed all the support I could get, says Frank. *I was a general secretary whose [own] church was not a member of SACC, and my church had just suspended me because I was involved in politics. I had to be strategic about how I mobilised the leadership of the SACC. None of the leaders presented themselves as an obstacle to what I believed the SACC should be doing, but Manas Buthelezi[3] wasn't a rabble-rouser or a radical and he was not always in the office. He's a bishop of the Evangelican Lutheran Church and he came for meetings.*

He was a good bishop who believed in justice but he was not a person who was ready to go and march in the street — he went because it had to be done. Khoza Mgojo[4]

[2] *Come Celebrate 25 Years of the SACC*: Chapter 12: According to Bernard Spong, *The bomb went off in the basement garage of Khotso House not long after midnight on the morning of August 31st. It ripped through the building using the lift shafts as a conduit of destruction on every floor and going as far as blowing off part of the roof. Windows of surrounding buildings were shattered as well as nearly every window of Khotso House itself. Rubble and broken office furniture, scattered files and broken equipment lay everywhere*: www.sacc.org.za.

[3] SACC president 1983–1990.

[4] SACC president 1990–1995.

was more on the radical side, but he was in Durban. Sheena was close by in terms of what we could do; I could interact with her whenever there was an issue — any issue.

I had been in the United Democratic Front (UDF) before I went to the SACC so I understood that you may have your ideas, but you don't impose them on people. You need to carry people along and you need their support. You don't prove your effectiveness by breaking out and dealing with radical concepts that don't make sense to the body — in this case, the SACC.

Before his term as general secretary of SACC, Frank had joined the Institute for Contextual Theology, a theological think tank that was highly receptive to liberation theology, and he became its general secretary in 1983. In 1985, he was part of a group of 151 clergy who released the Kairos Document, a Christian indictment of apartheid, which helped to mobilise significant support from churches overseas and formed the basis for a united church front against apartheid.

By the time we reached 1988, most organisations were banned and the trade unions and others were restricted, so the SACC was in effect forced to provide leadership, but church leaders did not always agree with each other. In the sixties and the early seventies, for example, there had been a big struggle within the SACC about the position it should take in relation to the liberation movement — the 1960 Cottesloe experience and Spro-cas material out of the Christian Institute in the early seventies testify to this process.

Through the Institute of Contextual Theology we had dealt with the issues of legitimacy of the state, tyranny, and when can you remove a government. For the average Christian it was a difficult concept, but once we reached a stage where we declared the regime illegitimate, it qualified to be removed.

It was a question of how.

Sheena's life was in this space of rights, justice, stop the system and minister to victims, but the debate that never went away was whether or not you would have armed struggle as part of that. The 'just war' theories were debated as part of the theological perspectives but Sheena would have been more of a non-violent person, close to what you call pacifist in a sense. Resist the system but do it in pacifist ways: protest, resistance and defiance.

Sheena was a key moving factor in the changes happening in the SACC. Even when people were relaxed and wouldn't take an issue seriously, she would take it on. If you were dealing with any issue about victims, whether forced removals or whatever, Sheena would be on the leadership of that, she would argue for that; if you talked about conscientious objection, if you talked about the army, the military, she was there.

At a church leaders' meeting dealing with a legal issue you could be sure that Sheena would know what that was about, she would have an opinion and she would be able to motivate what the churches and the SACC needed to do. But I don't think that Sheena drew lines. My sense of her is that there was no line — when she was doing Black Sash work it was the same as church work and when she did legal advice she operated like a lawyer, but she was also able to deal with all the issues based on experience.

Sheena's contributions in the SACC were not limited to leadership and legislative guidance; she had no delusions of grandeur. She was an informal 'personal assistant' from time to time to Desmond Tutu, Beyers Naudé and then to Frank for the first three months of his term as general secretary. In this capacity, Sheena took on ad hoc tasks such as organising delegates and travel for international conferences and handling some basic correspondence, including the SACC's responses to numerous requests for funding.

Sheena preaching at St Mary's Cathedral, Johannesburg

'Being SACC vice president does not mean a great deal more work,' Sheena wrote to her daughter after a week in the role. 'All meetings of the executive are in Khotso House [the same building as the Black Sash offices] and helping Frank Chikane will come to an end once he gets a proper staff. I am actually enjoying it and it will be difficult to find someone to fill the position. I know so many of the people who write to SACC from all over the world and it is nice to be able to write personal letters back to them.

'I have spent this evening writing to bishops. They have been writing to congratulate me on the appointment; I think they are just pleased to have an Anglican on the Presidium after all those Lutherans, Methodists and assorted Dutch Reformed Church dissidents.'

Much as she enjoyed this intense period of work, however, three months later, at the end of September 1987, Sheena wrote, 'I feel I have a new lease on life today. Frank Chikane has taken Marj Brown on as his personal assistant until the end of the year, when a permanent appointment can be made and I can thankfully relinquish this temporary voluntary job. It will be a great relief and I was beginning to be afraid that they had forgotten that it was supposed to be an interim arrangement to help out in a crisis. It will be nice to be back full-time in the advice office and it will also be nice to be able to compensate for having to have ghastly committee meetings at night to be free to work and concentrate at home on Wednesdays.'

An aspect of her SACC work that Sheena valued immensely was her participation in the Justice and Reconciliation (J&R) division. *Sheena came with experience connected to due diligence and she headed Justice and Reconciliation. I remember,* says Thudiso Virginia, *that she introduced what I don't think any one of us would have thought of, a 'round table leadership'. This means that every member of the division had almost equal status as, seated at a round table, you never know who is at the head and who is at the bottom. So she was trying to encourage the group to know that we are all equal and equally responsible for whatever we do.*

Sheena herself did not claim full credit for this: 'Dr Kistner laid the foundations for shared responsibility well and the J&R advisory meetings are the most enjoyable I have to attend. There does not seem to be any backbiting or underhandedness.' The creative ways of working together were picked up with enthusiasm by Emma Mashinini, with whom Sheena worked closely. In March 1988, Sheena wrote to Anne Hughes. 'Emma is remarkable. She is doing very good work and is holding steady against the onslaughts of the PSC,[5] which wants provincial offices to achieve the impossible. She has created a whole informal network with J&R divisions in other denominations, is very active in SACC work and manages the Bishops by drowning them in paper whenever they want to know what the use of Provincial departments is. PSC abolished all the Boards in November in the interests of the economy. Emma has quietly gone about setting up a small advisory committee for herself of local people who do not have to have the authority of their Bishops. It is a very free way of working and much better. PSC's assaults on the work of the church continue but somehow we manage to get around them.'

Another of Sheena's colleagues was Ishmael Mkhabela. In the face of much scepticism, and even criticism from many of his fellow Black Consciousness activists, this young black leader — founder member of AZAPO and husband of radical activist Sibongile Mkhabela (nee Mthembu) — quickly saw that Sheena was not condescending, as were many 'liberal' whites. He recognised her as an ally of the Black Consciousness project of creating an environment in which people could organise themselves, claim responsibility for their lives and make the most of what they had to offer.

When Sheena saw facts speaking for themselves, says Ishmael, *she would be influenced and change. If you presented and Sheena didn't say anything, you knew she just didn't have another opinion. She was not one who would say one thing in my face and then when I'm gone change her tune and say something behind my back. She gave us that sense of certainty and assurance that we could put an issue on the table, debate it and even where there were differences we could talk about those things and find one another — and then if we still didn't like it or agree, we could live with the difference.*

What struck me was her energy, her presence of mind and that she was a very strong person. She could argue her position, she could articulate what she thought — always

[5] Provincial Standing Committee.

with an eye on what we could do against the injustice of the system. I also always remember her writing notes and passing them around. If you dropped a pile of notes in front of me today and said, show us Sheena Duncan's handwriting, I wouldn't hesitate to say, 'Sheena wrote this little scrap.' I also came to realise that working with her, we did not just go for propaganda or sensationalise anything. We had to do our homework and back our utterances with fact. That was the influence of Sheena for me, and for other people I worked with. What's more, you were dealing with Sheena based on her values and her beliefs, not because someone gave her an instruction to behave in a particular way. I've worked with people, including some of her associates in the SACC, who left me deeply emotionally wounded because they had no standpoint of their own. When they work with you, it's because they believe it would be acceptable to one political party or another. It could be ANC, or other underground structures. In my work with Sheena, I'm pleased to say I never spent a sleepless night.

Typically, Sheena did not try to hang on to her leadership role in the SACC. On 18 July 1993, Sheena wrote to her family that 'the SACC conference was fine. I withstood all attempts to nominate me as president and ended up being elected as an honorary life vice president which is okay as it does not have any regular duties but enables Frank to call me in when he needs support and enables me to pick and choose what I am prepared to do — starting with tomorrow when he has roped me in to a meeting with the National Peace Accord to discuss our critique of them. I don't mind that because it is more interesting than the regular finance committee etc but it is a fact that my diary seems no less full than it was before.'

Once again expressing a degree of relief, this time to one of her advice office colleagues a few months later, Sheena wrote, 'One thing about not being a vice president of SACC anymore is that I am now free to say what I think again. I had not realised what a restraint it was on me until it was removed.'

Yet, even within this feeling of restraint, Sheena's SACC colleagues speak with one voice about the scale of her contribution. In her, the SACC found someone who could craft resolutions, develop a constitution, know who to contact for what purpose, interpret legislation for church leaders and community activists alike, advise and encourage well-informed protest and solidarity actions, write user-friendly booklets and enable people to put them to good use, travel and speak nationally and internationally on behalf of the council, assist with evaluations of regional councils of churches and in many more ways respond to the needs of others when asked to do so.

Throughout her association with the SACC, Sheena ensured that the organisation and the church leaders were well briefed about any apartheid legislation that was likely to affect them, either directly or through their constituency. Her analysis was careful and strategic, and its usefulness is evident in a March 1988 letter to her friend Anne Hughes:

'SACC gets specifically named in the new legislation to stop foreign funding of any organisation the minister chooses to name. With legislation come the new provisions which will affect every organisation's day-to-day work. I am sending you under separate cover a paper I wrote in a great hurry for Episcopal Synod. The Bill removes the church's exemption from the fundraising act for money collected outside the Republic. We will still be able to collect money inside the country for our religious work but we will have to register as a fundraising organisation in order to receive money from outside the country. Even if an organisation is registered as a fundraising organisation and receives money perfectly legally from outside the Republic it may not use that money for any political purpose. A political purpose is to promote or further or oppose any political aim or object.

'The churches could legitimately claim that they are not promoting political objectives because they are pursuing the biblical imperatives of justice and peace but we certainly do oppose all the political aims and objects of apartheid. In any prosecution the state must prove that foreign money has been received and that the organisation does further or oppose a political aim. The organisation must then prove that none of the foreign money was used for any political purpose. Penalties are 10 years or R20,000 or a fine of twice the amount of the money involved. It is a huge problem for the church to even contemplate applying for registration as a fundraising organisation because you will remember how many controls the state may then exert over the activities of the organisation. It raises huge theological problems about the relationship between the church and the state. You will have noticed that the relationship is hardly at its warmest at the moment. There is a concerted attack on Desmond, and now the bishops, Allan [Boesak] and SACC. It will get much worse and we are thinking deeply about responses. If SACC and its member churches are prevented from receiving overseas money we must be prepared for a whole lot of innocent seeming applications going to our partners and other funders overseas so that the front organisations will be able to deliver the goods. We are worried but I think the first task must be to oppose the Bill in whatever way we can. This country needs foreign money desperately. If government intends to stop foreign money coming in for humanitarian purposes which it does not approve of then I think it must be made clear to them that if they don't want foreign money it will ALL be stopped.'

Sheena travelled as an SACC representative more often than she wanted to. In mid-September 1989 she wrote to her daughters, 'I am going to meetings in Brussels with the European Commission from 27 to 30 September. I do not want to go but no one else from the SACC executive is available and these are important meetings regarding the European "twin track" policy when they have deliberately lost sight of the other track and now the threat to their funding by the promulgation of the Disclosure of Foreign Funding Act. I'm sorry I cannot take the opportunity to duck across to Britain to see you Lindsay and Jeremy, but I used up all my foreign exchange on our holiday.'

Another of Sheena's greatest strengths as an activist was the manner in which she could write and speak to a conference audience; she could bring participants face to face with realities in what otherwise might have been 'grey' areas, but where the need for policy decisions or well-considered protest lay in wait, if not at that particular conference, then in the near future. As was the case in her leadership role in the Black Sash, this happened frequently in service of the SACC, both in her home country and when she engaged with international audiences. Internationally and locally her words offered crucial insights during the worst years of repression, but in the years just before and after 1990 it was just as important to ensure an awareness of the dangers of succumbing to disingenuous promises of transformation.

Delivering her paper 'In Humble Submission to Almighty God — Church, State and Conflict in South Africa',[6] in Sweden, Sheena left no room for the international community to be seduced by apartheid's distortions of theology in an attempt to justify racial discrimination, or by the apartheid regime's talk of reform: 'The "reform" process,' she writes, 'is as necessary to the maintenance of that power [in the hands of the ruling white minority] as is the system of repression.'

The minutes of the 1992 SACC national conference read, under the topic 'The Use of Indemnity to Release Criminals and the Demand for Justice': *The Senior Vice President [Sheena] reported that the Conference of the Human Rights Trust had been very interesting, attended by lawyers and human rights groups. The conference was adamant that truth was more important than justice. There was a consensus that there would have to be trials but that provision may have to made for amnesty once a trial and conviction had taken place. This was the beginning of on-going discussions. It was important that the churches think very carefully about their approach to this issue.*

In October 1992 at Diakonia's Socio-political Developments Programme breakfast briefing, headed The Church's Role in Preparing for Free and Fair Elections, Sheena said, 'In the struggle for justice, we can't just let the politicians make a constitution without watching very carefully what they decide among themselves. We have to ensure that those decisions are not going to deny people justice, and to remember at all times the question of economic justice which is simply not being discussed as it should be in the churches.

[6] Hallencreutz, Carl Fredrik and Palmberg, Mai (eds): *Religion and Politics in Southern Africa*, Seminar Proceedings No. 24, The Scandinavian Institute of African Studies, (Uppsala 1991).

'South Africans of all kinds are accepting that socialism has failed and capitalism is the only alternative. I don't believe that's true. I don't believe that we've got to get swept along by the "reaganomics" of Mrs Thatcher. Look what Mrs Thatcher has achieved for Britain. We have to decide for ourselves what economic justice requires for this very unequal society. We mustn't let the politicians get away with agreements on things like land distribution and so on without making sure that we have done our level best to prevent them from further impoverishing the majority.

'Now all that sounds like an enormous task but we have to remember that if we're all in it together, it's broken down into very manageable pieces. The churches have the advantage that if you want to do it, you don't have to travel miles away or do it somewhere else. We can do it where we are, in our congregations, in our parish churches on Sundays. It's something we can build into our ordinary daily tasks.'

Ishmael encapsulates a sense of her presence when he says, *I don't remember any major campaign of the SACC where Sheena would be a bystander. She would always be at the centre of discussion and at the centre of action. For that matter, even if her name was not on it, I don't know of any resolution or any major press statement which would see the light of day without having had the benefit of having been seen or influenced by Sheena Duncan. She would not just jump on the first thing that was proposed; she would question and examine with that strong sense of discernment which was a talent she had and a gift she shared with all of us.*

I actually believe that Sheena was God's instrument in a particular era of our history.

CHAPTER 6

Engaging the Church

Some of [the conference] decisions will have far reaching consequences. Not only in terms of [SACC's] relationship with the Government, but also in terms of its relationship with member churches and with Christians in general.

Ecunews, 'The SACC 1985 National Conference — an historical watershed'

The 1985 conference offered several examples of matters on which delegates took decisions — although not necessarily unanimously — that caused discomfort to a range of member churches and contributed to the often uneasy relationships between the SACC and its member churches, or which prevented some churches from associating themselves with the SACC. The decision to call for disinvestment as an instrument of non-violent change was one; it received overwhelming support at the conference, but not back home in the parishes and even the broader church 'constituencies' of many of the delegates. The stated intention to devote a good deal of time to the conference theme, 'Women, a Power for Change', was another example. Fortunately for those who thought this an unworthy theme, it was smoothly swept aside when news of violent events intruded, and the agenda was radically changed to deal with *life and death issues*. On the third day, conference business was suspended to allow discussion of the killings of young blacks in incidents of 'unrest' on the East Rand, without even a moment's pause to take into account that life and death issues were, and still are, a daily feature of women's lives.

Aside from specific conference matters, there were recurring points of dissent among the churches, including violence (whether structural, oppressive or liberatory), resistance to violence, white liberal hegemony, black and liberation theologies, engagement with government, the ordination of women, the peace process, political prisoners, the death penalty, and the return of exiles. All were weighty moral matters, worthy of feisty discussion and dissent, and each had the potential to enlighten parishioners on the one hand or, on the other hand, to cause friction and even divisions between the SACC and at least some of its member churches.

There were several possible reasons for the tensions. One was that church 'representatives' on the structures of the SACC were often not at all representative of the views of the church to which they belonged at parish level, nor even at the level of council, synod or any area or regional structures in which the various denominations participated. Another reason was that there were generally few prior consultations or opportunities for pre-conference discussions. Policy and programme decisions as well as media releases and resolutions emanating from SACC conferences were frequently informed by the executive's views, combined with expressions of individual ideas and conscience. 'Delegates' to conferences were usually no such thing — they were not delegated with a mandate that had been developed in a process of inclusive preparations. Sometimes the reasons were circumstantial but mostly they were attributable to the nature of structured hierarchies and bonds within and between SACC and its member churches. Consequently, many member churches could be obstinately resistant to the progressive — and what they saw as inappropriately 'political' — ideas, programmes and actions of the SACC. There were some notable exceptions to such lack of consultation, one of which was Sheena's painstaking development process of the SACC constitution — and subsequent SACC contributions to the post-1990 Constitution of South Africa.

Recognising and respecting the relevant role of the SACC in the anti-apartheid struggle, as well as the desperate and oppressed circumstances that characterised the lives of the majority of South Africans — and thus the majority of South Africa's Christians — church leaders and worshippers may have been reluctant to express openly their dissatisfaction with the SACC. But their resistance sometimes simply made it difficult for 'progressive' anti-discriminatory views to be woven into the words of ministry that were offered for solace and moral guidance. In some rare cases, like those of Beyers Naudé and Frank Chikane, their views — acceptable and worthy within the SACC — were so intolerable to a specific church or denomination that the individual was punished with isolation from his or her familiar spiritual home. In other cases, however, such as during the Eloff Commission,[1] the SACC received support from a significant number of member churches.

Sheena herself did not experience such tensions. In addition to the respect accorded her in the SACC, she was valued by her own Anglican constituency as a regular congregant as well as at the highest level of the Anglican Church. In 1986, after serving as Bishop of Johannesburg for just over a year, Desmond Tutu was elected as Archbishop of Cape Town and became the first black man to lead the Anglican Church in South Africa. Within a year, he had done what Sheena saw as a most sensible thing. 'He summoned a few of us together,' she wrote to Anne Hughes, 'mainly laypeople, to form a kind of informal task force to advise him on issues: Michael Corke on education, Shirley Moulder and Mamphela Ramphele on development issues, Emma Mashinini on labour and anything J&R which is not covered with Syd Luckett locally, and myself on structural/constitutional/legislative

[1] An all-white judicial enquiry into the SACC (membership of which was 80% black) set up in 1981 by the government in, inter alia, an attempt to discredit the SACC and disable its financial viability by trying to prove that it did not in fact have the support of the majority of South African Christians.

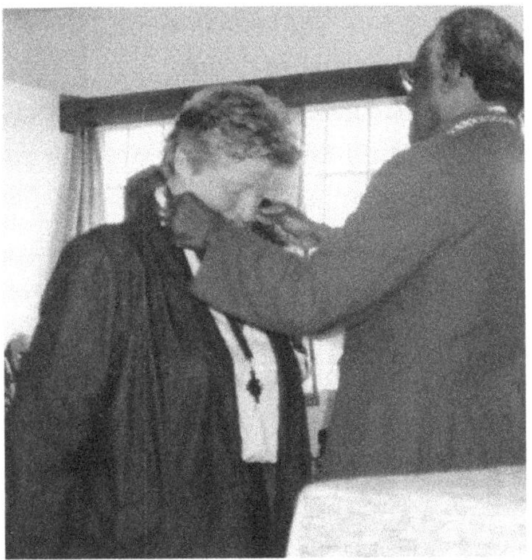

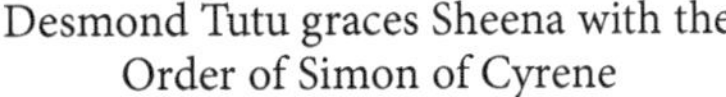
Desmond Tutu graces Sheena with the Order of Simon of Cyrene

Sheena as a lay canon of the Diocese of Johannesburg

issues etc. This gives us a direct line to him through Winston[2] and will be a great help. Emma and I feel we will not have to pussyfoot around any more through the J&R board all the time and the Synod of Bishops. We have a kind of officially recognised immediate channel now and perhaps that will help Desmond. He is a great man under great pressure and if he can find ways of short-circuiting the impossible processes and structures of decision making in the church, good luck to him. The situation is too critical to be managed through those ponderous formalities.'

Just a few months later, Sheena wrote to tell her daughters that 'Desmond Tutu phoned me from London last week to tell me the Anglican Bishops of South Africa have decided to make me a member of the Order of Simon of Cyrene. That is the ultimate they can do for a layperson. I was speechless. Dad says, what's that? And no one is properly impressed. It is the highest accolade that can be given to an Anglican lay person in South Africa. Like the MBE or something — an honour to which I will no doubt have to be installed in some ceremony to which I don't think I will bother to invite your father. I shall have to be made Pope before any of you are properly impressed.' In 1992 when Sheena was made a lay canon in the Anglican Church, Neil wrote to their daughters, *Ma's canonisation was quite a do. There were five of them, all put into magnificent capes as part of the proceedings. The Bishop had organised the brass section and the drums of the National Symphony Orchestra. Together with the cathedral's own organ, which makes St George's one sound like a toy, it was a feast of reverberating sound and very moving. But the service took two hours and we had to be half an hour early so it was a long morning; the acoustics are so bad you couldn't hear a*

[2] Winston Njongonkulu Ndungane, at that time the executive officer of the Anglican Church of Southern Africa, appointed by the Archbishop of Cape Town, Desmond Tutu. One of his major responsibilities in that role was as secretary to the various synods and committees of the church.

word that was said and there were hordes of screaming kids. The cathedral was packed, but that's probably normal, and the Bishop came over and said hi to me.

Sheena was acutely aware that by its very nature, the church is the place that is everywhere in all communities and that it could do an enormous amount to change the country. It was a source of some frustration to her that it was so difficult to persuade ministers that not only were the actual church buildings incredibly important community development and care resources, but also that a mere five minutes at the end of a service could make the world of difference — particularly in a country where verbal communication and visible example were so important. As she put it, 'Wherever you are there is work to be done to make life better for people or, if I am to put it in terms of my belief, work to be done to bring about the kingdom of heaven here and now.'

This is not to ignore great work done by the churches. In Sheena's own diocese, for example, under the Diocesan Social Responsibility Team (DSRT) — of which for many years Sheena was the chairperson and Douglas Torr the coordinator — there were several initiatives. COACH, an integration in 2003 of three children's homes, was completed with a lot of energy from Shirley Moulder. The homes merged their traditional roles into a framework to work — in full partnership with the diocese — for a holistic and multilayered continuum-of-care approach to orphaned and vulnerable children and their caregivers. The Johannesburg Anglican Environment Initiative (JAEI) followed, drawing extensively on the energies of young people at parish level throughout the diocese. An HIV and AIDS service was operated from the diocesan office, coordinated by Tshepo Matubatuba; Barney Curtis was involved with street children; and Tim Grey had oversight of environmental initiatives. Wherever possible the DSRT worked in cooperation with government and other resource agencies.

Douglas sums up Sheena's key role in the first words of his Coordinator's Report of 2007: *I would like to begin this report by thanking Sheena for her support and sage wisdom. If Madiba has the elders to combat poverty, war, and injustice, then I am thankful that in this diocese on a far more local level we in the DSRT have you* — directing himself to Sheena — *and your wisdom to guide us.*

Although Sheena remained exasperated with many aspects of the Church, she also found much to appreciate. In May 2008, for example, after participating in a non-violence training workshop with Walter Wink and Richard Deats[3] in Lesotho,

[3] Walter Wink was an American Methodist biblical scholar, theologian and activist. He was just a few years younger than Sheena and is known, among other things, for his work on power structures and disorders, pacifism, and political and cultural matters of the time. Richard Deats is an American United Methodist minister and writer, who worked for the Fellowship of Reconciliation (FOR) for over 30 years. He is valued for his workshops and lectures on active non-violence in many countries, including South Africa. His writing includes biographies of Martin Luther King (Jnr) and Mahatma Gandhi. He has also contributed important work on the death penalty and Christians and homosexuality.

sponsored by the SACC and the Fellowship of Reconciliation, Sheena wrote to Anne Hughes: 'It was incredibly inspiring and we came back all lit up into the Church Leaders Emergency Convocation, which rapidly reduced us to normal. It was so disappointing. There is enough to go ahead with — at the church's usual slow pace — but it did fail in providing the kind of inspiration we had hoped for. One day I expect I will learn not to expect too much from the church but one cannot help going on just hoping that they will get their act together however belatedly.' Sheena also appreciated what Sue Brittion had referred to as the 'subtext' of the religious context, in this case a Saturday afternoon at Masite after the Lesotho workshop. 'I have never been there before,' wrote Sheena, 'but I do hope there will be opportunities to go there again. The nuns all came to the guest house in the afternoon to ask us questions about what is going on and I felt very strengthened by the knowledge that they are there just praying for us.

'I expect you will be seeing something of some of the Bishops while they are at Lambeth. I think we must mount a revolution against the church structures while they are away. The opportunity does not happen too often and I suppose we should use it to reorganise things! Unfortunately there are too many clergymen who would prevent any kind of innovative thinking. I have little hope that the church will ever be able to break out of its structure or the weight of its tradition.'

One of the issues under the weight of this tradition was the role of women. Sheena did not think of god as a physical being: 'To struggle with God language is a pastoral and deeply spiritual exercise. I do not regard God to be a person of some kind. God is more of a spirit, a dimension to life.' [4] Sheena and many others — both male and female — have over the years unravelled bits of the stubbornly gendered intricacies of the words and images, or symbols, used in relation to god. Marginal and feminist scholars have presented notions and — in their view — evidence of prehistoric matriarchal religions, with god symbolised as female. Their ideas are mostly rejected by modern anthropologists and are certainly given no scriptural credence by Christians.

From way back in ancient Hinduism, Judaism, Islam and Buddhism, it seems indeed that all other expressions of dogmata and doctrines, whether or not they actually name god, have passed god into common forms of thought as male. Even when this might be considered simply a linguistic misunderstanding, the god image is indisputably conjured up in male terms. Sometimes overtly and sometimes most subtly, this tends to influence the way men in the Church respond to women in the Church, no matter at what level. That, in turn, has embedded a culture of spiritually justified male superiority, which is at its most obvious in the teams of 'holy' men who through the ages have appointed themselves as the legitimised interpreters and the

[4] Villa-Vicencio, Charles: *The Spirit of Freedom*, chapter 'Sheena Duncan: Surprised by Joy'.

acceptable intermediaries between human beings and god. With notable exceptions and so terribly slowly, this started to change in some denominations of the Christian church during Sheena's lifetime. However, even in the 'progressive' SACC, in the more than forty years following its establishment in 1968, Brigalia Bam and Charity Majiza[5] were the only women to serve as general secretaries and, without exception, all the presidents have been men. This despite the reality sketched by Frank that *if you were a child growing up in Soweto, the fact that a woman was a leader wasn't a big deal. Although culturally and traditionally, men oppress and discriminate against women, that didn't stop women from playing certain roles within the society. The strong characters and personalities a child remained with at home were the women. You didn't see your father much and, anyway, when he comes home he becomes like a dictator.* Maybe children really do know best. Brigalia tells a story she heard about a Sunday school teacher who asked the small children in the class to describe God. *Oh,* said one of the children, *God is like my mother. Why?* asked the teacher. *Oh,* said the child, *my mother knows everything; she is always with me; Mama takes me to school, cooks, dresses me up and laughs with me and says, 'Oooh I love you very much!'* The teacher thought about this person who this child loved so much and who was doing everything and was everywhere, and then asked, *What about your father? Oh no,* said the child, *my father reads the newspaper.*

In her work and prayer, Sheena rubbed shoulders on an almost daily basis with men of great moral and spiritual stature. She cherished these fine men and through them deepened her understanding of the extraordinary tenacity of conservatism and of the fear that underpins patriarchy. The magnitude of her faith, her humanity and her compassion found new dimensions. Intrinsically unintimidated, Sheena risked nothing of her own sense of self by being open and humble in her acceptance of what she could learn from the men around her. Willing to engage in argument when she disagreed, she remained courteous and an 'Ag no man, Desmond[6] …' may have sounded irreverent in relation to the status of one of the world's greatest church leaders and internationally celebrated peace activists, but it was never said without respect and affection, nor did it ever precede a point without relevance to the issue at hand.

Many members of staff of the SACC outreach programmes were also men, and Sheena — despite her seniority in 'rank' and age — engaged with young men like Ishmael Mkhabela and Joe Seremane in an open, mutually respectful way and with a willingness to listen and learn — just as she did with their female colleagues.

The pragmatism of black theology had obvious appeal to an activist of Sheena's nature, and she deeply valued its characteristic intellectual and spiritual questioning

[5] The first woman ordained as minister in the Reformed Presbyterian Church of Southern Africa.
[6] Sheena was frequently overheard prefacing a point she disputed with Desmond Tutu in this way.

of establishment assumptions about white hegemonies brought to South Africa astutely embedded in Christianity or violently enforced. Black theology was, of course, yet another male-dominated ideology and practice, but Sheena did not concern herself with this aspect in her interactions with men like Barney Pityana and Allan Boesak, both of whom she admired enormously as thinkers. Her relationship with other black men in the SACC, who might not necessarily have associated themselves directly with black theology, also offered wonderful opportunities for interactive questioning or thought-provoking observance; and then there was Sheena's unwavering loyalty and loving respect for Desmond Tutu and Frank Chikane, which went way beyond the boundaries of theology. She worked particularly closely with both men and much admired their courage. During the detainees' hunger strike of 1989, for example, Sheena wrote to Anne Hughes: 'Great credit must be given to Frank. He has been criticised by the mainly white radical left most vociferously for negotiating with the Minister without "consulting with the community" but he has maintained close contact with the hunger strikers' lawyers and with the detainees whenever he has been allowed to visit them and they are the community on this issue. One would not have thought even three months ago that the church leaders would be able to conduct such serious conversations and win their points with a member of the government. Frank is absolutely steady and understands very well the point that the opponent must be allowed to save face. He is very courageous and very brilliant and his leadership qualities are incredible.'

The work and words of many other fine men intersected closely with Sheena's work in the religious community and in the struggle against apartheid. Some were also friends, and all were allies in the search for moral and socially transformative religious leadership at whatever 'level' or in whatever faith definition they worked. She quarrelled with several, she intimidated a few, others found her opinionated beyond her sex and position. Without any need to invest in them the god-intermediary persona that tradition and culture accorded them — and which some of them might have wanted — Sheena was able to appreciate how much these men enriched her understanding of gender relations, power and her own spirituality. Undoubtedly she enriched them at the same time, whether they all acknowledged it or not.

I wish I could remember my conversations with Sheena about women, laments Denise Ackermann. *I don't think she ever disagreed with me. I have no memory of her saying to me, 'Oh Denise, well that's going a bit far' when I would put my feminist theological perspective to her. I can't remember her disagreeing with me but I also can't remember getting that perspective from her. All I have is a sense that in our context this was not the burning issue. The women's issue was second to the race issue. Gender did not feature on the top of the agenda. The race issue was so overwhelming that it drowned out a lot of the other stuff. Hierarchies of oppression were chosen. It was also about energy.*

gille de vlieg ©

Sheena bestowing an honorary sash on Denis Hurley; Beyers Naudé, who was 'sashed' on the same occasion, and Ann Colvin applaud

Perhaps it is ironic — or perhaps just strangely contradictory — that although Sheena expressed sureness that she herself had not ever been oppressed as a woman, she nevertheless felt that being a woman had given her some understanding of what it meant to be an 'underdog'. Furthermore, simply by virtue of being married to a man, she expressed herself able to enjoy her material privilege without a burden of guilt; the wealth and possessions were not hers, they were his.

Sheena certainly stood her ground as a woman among men in the church: *Sheena was beyond most of the denigration a lot of women endured in the church. She was too big for that. You couldn't put her down,* confirms Sue Brittion.

When she returned from overseas, Brigalia found that *Sheena was very active in the SACC, already a vice president and she was the most outstanding leader in that whole circle of mostly male church leaders. I remember distinctly her role in the first annual general meeting I attended in 1988. This woman was speaking in an amazing manner, yet with a lot of respect. There has been a tendency sometimes with us, when we are angry in the church, to be cynical — even be cynical about the gospel itself — but one of the things I liked with Sheena, she never used the gospel, the theology, for this. I liked her style very much because I was coming back from Europe where I had been working with a lot of feminist theologians and their approach was very different.*

I heard only after I had joined the SACC that Sheena had been part of the group of women who had lobbied for and supported the idea of having a woman as a general secretary of the SACC. It was another complex matter. Sometime in its history, the SACC had made a decision that the general secretary should be an ordained person. By implication, this would be a man because at the time most of the churches were still against the ordination of women. Thus, without it being explicitly stated, women were excluded from appointment as the most senior employee of the SACC. The constitution was silent, however, on the matter of deputies. *So, lo and behold, I worked as deputy to Frank Chikane; the debate was never raised and people pretended it didn't matter. Then when Frank was leaving [in 1993], they had to appoint a general secretary and Sheena challenged me in an interesting way; a gender thing, as it relates to me.*

I was genuinely active in thinking about this appointment because at that time I was clear on the kind of person the SACC needed to take the organisation forward, post-apartheid. I had a lot of ideas of what I had seen other countries do, countries which were not dealing with apartheid, and so I knew we needed to change the complete approach of our work in the ecumenical movement and move almost away from the welfare — we were more in welfare work, apartheid work, dependents' conference and so on. Brigalia shared her ideas with the 'search' committee, including thoughts on resources and funding. A lot of SACC funds at the time had been coming from overseas donors and this was changing, too, as the donors started thinking about how best they might channel their tax money through the development projects of a new South African government. The committee interviewed a number of people and Brigalia was hopeful that they would take Barney Pityana. *We had been together in the World Council of Churches, although he came after my time. He was very well trained, a lawyer and an activist, and he had everything you can ask for.*

The executive committee interviewed three people and that afternoon sent Sheena to ask Brigalia if she would consider staying. *Now let me tell you the absolute truth,* says Brigalia, *I was looking forward to leaving the SACC because I genuinely felt that a new person should come with new vision. Secondly, there were so many other opportunities; I had been offered just about everything you can imagine by the government because there were not many of us women who were going to be in government. I had been removed from the list for parliament because the ANC felt that of the number of us women and men who were working in the communities, not all should go to parliament. So, with all these offers I was ready to enter into a new exciting world, get a better salary and really be a government official. I was so ready — and then here comes Sheena.*

'Oh Sheena,' I said, 'it can't happen.' Deep down I really was thinking Sheena is wrong. I said, 'Sheena have you forgotten the constitution? The constitution states clearly that it

has to be an ordained person.' Sheena said, 'I have told the executive committee that they should make an amendment to the constitution.' Well, I can tell you, I was not amused! Because for me, it would have been a graceful nice way of leaving, with dignity and so on, not look like somebody who is greedy for power and importance in government. But the Anglican Church had recommended my name in spite of the constitution, and the Presbyterians had recommended my name, and I thought how could ... why would Sheena challenge me on this thing? It has now become a moral question, not a job. Am I now going to sacrifice this organisation, where Sheena is one of those people who fought that we should have a woman, and Sheena, knowing her, is now waging a war on an amendment of the constitution and then I have to say, 'No, I have to leave.'

So that was the greatest challenge of my conscience from Sheena ever in my life, but of course I didn't have much of a choice. I stayed on at the SACC for another five years as general secretary and I liked it very much, by the way. But I did tell Sheena a few times, 'Sheena I would be doing something very important in government now, earning a lot of money and look what you've done to me — and we are struggling with funds now.' I have never forgotten that, where I felt a moral obligation to a person first and foremost, and then a bigger one, really, to my own integrity. Yes, it was only Sheena that could do those kinds of things.

According to Bernard Spong, *The women in the SACC knew who they were and they were strong. Sheena already had this particular place, because she was white and she was knowledgeable and she was willing. She was powerful enough to make herself heard wherever she was. Virginia was much more gentle and did much more for women's development in the Council of Churches. Sheena was there as a vice president that would go into the meetings with her knowledge but Virginia, also vice president, actually got down to saying, 'These are the plans for women's development and these are the ways we need to go.' I think Sheena might even have looked down on these plans for women's development — sort of, 'Why bother — we're OK — why are we telling men we're not?' She didn't ever actually say this, but her attitude was such that there was no need to talk about women's development; she was developed and knew her place and who she was. Somebody with Virginia's experience and background understood discrimination against women much better.*

Bernard would certainly have been right that Thudiso Virginia understood some of the challenges facing women better than Sheena did, and Sheena was always one to leave things to others when she saw their competence. But when she was needed, Sheena was without question in the women's corner.

Sheena was a fighter, and quite a vocal one, says Thudiso Virginia. *I remember an ecumenical conference held to discuss where we were politically in South Africa. The women had a slot in the programme, the second last session of the conference — the last being closure. We decided, as women, that we must show in some way that we were protesting against that. So Sheena suggested that we should go on stage as expected, and I was to do the introduction but that not one of the women there should make a presentation. Instead, we would just stand up and say, 'Well we are here,' and sit down. Then at the end we decided we would walk out of the conference room. Earlier, I had heard somebody say, 'You know, we don't even need to take the time, it's just the women's session.' So as planned, when our slot was due to start, I stood up and said, 'Good evening' — although it was late afternoon. They said, 'Yes, yes good evening.' I said, 'Yes it is the evening of the day and the evening of the session and the women are only being brought in to have a say at this evening of the session.' I sat down. Then Sheena was the first one to stand up and do only the usual salutations and sit down. Then I did the same and then the next presenter did the same and so on. The other delegates began to wonder what was going on, the women are not saying anything. Just after the last woman had said her name and greeting, we all stood up and walked out.*

Sheena was sensitive and compassionate about the ego needs of most of the men in the Church. She was enabling and polite when men postured and pontificated within the boundaries of the male laager of spiritual superiority, which they had constructed for themselves through the centuries. *The way she conducted herself at church leaders' meetings was interesting,* says Marj Brown. *Sheena would be quite deferential. The church leaders would all arrive and Sheena would be so incredibly courteous. They were all men and then there were Sheena and Virginia Gcabashe as the deputy heads of the SACC. Sheena would never try to put herself forward in any way in those meetings and yet she had a greater mind than most of the men there. She had the ability to sit with these men very respectfully but was not in any way prevented from speaking out, although she would never use meetings as her soapbox. When she worked within that church environment, she showed the respect that those men expected without ever compromising herself or being ingratiating. I don't think she ever tried to belittle or show up any of the leaders, although personally she would probably have had a lot of axes to grind with a lot of those men. I remember when CPSA[7] had this whole debate about whether women should be ordained and Sheena wrote a very strongly worded email where she said this is all simply about power: people will cloak the debate in theology and the debate will go around in circles, but at the end of the day the essence of this debate is men holding on to their power within the church.*

Sheena was a vigorous lobbyist for the ordination of women, in a culture that definitely wanted to keep them in their place as a backdrop to men in this role — a culture that had support from women themselves, some of this support finding expression through a group that called itself Women Against Ordination of Women. This group accused women who promoted the ordination of women of being rabid feminists — *both* words intended as an insult.

[7] Church of the Province of South Africa.

Sheena remained firm on the matter but could also make the most of lighter moments and informal opportunities to shift people and change an attitude with a small intervention, an idea or a new perspective on a fact. Even so, sometimes with the 'best intentions', when it came to the point of making a decision about women's ordination, many men continued to prevaricate. Sue Brittion remembers how she and Patty Geerdts had to insist on their right as 'public' parish members to attend one of the Natal synod meetings at which the Anglicans were going to vote on the issue, and there they saw one of the senior church leaders who had assured them the previous week that he would be voting *for* women's ordination voting against it.

After many years of painful, mainly theological, arguments, Anglicans across the world slowly but surely started to allow for the possibility that God might not have a problem with women priests. Women's ordination was already a practice in several countries when Dean Colin Jones of Cape Town proposed the ordination of women priests at an historic provincial synod held in Swaziland in 1992, presided over by Archbishop Desmond Tutu. In his proposal, Colin Jones had shifted the argument significantly by saying firmly: *We are not dealing only with issues like traditions of male leadership, the prohibition of cultures, the role of men and women in the Church and society, matters of unity and faith and order, outquoting each other using scripture. We are seeking God's will for members of the body who happen to be women.* The motion was passed with a 79.2% majority and 17 abstentions. Only six of the then nineteen dioceses had actually voted in favour of women's ordination, however, and each diocese could decide for itself whether or not it would ordain women.

Bob Clarke in *Anglicans Against Apartheid: 1936–1996* makes no mention of the ordination of women in South Africa, despite the fact that the year 1992 falls within the scope of his book and he was a member of the diocese of the Cathedral of St Michael and St George in Grahamstown, which is where Bishop David Russell ordained the first Anglican woman priest, Nancy Charton, together with Sue Groves and Bride Dickson, in September of that year.

Nancy is mentioned only once in Bob's book, in a paragraph on page 408. After an expression of gratitude to the legal profession, the paragraph reads, *This sense of gratitude must also be extended to courageous members of the Black Sash like Rosemary van Wyk Smith, the Revd Nancy Charton and Priscilla Hall in Grahamstown and Di Bishop with her after-care as well as concern for the widows of the Cradock four who were murdered by the Security Police.* Sheena's name is mentioned four times: as a member of the delegation to the World Council of Churches Programme to Combat Racism meeting in Lusaka; as a person who asked a question regarding an SACC conference resolution of civil disobedience; as one of 242 arrested during an illegal protest march; and in a slightly more substantial paragraph on page 499.

As rector of St Bartholomew's Church and also ecumenical officer of the Albany Council of Churches, Bob knew Sheena personally. He knew her as an Anglican, as an anti-apartheid activist and, together with his wife Maggy, as a houseguest. Bob would have known Nancy even better and certainly must have been aware of the significance of these two women — and many others like them — in the Anglican community, for they were indeed 'Anglicans Against Apartheid'. It seems that many otherwise sensible men remain ambivalent about women's equality in the church and silence is one of the best ways to hide 'politically incorrect' ambivalence.

The tenth anniversary of women's ordination was joyously celebrated in Pretoria at a conference called Anglican Women Breaking the Silence. As reported in the Christian social justice magazine *Challenge*:

It was a historic moment. Anglican women from Namibia, Lesotho, Swaziland and South Africa, younger and older women, students and community activists, women priests and leaders of women's organisations, gathered in Kempton Park from 12-16 May to boldly break the silence about women's issues in church and society, to bring women across the church spectrum together to dialogue and share their stories, and to strategise to mobilise women in their own dioceses to move forward.

The conference ended on a high note, with the delegates joining many others in St. Alban's Cathedral, Pretoria, for a eucharist celebrating ten years of ordination of women priests in the CPSA. The theme for the service was 'Women Breaking the Silence: Celebration and Struggle'. The service began with short stories of particular women struggling for ordination. Sheena was delighted to be asked to do the service. *Ms. Sheena Duncan was the preacher and continued to remind us of our own history within the CPSA. It is not often that these stories and our history are told, and it was a privilege that many young women present enjoyed.*[8]

But four months later, at the CPSA provincial synod in Bloemfontein, several concerns were raised, including that there were very few women in positions of real leadership in the CPSA. All bishops and deans in the CPSA were still male. A further ten years later, in November 2012, twenty years after the first South African Anglican woman was ordained, Ellinah Wamukoya was consecrated as the first Anglican bishop in Africa. She is from Swaziland. South African Anglicans were still waiting.

Brigalia agrees about the difficulties of the 'second stage' for ordained women: *I recently had a conversation with a presiding bishop of the Methodist church here in South Africa, the first church that had the courage to have the first woman bishop, and he was saying things are more difficult than ever. It's absolute backlash. In the Anglican*

[8] Jakobsen, Wilma: article in *The Witness Magazine*, A Globe of Witnesses website: www.thewitness.org/agw/jakobsen012303.html

Church, our own church, the men tell you frankly — even bishops — that we are not ready for a woman bishop.

I'm talking of the year 2012 in South Africa, a country where the secular society has made attempts to put some women as judges here and there, in parliament here and there as ministers, in boardrooms and so forth, here and there. Yes, it's still tokenism but at least the courage has been there. In the Church on the contrary, it's backlash. I think it is about many things, mostly power and fear. Fear of power sharing. I think the male world is afraid of this new power that has never been tapped. They realise that these people who have been considered for centuries to be inferior, subordinate to men — their major role motherhood — can actually succeed at anything. I think the successes of women in some areas have created more fear in men. They do not want to share power. They realise there is something untapped, something deeper to these people who have these 'strange' gifts. I call them strange because I don't think men fully understand the humanness of a woman, nor the scope of her spirituality.

As women, we have our given deeper privilege of growing human life, of nurturing human life, of preserving human life. Something tells me in a manner I can never articulate that this person who has all these potentials is now moving into a bigger secular world, but I also think that religions — our faiths — for all of us, are much stronger than we realise. Maybe it is the religions that are holding us back as women because we anchor ourselves — even if not consciously — to some form of faith or religion.

We must also stop thinking ourselves into a box. I remember looking at the first woman bishop from Canada and feeling sorry for her. There's something wrong here and we must fix it. It's inside me too. There's my own example when I was flown by a black woman pilot! I said to someone on the plane, 'Our pilot is a woman, isn't that nice,' but I was scared, even as I knew that it was wrong to be scared. When the plane landed in Nairobi I asked if I could greet her, and when I finally saw her, I got even more scared. She was so small, and she had all the young braided hair, and then she put on her cap for respect — well I'm glad I didn't see her size before I was safe on the ground. Those are the things we must still do something about.

Sheena came from a different base, so she was articulating herself differently from the European feminists. If you come from a society like ours, which at that time was very politicised in terms of class and race, there's no way you can separate your understanding of the gospel or feminism — feminist articulation in theology — without looking at the context. That's where the South Africans always were different, very different. Class with us was a problem, but we also have racism and strong traditions still existing in all our societies, much more than we realise.

It's almost as though behaviours have changed because they have to, but actual attitudes, if anything, have hardened against women's equality. Along with a minority of remarkable men of all faiths, Desmond is a glorious exception and women are rightfully proud and appreciative that a man of his spiritual, moral and political calibre, his intellect, humour and inter-personal warmth, can see clearly that as human beings, they are his equal. The world can only hope that the future will see many more like him.

Sue Brittion observes that *Desmond, I think, really understood the quality of spirituality that was driving Sheena. Analysis is good, but in itself was not the guiding force that made her an activist. A lot of activism starts when people see things and decide with their 'brains' that things are wrong. Sheena's activism seemed to come from her heart, from the gut. She was an amazing embodiment of deep spirituality.*

CHAPTER 7

Advice Offices and the Law

In this century, having lived through two major global conflicts, and seen at first hand the hideous end results of racial persecution, we might be expected to be a little disturbed at the herrenvolk doctrines of our rulers. The moral debasement of our people has, however, been accomplished with such cunning, with such calculated management of group psychology and the inherent weaknesses and fears of the human animal in society, that hardly a voice has been raised in protest, and each new infringement of our rights has met with less and less response, until today it has become the silence of acquiescence.

JEAN SINCLAIR, National President Black Sash —
Opening address, Black Sash National Conference: 1964

When Jean Sinclair spoke of this 'we' and this 'silence of acquiescence' she was referring to the white electorate. Black South African citizens (although at that time they were not recognised as South African citizens) were certainly not apathetic, or silently acquiescent, despite the systematic and violent assault on their human rights and dignity. By 1964, organised black groups and brave individual disenfranchised black South Africans all around the country had already expressed countless courageous acts of resistance to the pass laws and to racism in many of its legislated and social forms. They did not need to understand each harsh and oppressive new apartheid law in all its detail, they experienced it firsthand.

Sheena, who applied her mind to the nuances of each law that brought people to the advice offices, whether as individuals or as communities facing forced removals and other human rights violations, soon realised three crucial things: first, that as surely as guns and bombs, apartheid law was being systematically used as a weapon of violent oppression; second, that as a society, most people were ignoring — or, at best, not understanding — the implications of the legislative horrors that were unfolding around them; and third, that there was a cadre of progressive lawyers who cared very much about what was happening, needed to be nurtured but could not always see past the word of the law. Moreover, their numbers were small and they were struggling to keep abreast as each new law wreaked havoc and created desperate situations that required urgent responses. Sheena herself had a deep-rooted respect for lawfulness and its intended outcome — justice for all citizens. As Jillian Nicholson observes, *Sheena never broke the law, but she excelled at exploiting it.*

Sheena was able to read a bill or an act with remarkable skill, understand it intimately, reduce it to essentials, highlight where and how it contradicted the

gille de vlieg ©

Sheena taking statements

political propaganda in which it was inevitably packaged, show up its deceptions or expose its naked brutality and, most importantly, pick out the loopholes through which it could be thwarted and some semblance of justice might be pushed by activist paralegals and human rights lawyers. Alison Tilley confirms, *I think of myself as a quick reader, but she was often ahead of me, with a battered set of documents, annotated in her sloping quick handwriting. Sheena knew her law: she read laws and bills as if they were novels, ploughing through reams of paper every night with a small whisky at her side. OK, a large whisky.*

Sheena absorbed information like a sponge, retained it as knowledge and shared it broadly. *Sheena was one of the most intelligent people I have ever known*, says Geoff Budlender. *She had an enormous amount of knowledge and factual information, and she understood it and could apply it. She knew that if you work with people who are not used to intellectual constructs, complicated explanations and fancy words — which a lot of the law is — you have to learn to boil things down to essentials. Sheena had a great ability to take a complex subject and deal with its essential elements. With lawyers, she could move skilfully into the legal mode and adopt it and analyse and debate it, yet she was not stuck there. Talk about working with people! That is part of what made her so versatile. She learned that formal education has little connection with intelligence. Her ability to identify and articulate essentials — no matter how complex the matter — came from working daily with people who didn't speak the same*

gille de vlieg ©

Sheena in the Sakhile community

language. She learned to listen and speak and think, through an interpreter, in a way that made it absolutely crystal clear what to say.

Sheena also took great care in translating legal jargon for others. *The thing that stands out for me about her incredible brain and intellect,* says gille de vlieg, *was her ability to read laws and Hansards, sift through them and simply, without condescension, make them accessible to all of us — people like myself who didn't have that type of brain, and people who had only basic English. I once asked one of the COSAS members from Thembisa that I got to know quite well, 'What is the main benefit of the Black Sash?' and his immediate response was, 'Those small booklets.' I realised that imparting information is empowering and so valuable.*

Sheena's skill in this regard was also a great asset in raising awareness among the Black Sash members. When the apartheid regime again wanted to change the constitution, this time to allow for the establishment of a race-based tricameral parliament, 30 000 copies of her booklet *You and the Constitution — Vote NO* were circulated to regional offices throughout the country, together with a personal memo from Sheena clarifying the reasons for the Black Sash campaign for a 'no' vote. The government propaganda around the referendum created a great deal of confusion in the minds of people and the booklet was used as a reference book by many speakers to dispel this, as it explained with clarity the implications of the proposed new constitution.

Joyce Harris, writing in a 1984 Black Sash headquarters report, shows how Sheena used the Rikhoto judgement[1] not only to help affected people but also to highlight the lawlessness of the apartheid government. *Sheena wrote a dossier on the judgement, and 250 copies were sent to the press, legal bodies and businesses, calling on them to make a statement of intent regarding their support of the points confirming the manner in which the government sidesteps or evades or manipulates or ignores the rulings of the courts. There was a favourable response from a number of recipients, plus press publicity.*

50,000 copies of her book You and Rikhoto *were printed, containing details of the ruling, who will or will not be affected by it and what they should do to establish the rights. Sheena stated that the South African government did not like the ruling of the Supreme Court, and that 'when officialdom makes up its own confusing rules and regulations to harass people and prevent them from obtaining redress ... when the administration refuses to pay attention to court rulings ... when government proceeds with utmost ruthlessness to reach the desired end ... then there is no rule of law. There is only administration. And that is the most dangerous prospect for our common future.'*

As well as forming the basis for many more of the Black Sash's illuminating pocket-sized booklets in the series *You and ...*, Sheena's legislative interpretations often featured in the organisation's magazine and in other resources that helped people find the practical realities in a maze of treacherous words. An example was her article on black local government in South Africa, which showed up one of the iniquitous burdens of votelessness that forced blacks to 'pay the same taxes as whites — but end up paying more for inferior services.'[2] Ishmael Mkhabela admits, *I still have the one about* You and Your Local Government *that I've kept just sentimentally.*

In the advice office, *Sheena was fantastic*, remembers Laura Pollecutt. *At that time, you couldn't just look on the internet. You had to get the physical paper legislation to look at a law, and also to track changes. Sheena was very incisive about legal things. She always made sure that she was on top of things even if that meant very late nights and very early mornings. She could probably have been a lawyer.*

There is no 'probably' for Alison Tilley, who experienced Sheena's dedication in the same way: *She stayed up late, I think every night, just sitting at her desk making sure she had a grasp of the brief whatever it was; that she had read everything and*

[1] The Rikhoto judgement in the Transvaal division of the Supreme Court established the rights of migrant workers to acquire urban residential rights. It held that ten consecutive annual contracts with the same employer, or fifteen with different employers, did indeed constitute 'ten years of continuous employment', and thus legal entitlement to Section 10 (1) *(b)* rights, allowing him and his immediate dependents to live permanently in Johannesburg. Although he was a single litigant, assisted only by the Black Sash advice office and the Legal Resources Centre, Mehlolo Tom Rikhoto's victory was relevant to the rights of potentially more than one million migrant workers.

[2] Duncan, Sheena: 'Black local government in SA', *Sash*, vol.6, no.4, February 1984.

understood exactly what was going on. She was one of the best lawyers I've ever worked with — she wasn't a trained lawyer but she was one of the best.

Domestic science! What a waste! Sheena should have been a top advocate, says Kathy Satchwell. *What is fascinating of course is that, without being a top advocate, look what Sheena achieved. That, in a way, is even more remarkable. I suspect that if Sheena had done law, there would not have been as many achievements because there wouldn't have been the kind of advice offices that the Black Sash advice offices became. I don't know who would have run them, who would have worked in one. I mean, Sheena wasn't a boss, she was a worker. I remember going to her house — you remember that sort of study in the middle — and there were all these papers and things lying all over. She worked everywhere and for much of each day. It was so impressive.*

Among the Black Sash members there were other brilliant, articulate and courageous women. Yet in her time, Sheena was undoubtedly the one who could best pinpoint not only the duplicity of government promises but also the racism and injustice in legislation and then alert members — particularly the more conservative ones who wanted to believe that reform of apartheid was possible. Even they could not ignore the human situations revealed unequivocally by the people who came to the advice offices. Sheena was also the person who made sure that the Black Sash workers and volunteers in the advice offices were kept up to date about legislation that would affect the problems people would be likely to face. There were many such examples, but two of those that poignantly affected black South Africans centred on their citizen rights.

In 1986 President P.W. Botha announced the repeal of the pass laws, together with 34 related laws. With good public relations, the government fooled a lot of the people for quite some time — the draconian pass laws repealed at last! Yes and no. It was expediently done and prepared for with diabolical cunning. New influx control strategies and regulations were quietly slipped into the remaining body of apartheid law on the wave of new measures encompassed by the second state of emergency, which was declared throughout the country on 12 June 1986. In the brutal tempo of the state of emergency, it would have been easy not to notice these new forms of control and exclusion because the police had free rein to do whatever they wished anyway, including prohibiting media coverage of their actions. Sheena noticed.

On Thursday 30 June 1986, Sheena walked into the Johannesburg advice office and told all the men and women sitting there that from the next day, 1 July, they would never again be required to carry the dompas — after nearly twenty million of their grandfathers, grandmothers, mothers, fathers, sisters, brothers, sons, daughters, aunts, uncles, friends, or even they themselves, had been arrested for so-called transgressions.

'There was a total non-reaction.'[3] The waiting people were more concerned with their daily realities as they encountered the state of emergency, declared just two weeks previously.

[3] Sheena Duncan quote from *The Burden of Privilege.*

Sheena had tears in her eyes as she turned to her desk. But she would probably have wiped her eyes, sat down and, before calling in the first advice seeker, lit a cigarette, picked up the Restoration of South African Citizenship Act, which would also come into effect the following day, and done a final check of her article for the next *Sash*[4] magazine.

In this article, Sheena pointed readers to the fact that the so-called restored citizenship would apply to less than two million of the more than nine million black South Africans who had been denationalised. Those who did not qualify to get their South African citizenship back would be worse off than before and excluded from all the benefits of the new reforms.

The Abolition of Influx Control Act had completely removed the system of pass laws and influx control: those black people who were considered to be South African citizens would no longer be required to have permits in order to work and look for work. However, their mobility would remain limited by the provisions of the Group Areas Act, the Land Acts, the Trespass Act, the Prevention of Illegal Squatting Act, and by the shortage of housing for black people. And now, because some would remain excluded by the so-called reforms, as Sheena put it:

'The barrier between insiders and outsiders has been redrawn, not removed. The old insiders were the people with urban residence rights with Section 10 qualifications. The outsiders were everyone else. Now the insiders are those who can get IDs and the outsiders are those 'aliens' who cannot.

'Apartheid is not dead. It appears in a new form.

'It is such a pity that the undoubted benefits of the new system to two thirds of the people cannot be welcomed wholeheartedly because of the dreadful position of the other third who increasingly will be excluded from participation in our common society because of the preference given to those people who carried South African identity documents. These can work without restriction and there will be no red tape involved for those who want to give them work.

'The rest have to seek permission to be in South Africa, and a work permit to work in a specific job. If the permit is not granted, an employer who gives them work or a person who gives them accommodation is liable to a fine of R5000 or to imprisonment for up to two years. This cannot be called reform.'

The so-called repeal of the pass laws was by no means the first example of the cunning and subterfuge practised by the apartheid regime. In an article titled 'The Big Cheat',[5] Sheena highlighted the key implications of the Aliens and Immigration Laws Amendment Bill, not only for 'real' foreigners but also for South African citizens who had been rendered 'alien' by their apartheid-legislated citizenship of 'independent' Bantustan homelands. She reminded members and other readers of *Sash* that:

[4] Duncan, Sheena: 'What the new laws say ...', *Sash*, vol.29, no.2, August 1986.

[5] Duncan, Sheena: 'The big cheat', *Sash*, vol.27, no.1, May 1984.

> An alien is defined as a person who is not a South African citizen.
>
> Permanent residence permits are not issued to black foreigners who come to South Africa.
>
> The Act lays down in section 4 (3) that the Immigrants Selection Board shall not authorise the issue of a Section 4 permit unless the applicant is 'likely to become readily assimilated with the European inhabitants of the union.'
>
> A 'European inhabitant' is defined as being a white person as laid down in the Population Registration Act of 1950.
>
> In South African language black people are not 'readily assimilated' with white people.
>
> There are many thousands of black people who were born in South Africa and who have lived in South Africa all their lives who are still foreigners. They have no claim to South African citizenship if both their parents were born in another country because their fathers never had a right to permanent residence in South Africa, even if they have been living and working lawfully in this country for decades.
>
> This is in marked contrast to the children of white immigrants who are automatically deemed to be South African citizens if they were born in South Africa. The difference is, of course, that the white fathers are granted permanent residence permits.

Sheena also spotted the racist injustice in relation to foreign migrant workers:

> It must be remembered that white South Africa actively encouraged and recruited black people from neighbouring countries to come to work here on the mines, the farms and in industry, impoverishing the sending countries in the process.
>
> Now that we do not need them any more, we push them back across the borders.
>
> This is a gross injustice.
>
> It is for these people that the amendments to the Aliens Act promise disaster.

Sheena showed how the additional prohibitions in the proposed amendment were disastrous not only for the so-called foreigner but also for his or her employer and that the penalties were ten times higher than before. Furthermore, she pointed out the effect on South Africans who were now also classified as 'aliens': 'The law has denationalised at least eight and a half million black South Africans since October 1976.'

Sheena circulated a note to all advice office workers on 1 July 1984, less than two weeks after publication of the legislation, alerting them that:

> The Aliens and Immigration Laws Amendment Act became law on 18 June 1984.
>
> This means that any person who shelters (gives accommodation to) or gives employment to an 'illegal alien' is now liable to a fine of R5000 or imprisonment for 2 years.

NB Xhosa, Tswana or Venda people who have no permit to be in any place outside their respective homelands are 'illegal aliens' as well as the Lesotho, Zimbabwean, Swaziland people etc.

Please tell me about any cases you may have where the new penalties are invoked.

This makes the whole issue of 'foreigners' in South Africa of the utmost importance. Please be very careful when dealing with such cases and refer to me if in doubt.

The government says it is not the intention to use this amended legislation against the citizens of independent bantustans.

We are not reassured by these statements.

It is not good enough that government makes statements about its intention to use this draconian measure only against certain groups.

There have been many broken promises in the past. The law is not to be made into a matter of selective executive decision.

As much as the legal administration played an important role in establishing and then maintaining apartheid as a political, legal and social order, progressive lawyers were also brilliantly using the law to attack and dismantle the system. Some significant victories were won in the courts, often with a lot of assistance and even guidance from human rights organisations. The Black Sash was one of these, listening with attention and total respect to the stories brought to its offices and rural fieldworkers, defining issues and then providing the interface between the lawyer, the issue and the 'plaintiff'. This was where Sheena shone and her attitude is exemplified in Laura Pollecutt's memory of *being at her house once with Geoff Budlender. She was talking to him about land issues and conveying to him that what they (those who were not lawyers) were saying was, 'We don't want you to tell us what we can't do. We are going to brief you, tell you what we want, and then you need to find a way to do it.'*

Political activists also used court proceedings — even if they did not accept the applicable laws as legitimate — to publicly express their views. These statements did not all carry the weight of, for example, Nelson Mandela's April 1964 speech from the dock. Nevertheless, each was part of a small but steady chipping away at what Jean had called the *calculated management of group psychology.*

In May 1988 when the Delmas Treason Trial[6] resumed, Sheena was called as a witness by George Bizos for the defence, in the court of Justice Kees van Dijkhorst. She was on the stand for almost three full days. Her evidence runs to over 200 pages of court transcripts and she took the opportunity to state, for the public record, not only some key views and actions of the Black Sash but also their rationale. Of particular relevance with regard to the United Democratic Front (UDF) was the

[6] Case Number: CC 482/85 started in Delmas, concluded in the Transvaal High Court: Sheena's evidence 2, 3 and 4 May 1988.

call to vote 'no' in the referendum about the new constitution and the tricameral parliament. Much of the court record consists of Bizos reading from various Black Sash documents — many of them written by Sheena herself — and then confirming that they represented Sheena and the Black Sash's views. With reference to the referendum vote, for example:

'The answer must be "no" because this constitution is a recipe for conflict in this country. The constitution for any country must be one which will last. A constitution must not be unilaterally devised. A constitution must be generally acceptable to all citizens if there is to be peace. This constitution is totally unacceptable to the vast majority of the people in the country. This constitution cannot possibly work; it can only lead to an escalating conflict.'

Skilfully questioned by Bizos, Sheena's evidence affirmed her approval of the UDF (many of its leaders were on trial) and pointed out how the formation of the UDF, its policies and its actions were basic to the notions of human rights and human dignity, not treasonable. Sheena told the court that, although the decision was preceded by much internal discussion, some fierce arguments and dissension, the Black Sash had eventually agreed not to affiliate to the UDF. But, Sheena continued, 'The formation of the United Democratic Front was so welcome to us, and we did believe that united action on issues is of the utmost importance and therefore we wanted to offer them wholehearted cooperation wherever a campaign of theirs or an issue was also of concern to us.'

Bizos: *Were you aware of what was stated in the declaration of the UDF at the time that this discussion took place?*[7]

Sheena: Yes, we were.

Bizos: *What was your attitude to that declaration?*

Sheena: I felt very positive about it.

In addition to the vote 'no' constitutional campaign, there were numerous other Black Sash commitments to action that were the same as those of the UDF. Two further examples were the consumer boycotts as a strategy of non-violent resistance and the matter of a representative national convention. Using the Black Sash March 1982 national conference minutes as source, Sheena read: 'We commit ourselves to principled non-violent action for change towards justice and liberation. Such action, which includes the withholding of support for example as consumers, should be used as appropriate in particular situations.'

The court also heard how the Black Sash had initiated, under the leadership of Joyce Harris, a discussion forum as far back as 1977 to encourage a united front of opposition to the legislative process, including the so-called Koornhof Bills, that was

[7] No italics in original court proceedings transcript.

systematically stripping black South Africans of their citizenship and of any hope of future voting rights in their country and also to take forward the possibilities of a truly representative national convention.

Bizos: *Now were you aware that the UDF had called for — was calling for a national convention?*

Sheena: Yes, we were aware of this.

Bizos: *Were there any preconditions that you became aware of?*

Sheena: The ones I remember which are also agreed to by the Black Sash is that political prisoners must be released; there must be a free return of all exiles and organisations' representatives; all the banned organisations should be unbanned before it would be possible to enter into any process such as a national convention.

Bizos: *Was the call made by the UDF for a national convention substantially dissimilar to the call that you as the Black Sash and more particularly the ad hoc committee headed by Mrs Harris made?*

Sheena: It was not different at all. It was the same thing.

Court: *Did the Black Sash as such call for a national convention or only that ad hoc committee?*

Sheena: No, no, the Black Sash as such had done so many years before that. It was one of our accepted and agreed principles or policies.

The defence argued that the UDF's opposition to the tricameral parliament was driven by a belief in a united, non-racial, democratic South Africa. Black local authority structures were seen as administratively impotent because all their major decisions needed the approval of the relevant white member of parliament. They were thus seen as an unacceptable substitute for meaningful political rights for blacks. It is noteworthy that the UDF leaders were on trial for views that the Black Sash shared and had raised publicly for some time.

The trial ended with the conviction of eleven defendants.[8] In 1989 the case went to appeal and the judgement was set aside.

South Africa was on an inevitable road to change, and in the process of her participation in the journey along that road, Sheena proved to be skilled in assisting when new legislation was being drafted.

[8] Thomas Madikwe Manthata, Popo Simon Molefe, Mosiuoa Gerard Patrick Lekota and Moses Mabokela Chikane were convicted of treason. Lekota was sentenced to twelve years' imprisonment, Molefe and Chikane to ten years and Manthata to six years. Gcinumuzi Petrus Malindi, Morake Petrus Mokoena, Tsietsi David Mphuthi, Naphtali Mbuti Nkopane, Serame Jacob Hlanyane, Hlabeng Sam Matlole and Tebello Ephaim Ramakgula were convicted of terrorism. Malindi was sentenced to five years' imprisonment and the remaining defendants received suspended sentences with severe restrictions on their rights to freedom of speech and association.

Alison recalls how *my relationship with Sheena really developed when we started doing the work on the constitution [this time the proposed new constitution for a democratic South Africa] and the constitutional submissions. I regarded Sheena as a sort of touchstone as far as what Black Sash policy was — because of the length of time she had been in the organisation but also because of her impeccable political instincts. I felt that I could rely absolutely on her take on an issue; that it would both resonate with the Black Sash membership and would, if not resonate with the advice offices, at least ensure that there wouldn't be a lot of disagreement with the advice offices. I was in a situation where I sometimes had no idea what other organisations were going to do or say on an issue. It was important that we would find ourselves in a space that really — although we didn't talk about it in those terms at the time — represented the vision and the mission of the Black Sash and that this would be carried through into whatever the discussion was about.*

Sheena would be very quick to respond to any questions that I put to her, to any issues I was worried about. Certainly in terms of submission drafting — that became the big issue — I would draft submissions without an awful lot to go on because there couldn't have been a detailed policy paper on issues that nobody had really considered in detail before. So I would sit down and sort of 'channel' the Black Sash — what might we think about this? I would send it out and then Sheena would come back almost immediately — and was always very kind in her comments. I don't recall her being impatient or dismissive, ever. She might say, 'Yes, that's a logical submission and you've developed this part and that part well,' then she would look at sections of it and say, 'Well maybe that needs a bit of a rethink?' The Human Rights Commission (HRC) and its establishment was an example, although I'm not sure we got it right. Sheena felt strongly that the HRC should not have significant search and seizure powers — she said, 'That's not what we need. We don't need police kicking doors down. This is a hearts and minds institution to change the culture of the country and it's best from the beginning just to make that clear.' I can remember making the submission and I think there was a lot of disappointment from some members of parliament that we hadn't come in with a much more aggressive — kicking doors down is absolutely fine — position. It was interesting to me how much emotional weight was attached to the Black Sash submission on the issue. I really hadn't experienced before how important the Sash submissions were and how people were disappointed or pleased — one could feel the room's response.

Through processes like that I got used to taking positions that weren't necessarily always the 'right' line, the party line. Sheena would never do that but her recommendations were always politically sound. We had an interaction once on the child support grant when [the then minister] Geraldine Fraser Moleketi called us in. Black Sash had been making an unholy fuss about the child support grant and we were having an effect, changing views on how the new grant should be implemented. The minister called us in, with a number of organisations — in Johannesburg. Sheena had hurt her foot and couldn't wear a shoe on that foot. She had crutches and for some reason she decided it was better to go barefoot than with one shoe. Her glasses were stuck together with Elastoplast. I was just ... it's difficult to describe because my respect for Sheena was such that if that was the way she was going to the meeting, then that was the way. Yet, at the same time I couldn't help but think that we could really have put on a more professional kind of show. We went into the meeting with the minister and there was a lot of sparring around opposition on the grant.

I was pretty forward with our calculations and why the grant should be increased significantly and why the department had done its sums wrong. So we had technical discussions and then the minister ended up looking at Sheena and saying, 'Well you really have to understand you are either with us, or you are against us.' Sheena sort of settled into her chair and said, 'Minister, when you are right, we will be with you and when you are wrong we will be against you.'

That kind of concluded the discussion, and I took it as my cornerstone and have had it ever since, in terms of advocacy and policy work that I do. You've got to work out what your position is as a matter of principle, looking at your guidelines — the constitution, legislation, international instruments and you have to decide where you stand and you look at where the government is on a particular issue and if they are right you support them and if they are wrong you oppose it. So for me that was a really important moment.

Sheena really helped me look at legislation sceptically and with a challenging eye. I think before then I might have been frustrated with the law but I didn't understand the whole idea of challenging the way something was drafted — putting forward an alternative.

Then, in 1994, came an extraordinary situation for the woman who had studied domestic science but was about to receive her third Honorary Doctorate in Law from yet another of South Africa's leading universities. This is how Sheena herself described the new situation in a letter to her children on 1 August:

'I am on the horns of a dilemma. Yesterday the Black Sash said they wanted to nominate me as a judge on the Constitutional Court. When whoever proposed it, they all rose to their feet and cheered but I said I would not accept because I do not think I am competent and also because it would mean that I would have to cease all the work I do for the Black Sash and the churches and a lot of other organisations. If you are a judge you cannot push and shove and lobby people from the edges nor can you allow people to try to influence you other than in argument before the court.

'That was yesterday. Today the World Conference for Religion and Peace (SA chapter) and Independent Forum for Electoral Education also want to nominate me and are pushing me quite a lot because the nominations have to be in within the next two weeks. I have therefore begun to consider it seriously — not because I want to do it but because I think it may be my duty.

'I think I may be more useful remaining on the outside rather than writing minority judgements in the Constitutional Court but, on the other hand, maybe I should not so hastily shut the door.

'The thing is that the interim constitution provides for a Court of eleven persons — the President of the Court has already been appointed: Arthur Chaskalson. The other ten are four judges of the Supreme Court, and six others nominated by the Judicial Services Commission after public hearings. Four of those must be lawyers with at least ten years experience. Two of them can be lay persons who *by reason of their training and experience have expertise in the field of constitutional law …*

'Those who are pushing me say that I can bring a human dimension and understanding into consideration of the court which, if left entirely to lawyers, will be absent as they concentrate on the words and the technicalities of the law. They say that I have sufficient understanding of the law to know what the lawyers were talking about without getting bogged down in it.

'I have asked Dad to advise me. I think he might find it quite attractive because the Court will be seated in Johannesburg and it would be a regular job with no possibility of adding on any of the other things I do in flying around the country. It would obviously need thinking work at home but I do that anyway and enjoy it so that would make no difference. I suppose it would entail some horrible official functions and receptions but I suppose one would not be expected to drive oneself to Pretoria to find one's way and parking. There would also be a considerable salary such as we have never earned between us and some kind of lavish golden handshake at the end of the seven-year term to compensate for not already being a member of whatever pension fund long standing judges belong to.

'At this stage I just do not know. I have asked different people to think about it and to advise me honestly but I will, in the end, have to make up my own mind. Of course, even if I accept the nomination, I may not be appointed but if I do accept the nomination I am committed to do it if appointed.

Sheena concluded her reflections with a note to her grandson Samir Haouach:

'Hey Samir, how would you like to have to address your grandmother as Mr Justice Duncan?'

Writing in the same letter about her lifelong passion for books: 'I went to Exclusive Books, and ended up, as usual, coming home with a pile of books. It is like going to a stationery shop when I go into a sort of hypnotic state piling pens and different kinds of paper into my basket. Dad goes into the same state of suspended animation in food shops but doesn't complain about the bills. He does it once a week. I do it about twice a year. He has just complained about the Exclusive Books item which has come through on his card account and says he will be glad when I am a Judge and can pay my own bills! I do not value his advice on this because he is biased! — in favour of additional income.'

A week later, Sheena had made her decision.

'The thing is, if it were to happen that I got appointed, I would have to give up everything else I do. Judges become very isolated and in the case of the Constitutional Court even more so. For example, the Black Sash is preparing to bring the first "class" action in SA on behalf of black pensioners in terms of the right to procedurally fair administrative action. I really would not like to have cut myself off from all the discussion and it applies to the work I do in the churches as well.

'I also doubt my ability. I am not a lawyer and I do think they all need to be lawyers in order to fully understand the very complex issues that will be involved. Anyway I decided not to accept nomination and informed everyone who wants to put my name forward of that fact. I think I am more useful on the outside pushing.'

Push she did. 'Today I am sitting at home glued to the telephone,' Sheena wrote in a family letter on 10 September 2001, 'waiting to hear if I have to go to the High Court in Pretoria with Geoff Budlender tomorrow. It is the Black Sash case against the Minister of Welfare and in the end we had to force their hand because we have agreed to several postponements to accommodate them and tomorrow is the absolute final date so there has been a flurry of activity over the last ten days because the Government does not want to meet the Black Sash in court. They know they do not have a leg to stand on in terms of the right to social security in the Constitution. It got to the stage where President Mbeki set up a special cabinet task force to deal with us — the Ministers of Social Development, Justice and Finance which merely complicated things further, as the Minister of Social Development (Welfare) was always ready to settle, thwarted only by his bureaucrats.'

Geoff Budlender recalls that the minister, Zola Skweyiya, said, *What we were doing is wrong if Black Sash and LRC are suing us* and that in the end government capitulated; an order was taken by consent and government voted an additional R3 billion to the department. Zola's attitude at cabinet level was supportive and he said it was good that another R2 or R3 billion would go to poor people. He was a remarkable, big-hearted exception, with abiding respect for Sheena and the Black Sash and, according to Geoff, *a worthy comrade and opponent both.*

As, from the other side, was Sheena.

Over the years, Black Sash advice workers as well as those working through churches, civics and other community-based organisations — rural and urban — garnered a vast body of practical and intellectual experience. They were uniquely equipped to guide people through the maze of truly draconian apartheid legislation, helping to squeeze out a semblance of some sort of justice here and there. They had learned a lot from daily listening with attention to personalised accounts of oppression, from rubbing shoulders with some of the world's best human rights lawyers and from the various training opportunities to which they were exposed. They had learned about developing human capacity and they had learned about working with the law — albeit an unjust one.

Some had been trained in basic levels of paralegal skills and had grown used to thinking of themselves as paralegals — somewhere on what was later described as a 'ladder' of legal training and qualification.

Some had experienced other learning opportunities. For example, in response to requests from black community groups outside of the major cities — and initially due to Sheena's determination and personal enthusiasm to reach as many people as possible with useful and accessible information — the Black Sash developed easy-to-use materials and booklets and had these translated into appropriate languages. Starting with *You and the Pass Laws*, the *You and ...* booklets were carried around in pockets and used in the most remote corners all over the country for many years. These resources, and the Black Sash's experience in confronting unjust authority and situations, were crafted into the group training courses that characterised much of the Black Sash advice office work for more than twenty years. The most formally organised of these training programmes were residentially subsidised but facilitated 'at the work place' at the Black Sash advice offices in Johannesburg and Port Elizabeth. With a basic core content, both regional programmes adapted to the needs of the communities who used the service and to the changing laws and political activities exercised by the apartheid regime. Sheena enabled those with a passion to take ownership of the training programmes, and in Johannesburg, she also generously shared her own communication skills and knowledge, facilitating many of the workshops herself, including those on the philosophy of advice offices, the budget, the making of laws and the Government Gazettes.

In due course, the Black Sash's in-house training courses were formally accredited. Training was, however, also done and supported more widely in the rural areas by the Black Sash fieldworkers (including Sheena, who from time to time left her advice office desk and travelled with them). The fieldworkers each worked from a base at one of the urban Black Sash advice offices and other trainer-caseworkers also facilitated ad hoc learning and skills-sharing initiatives on request, sometimes in the advice office itself, and sometimes collaboratively at venues convenient to particular learning groups. For example, in July 1990, the Cape Town Black Sash advice office, working with various other rights-based non-governmental organisations through the Rural Advice Training (RAT) project, organised a three-day international paralegal conference that included substantial workshop and training components.

Following up on the conference, the RAT published — and then regularly updated — an invaluable and accessible resource manual for advice workers and paralegals, which extended its reach across many rural areas of the Boland, Karoo and Southern Cape. In Port Elizabeth the Black Sash training programme grew exponentially from 1991, when it held five three-week courses for rural participants. These were key interventions and the majority of advice offices whose workers participated in the training became firmly established.

In the historical apartheid context of 'bantu education' and abysmal post-matric educational opportunities for black citizens, the notion of gaining a recognised paralegal qualification on a potential career path was particularly attractive to some advice workers — those who Sheena sometimes described affectionately but also slightly condescendingly as 'baby lawyers'. Other advice workers saw advice work as an opportunity for party-political mobilisation, while some just wanted to serve their communities in the best possible way as human rights development activists, focusing on providing information and then enabling people and communities to develop their own sustainable solutions. Sheena favoured the latter approach, and steered the Black Sash training accordingly.

In the years following 1990, people and organisations involved in the anti-apartheid struggle began to think about the future less as a far-off ideal and more as an imminent reality. Advice offices had to consider how best they could survive and approach the new challenges. Marginalised people still did not have the resources to easily identify, understand and claim their rights but the country was changing. In 1991, Jenny de Tolly, in her first address to the Black Sash in the role of president, touched on some aspects of the reconstruction process, including the judicial process: *The law must become accessible to all. We welcome the setting up of small claims courts, and of a public defender system for people who cannot afford lawyers' fees in criminal cases. A very exciting development, and one in which the Black Sash is involved, is the growth of a paralegal movement.*

Funding became a major challenge in the nineties and in the decades that followed South Africa's first democratic elections — when international donors withdrew most of their funding of civil society. Such donors seemed to think that giving money directly to independent non-governmental organisations would not after all produce the same yield in economic and political connections — and influence — as would money streamed through bilateral government-to-government funding. Often this money was intended by the donor to reach civil society, but via the government. But once human rights work is funded by — or via — the government, whether at national, provincial or local level, it is trapped in a net of state policy, bureaucracy and, inevitably, political and economic expedience. So, not all non-governmental human rights organisations were willing, or able, to access or use government funds. Many weakened and others disappeared. A few grew strong and not only inspired successful constitutional litigation but also created a space and an information base from which ordinary people could grow in solidarity and assert their rights in creative and meaningful ways. Mostly these were well resourced in 'human capital' and geographically convenient to the 'corridors of power'.

'At the September 1992 Black Sash advice offices workshop,' Sheena wrote in her report, 'we discussed new questions arising from our training programmes. This was sparked by a request by social workers in the "coloured" own affairs administration in Port Elizabeth for paralegal training. There have also been problems with ex-trainees who fail to comprehend that a community advice office must be open to the whole community and cannot be the preserve of a particular group.

'An advice office in the Orange Free State provides an example. The local civic association had selected candidates for training. Some months after they returned home the office was running smoothly and the civic committee told us they were doing good work. Then an African National Congress (ANC) branch was launched in the area. The advice office workers declared themselves as Pan Africanist Congress (PAC) members and said that the services of the office were only for card-carrying members of the PAC. This caused the collapse of the civic, and of the advice office, as the committee was split down the middle.

'We agreed at the workshop that we will train anyone who asks, provided they are properly mandated by their community or organisation, that they demonstrate that they understand the importance of not disempowering the people who seek assistance, and that they fit into our normal training programmes. We will not do exclusive training for any group. We agreed that our training programme should be seen as part of our commitment to non-violent direct action, as a way of changing things, and our principal means of working to establish human rights.

'In Johannesburg, where we run two four-month training sessions per year, we decided that if the community is sending two trainees, at least one of them must be a woman. We have tried to achieve this by encouragement but it has not worked and the last group in 1992 included no women. The problem seems to be that community committees in small towns and rural areas consist entirely of men, and women present keep silent at meetings. The Johannesburg advice office brought together all trainees during the past two years at a workshop in November, to hear how they are coping and to equip them with basic knowledge of voting procedures so that they can teach this in their communities.'

In tandem with her own voluntary, almost daily commitment to the urban Black Sash advice offices, these 'community-based' advice offices and their workers, urban and rural, were close to Sheena's heart. In the nineties, these were the workers struggling most directly with political loyalties and frictions — their own and those of others. They also faced livelihood challenges in their personal lives and reduced or total loss of funding for their organisations and for the service they offered to their communities.

At a paralegal training conference in October 1993, Sheena expressed some thoughts on the matter of finances in community advice offices as follows: 'LHR [Lawyers for Human Rights] and other organisations present did not seem to see anything wrong in advice offices charging for their services. When I asked wasn't it illegal for paralegals to charge for giving legal advice, it was explained by LHR that they are not charging for advice but for "disbursements". I remain implacably opposed to charging because it excludes the poor who are the people that fill our queues, but it does explain some of the cases we have had in the Jhb AO [Johannesburg advice office] where people have come to us because the advice office they had first approached had asked them for a fee.

'My personal opinion is that there should be some kind of basic and equal sum allocated to all community AOs irrespective of where they are situated — perhaps in quarterly instalments on receipt of reports. This could come through the Legal Aid Board if it were a more representative independent statutory body. Other funding would be dependent on the fundraising efforts by the AO committees and if additional funds were sought from the state, they should only be allocated on a rand for rand basis, the first rand coming from community fundraising events. That would have the advantage of ensuring that the AOs are truly community based.'

There was still to be one short generous burst of money available to civil society ahead of South Africa's first democratic elections, when human rights activists and organisations, whether urban or rural, faced one of their first major, but internationally popular, 'democratisation' challenges. At grassroots community level, on factory floors, at churches, schools and sometimes even in boardrooms, they were called upon to introduce and to nurture the first emerging bill of rights 'sprout' — the right to vote. The work was to train adult men and women to fully understand and to use their right to a vote — by secret ballot — for the political party and leaders of their choice, to govern their country. The context was one in which no South African had ever voted in a democratic process before, and the vast majority of South Africans had never voted as citizens before. The country was fraught with the shifting sands of conciliatory negotiations, and party-political differences and ambitions were being expressed with extreme violence. It was also a context in which advice office workers and their governing structures, like so many other non-governmental anti-apartheid organisations, had to decide on their road ahead in the unknown landscape of a new and democratic South Africa. Each possible road had its share of sincere and committed fellow travellers, but was also littered with potholes and opportunistic hitch-hikers.

When the dust eventually settled on the euphoria of the 1994 elections, little had changed to mend the differences or curb the rampant ambitions and often contradictory plans that were hobbling progress in the advice office/paralegal sector. The backdrop was plastered with catchphrases and words, widely interpreted to mean whatever each entity wanted them to mean and most guaranteed to cause some friction if questioned. By the end of 1994, for example, '*Access to Justice*' was embedded as the catchphrase in circles of discussion among most of the organisations active in the fields of justice and human rights work,[9] which were also trying to consolidate resources and lobbying power.

The following extracts from correspondence dated 12 May 1994, from the Black Sash to LHR, highlight some of the issues in the advice office sector:

In terms of paralegal training and the roles of paralegals in South Africa, we think there is potential for paralegals to develop and serve communities in a diversity of ways.

One direction aims to prepare paralegals to operate with various stages of legal 'apprenticeship', involving accreditation and registration by some central and probably statutory body, and a series of steps along a path of paralegal qualification.

Another direction aims to prepare advice workers/paralegals/rights workers to provide those seeking advice with as much information as possible, relevant to their problems; this would include some legal and administrative information but also more broadly examine the socio-political, community context when exploring possible solutions. The focus here would be on enabling advice seekers to make their own decisions about how they will act to seek solutions to their problems, rather than acting on their behalf.

There are also differences between dealing on a case-by-case, individual basis, as contrasted with involving many members of a given community in trying to deal with the causes of the problems collectively.

The various ways require different skills, and training programmes are accordingly shaped in terms of the identified objectives.

In 2004, in response to the survival needs in the community-based advice office sector, the National Alliance for the Development of Community Advice Offices (Nadcao)[10] was formed. It was an alliance of human rights organisations supported by several key donors. Nadcao's overall objective was *to ensure that by 2013, access to*

[9] A fledgling Paralegal Institute (NPI SA), Black Lawyers Association (BLA), Black Sash, Commission for Conciliation Mediation and Arbitration (CCMA), Diakonia, Farmworkers Research and Resource Project (FRRP), Industrial Aid Society (IAS), Lawyers for Human Rights (LHR), Legal Aid Board (LAB), Legal Education Action Project (LEAP), Legal Forum, Legal Resources Centre (LRC), National Association of Democratic Lawyers (NADEL), National Community Based Paralegal Association (NCPBA), South African Legal Defence Fund (SALDEF), Women's Legal Centre (WLC), surviving urban and rural community-based advice offices and their workers, university-based law clinics, and community law centres and projects.

[10] www.nadcao.org.za

justice at the community level is not only a permanent policy focus but is characterised by an institutional model that provides structured, ongoing support to the sector, particularly the work of CAOs and community-based paralegals. The Nadcao view of a paralegal included the *non-lawyer* capacity that Sheena felt to be so important. South Africa by then had many more courts and many layers of potential court justice, a more representative and thus more skilled cadre of legal professionals and a brilliant constitution with a powerful Bill of Rights and significant 'chapter nine' institutions established as watchdogs to safeguard democracy. The Legal Aid Board was providing service at local level throughout the country at more than forty Justice Centres. However, not only was much of this courts-based system of justice clogged with unresolved issues of racism, sexism, one-upmanship and bureaucratic phlegm, but at community level gross injustices prevailed.

The majority of people did not live in the context of justice described by the constitution, nor did they enjoy many of the benefits promised in the Freedom Charter when it was drawn up in 1955. Despite unwavering voter support for the ANC, despite the political significance of their right to vote, millions of South African citizens still had no affordable access to healthy food, clean water, security of person, housing, adequate education, electricity or transport. They remained almost powerless to change the conditions in which they found themselves. Nor did they have a hope of the opportunity ever to work for and have the material resources to buy these basic rights — for bought they must be, in an increasingly corporatised private sector that used what amounts to a foreign language to many citizens and operated within an uneasy neo-liberal capitalist dispensation.

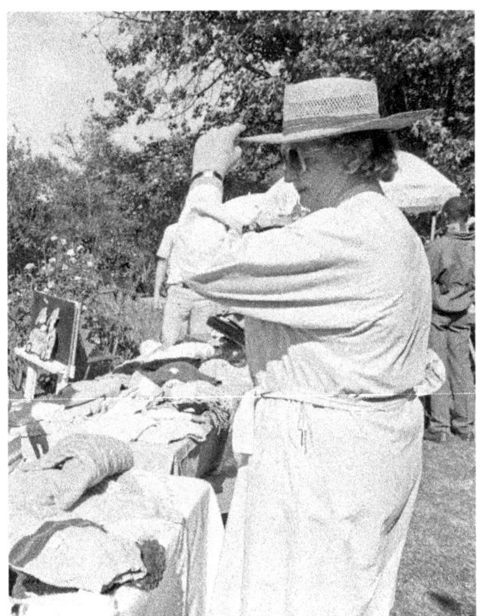

gille de vlieg ©

Sheena at the Black Sash morning market, the organisation's annual fundraising event

Is it reasonable to speculate that, twenty years into its democracy, South African society might have been different had there been less paralegal training with an eye on court-based litigation, but rather more dedicated *justice* training? If advice workers had learned more precisely and more extensively how to identify the practical implications of each new *just* law; how to encourage and remain constantly open to all possibilities; how to achieve and sustain authentic access to justice and reconciliation in the communities they serve; how to take into account all socio-political realities of the day; and how to be mindful at all times of gender discrimination? If the Black Sash had honed its training intentions to a fine art of activist human rights education, could the hope that Sheena embodied have been nearer fulfilment?

'We have a long hard haul ahead of us before justice is established in this land,' said Sheena in 1993.[11] Twenty years later, perhaps Nadcao — well-established almost a decade after its formation — will realise its vision and at last tip the scale.

[11] Duncan, Sheena: 'Going beyond advice', *Sash*, vol.36, no.1, May 1993.

CHAPTER 8

Land

Making a distinction between ownership and usage of land, Duncan suggests that ownership, as defined in laws inherited from Europe, is foreign to the people of Africa, who understand land as being something given in trust into the stewardship of the present generation by the ancestors for the benefit of future generations. Duncan links this to the biblical understanding of the use of land: 'Your land must not be sold on a permanent basis, because you do not own it; it belongs to God, and you are like foreigners who are allowed to make use of it.' (Leviticus 25:23)

'We need to note,' she continues, 'that the people we call squatters rarely move onto land that is being used. The land they occupy is indeed owned but it is not being used in any visible way. It is "empty" just as the history books have taught our children that the land appropriated and used by white settlers and trekkers was "empty".'

Charles Villa-Vicencio — *The Spirit of Freedom*[1]

The modest strip of land in Parkhurst in Johannesburg on both sides of the choked-up trickle of a stream had also stood 'empty' — until Neil and Sheena bought it and built their dream house on it. Once the Duncan family had settled into their new home, to the utter astonishment of many of their progressive friends, and with certain practical limitations and most basic 'ground rules' in place, Sheena and Neil continued to allow small drifts of homeless people to squat in corners of safety in still 'empty' spaces of the now exquisitely landscaped land. This should not really have surprised anyone — Sheena always was one to 'walk the talk', to make every possible attempt to adapt her heritage of culture and privilege to her pragmatic yet deeply spiritual understanding of how to be a simply decent human.

I remember Sheena always being able to accept the contradictions, and then being inclusive, says Aninka Claassens, *accepting these people living in her garden and also accepting her own beautiful comfortable house.*

Land dispossession is as old — at least — as colonisation. From the date of their first decision to establish settlements in South Africa in the seventeenth century, light skinned northerners grabbed at the 'empty' land that had been used by various indigenous peoples for centuries. The colonisers used guns, distorted Christianity and other cunning practices to stake out their 'ownership'.

In 1913, later generations of these same northerners took it upon themselves to declare laws that made it impossible for the later generations of the indigenous

[1] Villa-Vicencio, Charles: *The Spirit of Freedom,* chapter 'Sheena Duncan: Surprised by Joy'.

people to own land, except in a ludicrously small portion of the country — the exact whereabouts of which the whites also chose. As Margaret Nash[2] recorded in the August 1983 *Sash* magazine: *The legislation, not even mentioned in the Governor General's speech at the opening of the 1913 session of Parliament, was foreshadowed by a February 18 question concerning details of the registration of transfer of farms in the name of blacks in the past three years. To it the Minister of Lands provided a cut-and-dried answer, which later analysis proved to be grossly misleading but at the time provided the 'statistical scarecrow' needed by the white racist lobby.*

10 days later, in an impassioned address on the enormous danger of squatting, Orange Free State member J.G. Keyter called for a General Pass and Squatters Bill to prohibit coloured people (1) from wandering about without proper pass, (2) from squatting on farms, and (3) from sowing on the shares system. Transvaaler P.G.W. Grobler, later to be imprisoned as one of the 1914 Boer Rebellion traitors, moved the addition 'and further to take effective measures to restrict the purchase and use of land by natives.'

Minister of Native Affairs Hertzog responded by introducing a Natives Land Bill, with the unprecedented assurance that the Governor General would not withhold royal assent. The Bill led to a furore in Parliament and throughout the land, with deputations and representations from all quarters — South African Native National Congress, Transvaal Landowners Association, churches, missionary societies, etc. Yet within weeks it was rushed through both Houses of Parliament, signed by the Governor General on June 16, and gazetted on June 19 to take immediate effect.

Thus it was that, *awaking on Friday morning, June 20, 1913, the South African Native found himself, not actually a slave, but a pariah in the land of his birth.*[3]

For the next eighty-one years, if these 'pariahs' dared to stake any claim of their own outside of the small, designated areas — and many a bold man and woman did — they were removed with force. The main — and often lethal — weapons of choice of their oppressors were bulldozers, guns, legislative refinements, prison and torture.

Throughout the media-connected world, from 1950 onwards, South Africa was shamed year after year for almost thirty years by reports or images of brutal forced removals of countless thousands of families from their land and homes, both urban and rural, regardless of whether the families had titled ownership, rental rights or were informal settlers or occupants. Once the necessary apartheid laws were firmly in place, any black people who were living where new laws decreed they were not permitted to live were cleared away with varying degrees of force. The Group Areas

[2] Nash, Margaret: 'What happened', *Sash*, vol.26, no.2, August 1983.

[3] Plaatje, Sol: *Native Life in South Africa,* (1916), Gutenberg Project ebook, Chapter 1, www.gutenberg.org/ebooks/1452.

Act came to 'legal' life in 1950 and the first major forced removal in Johannesburg took place just a month before Sheena and Neil's wedding day.

In the early hours of 9 February 1955, despite a vigorous ANC protest campaign and worldwide publicity, the residents of Sophiatown were crudely awakened. Heavily armed police, accompanied by government trucks, forced what was to be a total of 60 000 people when the 'slum clearance' was completed out of their homes and into the trucks with whatever belongings each family could salvage. The people were taken to a site called Meadowlands, 19 kilometres outside the city centre and on part of the tract of land designated as the South Western Townships — Soweto. Their Sophiatown homes, schools, shops and places of worship and recreation were razed to the ground and the area triumphantly claimed for housing for whites. This was a brutal and tragic pattern to be repeated many times on many sites in South Africa over the following years.

It is estimated that by 1983, the white apartheid government had forcibly moved 3.5 million black South Africans because, by simple decree connected only to their skin colour, they were no longer permitted to live where they were living.

Influx control might look like a simple capitalist act of favouring those who could contribute meaningfully to sustaining the culture and infrastructure needed for the development of wealth, and excluding those who could not. However, even if viewed from this perspective, it would have to be acknowledged that in South Africa the contributions of white people were seen as worthy and were well rewarded, while the contributions of black people were deemed much less worthy and poorly rewarded. This situation led not only to systematic material impoverishment of black people and enrichment of white people but also to stern regulations to keep the number of (materially disadvantaged) black people in any town to the absolute minimum required by the (materially favoured) white population. The circumstances under which black people, who were required to work for white employers, were allowed to live in urban areas were severely restrictive in terms of, for example, distance from work opportunities, lack of housing, extremely poor health and education facilities, limited access to water, electricity and transport — and of course *documented permission* from the state.

In her advice office report from Johannesburg for 1984,[4] Sheena reached disturbing conclusions, noting that 'chaos and confusion in black urban townships has increased markedly over the last year. We do not refer only to the protests and unrest, which were the mark of 1984 but to the total lack of predictable and efficient administration.

'There has never been justice in local government for black people because the administering authority has never been representative. The government's attempt to

[4] Duncan, Sheena: 'Chaos in the administration of black townships', *Sash*, vol.28, no.2, August 1985.

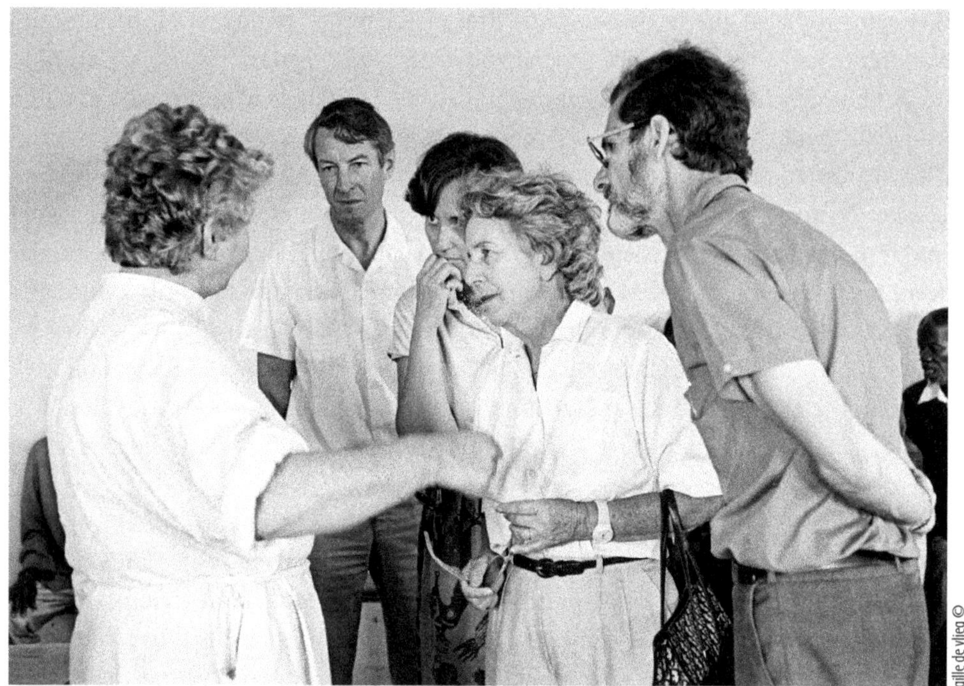
gille de vlieg ©

Sheena explaining to Helen Suzman and others about attacks on Moutse residents refusing to be moved

introduce representative local authorities has been totally rejected and is effectively inoperative in the Transvaal metropolitan areas.'

The report detailed — through advice office case studies — the bureaucratic confusion and corruption that prevailed: 'We have often reported in the past on bureaucratic inefficiency, of obstruction, maladministration and corruption but we had not before experienced such a complete state of disorderliness in administrative structures.

'The buck is passed from one office to the next, from one government department to another, from Town Council to Development Board and back again. People cannot possibly know with whom complaints can be laid or how they may obtain redress of wrongs done to them.'

There was legislative confusion, administrative confusion and particular hardships surrounding homeland 'nationals' and influx control. Sheena warned that 'It is not yet known what the Government's new Urbanisation Bill will be like but it will be a disaster if permission to remain in town is made dependent on possession of "approved accommodation." If this is what government intends, influx control will become even more severe and more rigid than it is now ... The current disorder will appear to be a Sunday school picnic ...

'Too many white businessmen are saying that influx control must go but must be replaced by a system of control based on work and accommodation. It sounds a very much more acceptable proposition. The words are softer and seem to be reasonable but it is a most dangerous delusion which must be abandoned at once.'

gille de vlieg ©

Sheena speaking on 'homeland' issues

Land issues had an impact in so many respects. Housing waiting lists had become chaotic and meaningless, subject to corrupt practices. Migrant workers — not workers contracted from foreign countries, but South Africans made migrant by virtue of their skin colour — struggled to make sense of their lives while earning a minimum wage, often in dangerous conditions deep underground. They were significantly affected by land dispensation; the curtailed land 'rights' they may have had in their 'homeland' were seriously eroded by economic imperatives and distortions. Their presence in and around cities and the enforced restrictions and limitations placed on them influenced South African society in ways that will reverberate for generations.

As far back as August 1973, Sheena had chaired a consultation on migrant labour attended by over thirty prominent people from all over the country, including Black Sash women and other thinkers in the fields of economics, sociology, philosophy, race relations, law and the church. They identified the centrality of the mining and farming sectors in the situation and considered how best to work for change at local, national and international levels. Their strategies included more in-depth research, engagement with the unions, putting pressure on employers, helping black workers understand and claim their rights — no matter how limited at any given stage — and working wherever possible to change the attitudes of white people.

In that same year *Sash* magazine[5] had published an article by Sheena called 'The Illegal Children'. In it Sheena wrote about the grim realities of the authorities' decision to demolish houses in Alexandra township, Johannesburg. The government's intention was to replace the houses with hostels that were intended to house 60 000 to 65 000 men and women in single-person accommodation. Regarding families with children, Coen Kotze, manager of the Peri-Urban Board's Bantu Administration commented: *We are giving them [these families] the choice;*

[5] Duncan, Sheena: 'The illegal children', *Sash*, vol.16, no.4, February 1973.

they must send their children back to their homelands and move into the hostel or must go back to their homelands themselves … this is the policy and we will enforce it.

The law states that they [the children] are illegally in the area so they have to go. It's as simple as that.

Sheena disagreed: 'Whatever the law says, these women have families with whom they now live and these families are being torn apart. Human decency demands that they be rehoused as family units, whether in houses, flats, or lodgings and that existing houses are not demolished until their occupants have somewhere else to live.

'It is a pretty rotten society where children can be described as being "illegal" when they are living with their mothers — mothers whose labour is being used by the white economy.'

The Black Sash had a cadre of members and a few fieldworkers who focused on land issues in urban, peri-urban and rural areas of most provinces. The SACC, through its leadership, its member churches and its staffed programmes, was also extensively involved in land and housing matters. In Gauteng,[6] through her consistent work in the advice office and her leadership positions in both organisations, Sheena provided a powerful resource link. She was closely connected to people like Ethel Walt, Ishmael Mkhabela, Josie Adler and other leading activists in this field; the Black Sash and the SACC both had offices in Khotso House; established relationships had developed with expert land rights lawyers and, for example, the Wilgespruit Fellowship Centre. In combination, these were among the factors that made for a strong, politically relevant, inclusive and interconnected body of support for people facing forced removals, land dispossession or race-based evictions and other threats to their homes, or their state of homelessness. As well as helping thousands of people with residential rights through the Black Sash advice offices in Johannesburg and Pretoria, the Black Sash, together with community-based or church advice offices, established various subcommittees to assist threatened groups to access resources with which to defend their rights.

There were several such 'removals' subcommittees in other provinces — not always directly under the umbrella of the Black Sash — but in Johannesburg two were. The Urban Removals and Homelessness Group was one. It was the committee, with Josie Adler as the driving force, set up in response to requests for assistance from urban and peri-urban people under threat of, or already subjected to, violent destruction of their shelters, homes or communities.

The second was the Transvaal Rural Action Committee (TRAC) with its home base also in Khotso House. *I don't think Sash intended to employ such a number of people,* says Aninka Claassens, *but there were so many pending forced removals at*

[6] Then known as the PWV (Pretoria, Witwatersrand and Vereeniging) region.

that point that Joanne Yawitch, Marj Brown and MamLydia[7] *soon joined the staff. We had wonderful support from Ethel Walt and extraordinary support from Sheena who had such clarity of vision and a very systematic way of approaching problems. We were dealing with risky and volatile situations where there were big risks facing people and at times we felt inadequate and had problems facing our own sense of futility. Sheena expected a lot from people and by expecting a lot and being very supportive, she created an enabling environment. Sheena made one feel there was nothing strange in thinking one could support people to stop a forced removal; she made it seem so inevitable and normal to go along with those people, stand with them and somehow stop it. In those rural communities people would not acknowledge the possibility of removal; they knew what they were going to do and it was not going to happen. We would come back and get the same sense from Sheena; whatever bizarre thing people thought of, she seemed completely confident that we would all work out strategies and deal with forced removals. We did. Somehow Sheena reinforced a sense that resistance was what was normal, what was human and that the threatened forced removal was an abnormal, unthinkable external thing we needed to keep at bay. Just standing together with people made it inevitable that people could change things. Put one foot in front of the other …*

TRAC works only with communities who approach it for advice, explains Aninka.[8] *In other words with organised people who have decided to take a stand and to achieve stated goals. From this it can be seen that the rural areas are more organised than is generally believed. There exists a misconception of rural people as apathetic and incapable of attempting to change their situation without education or help from outsiders. This imperialist concept of empowerment, essentially concerned with westernising people, is the generally accepted one. There is an empowerment which is more positive and evolves more from the people themselves. The community leaders are already powerful within their own situation, but they lack recognised power in the larger context.*

A field worker must be prepared to respect the ideas that come from the communities even though they appear initially to be strange or inappropriate. It is their ideas which give them energy and it is this energy which calls them out from under the crushing problems of rural life. The rural struggle is political, not in terms of alignment to political parties or ideologies but because the issues involved relate to a balance of power and to survival.

In October 1983 a woman called Rita Ndzanga arrived at the Black Sash advice office in Johannesburg to ask for help. She was from Mogopa and the bulldozers were lined up, ready to demolish. Although TRAC was to work with numerous other communities — including those in such places as Bloedfontein, Driefontein,

[7] Lydia Kompe-Ngwenya.

[8] Claassens, Aninka: 'Land policy: Seeking a common framework in local struggles', *Sash*, vol.33, no.1, May 1990.

Ekangala, Geweerfontein, KwaNdebele, KwaNgema, Machaviestad, Mathopestad, Moutse, Oukasie and Valspan — it is perhaps most appropriate to use the long-drawn-out struggle of the people of Mogopa to illustrate the resilience and determination of those South Africans who were being forced off land which was rightfully theirs, and the scope of TRAC's involvement. *Mogopa was terrible,* remembers Aninka. *It ripped those people apart, divided people terribly in the process.*

In a *Sash* magazine article 'Mogopa Rebuilds',[9] the story of one of the most well known apartheid-era land struggles unfolds.

The Bakwena BaMogopa own two big farms near Ventersdorp in the Western Transvaal. They bought the first of these farms, Zwartrand, in 1911 before the Land Act was made law. It is rich in minerals including diamonds, which are currently mined in the area on concession from the tribe. For over 70 years the tribe has lived at Mogopa and developed it without any government subsidy or assistance. They collected money and built two schools, a primary and high school. Both were beautiful cut stone buildings. They sank boreholes and put in windmills. They bought tractors and ploughed the land, selling the surplus produced to the Farmers Co-op in Ventersdorp. They erected fences and established roads. All of this was done so that the tribe could be able to maintain its identity and have a secure base in a world where its members were being recruited to work on white farms and in the towns.

Money is collected not only from the people living at Mogopa but also from migrants who work in town and who meet regularly as 'The Reef Committee.' All important decisions concerning the administration of the tribe are meant to be taken in general meetings held at Mogopa and attended by all adult members of the tribe who travel home from wherever they are working.

However, the previously peaceful existence of the tribe was shattered when Jacob More, an ex-policemen from Carletonville, was made headman in 1978. Soon after he was installed the tribespeople began to complain that he did not adhere to the democratic principles of the tribe. They say that he fined people large sums of money and even cattle for 'offences' which did not come before the Tribal Court.

Following a trail of evidence of Jacob More's corrupt 'leadership' the community decided — at a large and representative community meeting — to strip him of his office and replace him with a new headman, also electing new councillors. However, when they tried to inform the magistrate of Ventersdorp, a Mr de Villiers, of these changes, he refused to accept them. On taking legal advice in the matter, the tribe came face to face with the fact that *in terms of the Black Administration Act of 1927 the State President is Paramount chief of all Blacks* and, of course, through various ministerial and bureaucratic channels could 'legally' delegate to a magistrate the power to appoint and depose headmen, totally regardless of tribal preferences and

[9] 'Mogopa rebuilds: A story of resistance', *Sash*, vol.26, no.4, February 1984.

democratic processes. It was a devious yet simple path from there to corruption and collusion to suit the apartheid regime's purposes: the tribe were to be 'resettled' with arrogant disregard of their ownership rights, the graves of their ancestors, their citizenship, their safety and their collective will.

On June 24, 1983 the people at Mogopa were amazed to see bulldozers enter their village. Jacob More and his followers, allegedly ten families, were taken to Pachsdraai. As they moved, their houses were demolished. Then the schools were demolished, as well as the churches. Later the engines of the water pumps were taken away by the Magistrate. It is said that before Jacob More left he threw diesel in their remaining water.

The Bakwena BaMogopa called in the support of the Black Sash, Applied Legal Studies at the University of the Witwatersrand and other organisations and stood firm in their resolve not to move. Months of government bully tactics, lies and half-truths followed. A bulldozer and standby demolition squad set up camp, intending to intimidate. The tribe meanwhile mobilised resources through their own savings and support from others. Volunteer teachers were on standby to replace the teachers withdrawn by government. Their lawyers followed all legal avenues to stop the removal. The government blocked every move.

On 18 November 1983, an Order from the State President was read to those resisting forced removal and they were told that if they had not moved in the trucks provided daily by government between 21 and 29 November, they would be taken away by force. Further international attention and support was galvanised through a press and diplomatic conference, with a full statement from the Black Sash and members of the Mogopa committee present to answer questions in whatever detail was required. The article in *Sash* magazine continues: *Helen Suzman, in New York at the time, was contacted and asked to make representations and to use her influence with the US State Department. This she did with great effect — to Chester Crocker personally.*

The SA Ambassador in Washington was called in for discussion on the subject. Relevant information was placed in the hands of top government officials in London and throughout Europe. The overseas newspapers and television services were beginning to carry the story. [Foreign Minister] Pik Botha was at the same time on his European diplomatic tour, and was acutely embarrassed by the publicity.

The campaign gathered momentum as November 29 approached. Under the guidance of Bishop Tutu, clergymen of all denominations gathered in Mogopa for an all-night prayer vigil. This was one of those 'countless' days referred to by Desmond Tutu in his introduction, *when all you could do was to witness, be present and stand up to be counted there, with the people who would be losing their homesteads, their shops, their churches. I don't remember what Sheena would have said — but I do*

gille de vlieg ©

Priests including Desmond Tutu at a night vigil in Mogopa prior to the announced forced removal

gille de vlieg ©

Women at a community meeting to discuss the return to Mogopa

remember that she was there, a wonderful presence. On the morning of the deadline, with international press and TV presence in force, the removal trucks which had been there already for ten days made no move to carry out the order.

The responsible government minister, Piet Koornhof, received a deputation from Mogopa on 5 December, but excluded their lawyer. The community had prepared a short written memo with some questions. Koornhof answered none. They were prepared to meet him more than halfway, offering to move to a place approved by the tribe after proper negotiations concerning size of land and compensation. The minister did not agree. He had a joint press statement ready which the people refused to sign.

The people remained steadfast but the forced removal went ahead despite international condemnation, including a protest from the US State Department. On 14 February 1984, bulldozers flattened the houses and all remaining structures; people were loaded into trucks with their furniture and transported to Pachsdraai, more than 200 kilometres away.

Back amongst the ancestors' graves at Mogopa

gille de vlieg ©

They hated it there and over the years that followed, groups of those who had been forcibly removed moved several more times searching for a more suitable place. Then, as a result of continued and creative activism, the Bakwena BaMogopa received permission in September 1988 for a small group to return to tidy up the now overgrown graveyard where their ancestors are buried. The work itself did not require more than a few weeks but, when the task was nearly done, their hearts rebelled once more, work slowed down almost to a standstill, delaying departure. Others trickled back, built shanties in the ruins of their old stone buildings, planted cuttings from their fruit trees in small containers — to take with them if they were forced away again. The work on the graveyard proceeded at a snail's pace and remained unfinished. The white farmers who had been granted permission to use the land for grazing complained, and six months later, the government served the Bakwena BaMogopa with notice that the permission to restore the graveyard was withdrawn. The people ignored this, until the government went to the Supreme Court to get an eviction order; the people challenged it — and won. So it was that, in 1989, after six gruelling years of mayhem and destruction — of buildings, infrastructure and community relationships — the eviction was declared unlawful and the Bakwena BaMogopa were given the right to return to their own land.

In an article in *Sash*[10] Sheena explains another piece of legislation that affected the land ownership rights of Black South Africans: 'In 1970 the South African government passed the Bantu Homelands Citizenship Act. This act said that every black (African) South African is a citizen of one of the homelands. This applies to everyone even if they have always lived in the so-called white areas and have no knowledge of any homeland and no relatives in any homeland.

'Which homeland a person belongs to is really decided by the language he or she speaks. If he speaks Zulu he is a citizen of KwaZulu. If he speaks Tswana he is a citizen of Bophuthatswana. If he speaks Xhosa he is a citizen of Ciskei or Transkei — and so on.

'This act made no practical difference to people's lives because the homelands remained part of South Africa and everything went on as before.'

But, as from 1976 and starting with the Transkei, as each homeland was declared 'independent', the defined groups of people were systematically classified as foreigners — aliens — in the land of their birth and, Sheena writes starkly, 'By the end of 1981 almost 9,000,000 black South Africans will have had their citizenship taken away from them.'

Sheena's analysis then turns to some of the consequences, including that each of these millions of people will lose any chance of claims to political participation or to a fair share of the economic wealth; land ownership will remain a pipe dream; international travel will be impossible or at best a bureaucratic nightmare for them; their children, if born after independence of the designated homeland, will lose even the tenuous rights of residence the parents might have in South Africa; social grants and labour-related compensation would be fraught with complications; and all of these people, as 'aliens', would have no protection against being deported from South Africa at any time, without trial.

On 31 March 1992, the South African Native Trust, established in terms of the Development Trust and Land Act of 1936, finally came to an official end.

In recognition of the importance and urgency of the issue, the Commission on Restitution of Land Rights was constituted in less than a year after South Africa's first democratic election in 1994. Its tasks were to assist claimants in submitting their land claims, receive and acknowledge all claims lodged and advise claimants on progress. Various acts were passed to facilitate protection of certain land rights and three years after the election, in April 1997, the White Paper on South African

[10] Duncan, Sheena: 'Citizenship — the consequences of its loss', *Sash*, vol.25, no.1, May 1982.

Land Policy was published and outlined a strategy aimed at implementing land reform that would contribute to reconciliation, economic growth and stability. But, even after all these preparations, the process of land restitution ended up being ineffective and generated severe and painful backlogs — and ongoing hostility. Tackling the issue in a 1992 paper,[11] Sheena wrote:

> To enshrine the right to private property, subject only to the concept of *fair compensation* in the event of expropriation, in a constitutional bill of rights will, in the present situation in South Africa, enshrine and perpetuate injustice, an exceedingly dangerous thing to do.
>
> What, for instance, would constitute fair compensation?
>
> - Is it what the purchaser paid for the property at the time of purchase — with or without an adjustment for inflation?
> - Is it what the person or community which was dispossessed was paid in compensation, if they were paid at all?
> - Is it current market prices — grossly distorted as they are by the fact that land is being held unused for long periods and, in consequence, market forces have been manipulated to ensure a shortage of a finite resource?
>
> Has any person the right to own land which he or she does not use and to seek constitutional protection to keep those in need of land for shelter or food production from making use of it?
>
> Should any person be allowed the constitutional protection of ownership of property which was unjustly taken away from others (in the absence of any recognition of human rights or their constitutional protection) to the exclusion of claims for restoration, restitution or, at the very least, reparation?

After two decades of political democracy, although there has been some progress, many of these issues have not yet been adequately considered. A few key events serve to highlight some of the remaining challenges.

In June 2012, by which time less than 30% of the promised restitution had been accomplished with a woefully inadequate budget,[12] the ruling party announced its intention to institute a new policy, based directly on section 25 of the constitution which states that expropriation of land must be accompanied by compensation that is *just and equitable*. The *willing buyer, willing seller* principle was in disrepute. But what would constitute just and equitable?

In November 2012, in terms of the 2011 Green Paper on Land Reform, cabinet approved the establishment of the Office of the Valuer-General. One of the responsibilities of the office would be to assess fair and consistent land values

[11] Duncan, Sheena: 'The right to private property or the right to shelter', *Sash*, vol.34, no.3, January 1992.

[12] Over the nineteen years between 1994 and 2013, equivalent to about one-third of a single year's housing development budget. Visit www.africaresearchinstitute.org for more details.

and determine compensation when land is expropriated. Interpretation of the constitution suggests that such assessment, however, would not be binding unless agreed to by buyer and seller, or approved by a court.

In 2013, the centennial year of the notorious Natives Land Act, President Zuma announced that government, with cabinet approval, was considering reopening the process of lodging land claims, extending the previous application cut-off date of December 1998 to 2018.

In May 2013, the Restitution of Land Rights Amendment Bill was duly published for public comment. In addition to extending the claims deadline, the bill sought to align the land restitution programme with government's National Development Plan.

There are moves to ban foreign ownership of land in South Africa, *what should happen is that foreigners should lease land.*[13] In August 2013 cabinet approved a controversial Green Paper on Land Reform for public comment.[14]

Land ownership, use and distribution remain distressing unsolved problems, piercing thorns in the flesh of meaningful reconciliation. No one seems to know quite how to pull them out without causing excessive bleeding one way or another. But despite the difficulties, Sheena would not want us to give up. She would encourage us to 'look for creative ways in which we can address the problem of bringing into being a just social order'.[15] Most importantly, she would remind us that 'the debate must begin with the prior right — that of people to basic protection from rain, wind and heat, the right to privacy and security of tenure, to the use of land for the production of food for family, country and nation'.[16]

[13] Fin 24 quoting Land Reform Minister Gugile Nkwinti speaking at the National House of Traditional Leaders *lekgotla* in Durban on 30 July 2013. www.fin24.com.

[14] 'Land reform green paper approved by cabinet: Nkwinti'. Sapa, 24 August 2011: www.kwanalu.co.za.

[15] Villa-Vicencio, Charles: *The Spirit of Freedom*, chapter 'Sheena Duncan: Surprised by Joy'.

[16] Duncan, Sheena: 'The right to private property or the right to shelter', *Sash*, vol.34, no.3, January 1992.

CHAPTER 9

Abolition of the Death Penalty

If hangings were carried out in public, the public would at least know of the dreadful things that are done in the name of the people. The citizens would see that death is not always instantaneous. They would see that when men and women die in an extremity of fear their bowels may turn to water and they may defecate or urinate involuntarily. They would see that there are sometimes emissions of blood. They would know what the cold and deliberate taking of life means.

SHEENA DUNCAN, February 1988
'On hanging — a working paper: for Black Sash National Conference'

In her working paper on the death penalty, of which a few further extracts follow, Sheena presented a full account of the situation regarding executions in South Africa at the time:

> In July 1981 it was reported in the press that four men had resisted when warders entered the death cell to escort them to the gallows and that teargas had to be used to *calm down the prisoners.*
>
> In reply to questions the prisons department said, *It is of course always a possibility that a prisoner will refuse to leave his cell before his delivery to the place of execution — but this occurs only as the rarest exception. Naturally verbal persuasion as a means of handling the situation will be used in the first place. Only when this fails will other measures as dictated by the circumstances be considered.* The department did not comment on the merits of capital punishment but said, *This form of punishment does exist and the prison service is responsible only for the safe custody of a condemned prisoner as well as his delivery to the place of execution at the time determined beforehand. This task is fulfilled in as civilised and dignified manner and with as much humanity as possible.* One detects some repugnance in that statement. In the same reply the department disclosed that *the present facilities at the gallows make provision for the simultaneous hanging of up to seven condemned prisoners.* In August 1981 Mr David Dalling MP put a question on the Parliamentary order paper. He asked what was the average waiting time for condemned people from the time of arrival at the gallows to the hanging, whether they were given sedation, whether they were accompanied by a doctor, minister or anyone else, how many could be executed at a time, whether each man had his own executioner in multiple hangings, what procedure was followed and how many times physical force or teargas were used to get the men from their cells

> to the gallows. The Minister of Justice made earnest personal representation to Mr Dalling urging him to withdraw the question because the answers would be *too gruesome.*
>
> On 29 January 1988 seven persons were hanged in Pretoria. On 4 February 1988 seven persons were hanged. In the second week of December 1987 seven people were hanged on Tuesday, seven on Wednesday and seven on Thursday.
>
> 164 people were hanged in South Africa in 1987, the highest rate of execution since the Act of Union of 1910. The annual statistics are as follows but they are not entirely accurate. In the years since 1976 it has not always been possible to obtain the statistics of hanging in Transkei, Bophuthatswana, Venda and Ciskei, which each have their own gallows. The actual killing rate may have been higher in some years than those shown below.
>
> 1978/79 148 persons
> 1979/80 130 persons
> 1981 96 persons
> 1982 100 persons
> 1983 90 persons
> 1984 114 persons
> 1985 137 persons
> 1986 121 persons
> 1987 164 persons.
>
> Including the 14 persons known to have been hanged already this year that means we have hanged 1114 people over the last 10 years.
>
> At the end of 1987 there were 268 people on death row awaiting execution.

Sheena would have agreed with the saying that *not everything that can be counted counts and not everything that counts can be counted.*[1] The statistics were important for campaign work, but for her it was not just about numbers of people, or about what had been proved about their actions, but also that:

> The deliberate, planned killing of any human person debases those who carry out the hanging, those who must witness it, and all those who are members of societies which authorise it. It is the responsibility of all of us. To remain silent makes each of us a party to each judicial killing …
>
> Is there a way forward?
>
> Secular organisations and churches have passed resolutions from time to time calling for the abolition of capital punishment. We need to go beyond that now. There is a greater public interest in the question now because more than forty of the people currently on death row have been sentenced for actions arising directly

[1] Attributed to sociologist William Bruce Cameron.

> from the political conflict in this country. Concern for them in particular is being translated into a wider concern for the many more people who are awaiting the day when they will be put to death. More people than ever before are questioning whether or not there should be capital punishment.
>
> We can, as a means of raising public concern, push for an independent commission of enquiry. We can intensify efforts to persuade the State President to exercise his powers to grant clemency in all cases, not just in the case of political prisoners. We can do these things as part of the struggle to get capital punishment abolished altogether in our country.

Exactly two years after Sheena wrote this paper, in February 1990, along with other breathtaking announcements, President F.W. de Klerk declared a moratorium on capital punishment. This was certainly a step forward, but as Sheena wrote on the matter in a family letter, quoting Robert Frost, *The woods are lovely, dark and deep, but I have promises to keep, and miles to go before I sleep, and miles to go before I sleep.*[2]

Throughout the years of Sheena's activism, the broader church movement struggled to find its voice on the issue of the death penalty. In September 1969 the General Assembly of the Presbyterian Church of Southern Africa concerned itself with the question of the death penalty. In 1970 the SACC decided to print and disseminate among the council's member churches an informative pamphlet on capital punishment in preparation for discussion at that year's national conference.

The reasoning of the majority who wanted to retain the death penalty was that the threat of death would deter others from committing similar crimes. Yet, various studies over the years had not been able to provide substantial proof that capital punishment was in fact a deterrent in terms of the crimes to which it is applied.

'Extenuating' circumstances, which tend to be offered by retentionists as a humanitarian safeguard, are often connected to the personal and political disposition of the judge, or to the particular culture or socio-political system that supports the death penalty, or to a combination of these factors.

In South Africa the death penalty was irrevocably linked to race: the race of the people who created the law, the race of the people who powered the economic systems that created extremes of wealth and poverty, the race of the judge, the race of the prosecuting and defence attorneys, the race of the victim, and the race of the perpetrator.

In South Africa all death sentences were handed down by white male judges. All appeals against these sentences were considered by white male judges. All pleas for clemency were considered by white male state presidents.

[2] Frost, Robert: 'Stopping by Woods on a Snowy Evening', www.poetryfoundation.org/poem/171621.

gille de vlieg ©

Sheena speaking against the death penalty

These white men were part of the 'elite' in a society in which the Lansdown Commission[3] could declare that the death penalty should not be abolished because the bulk of the African population *has not yet emerged from a state of barbarism* and that, *in the mind of the undeveloped Native but recently brought into contact with Western civilisation and ideas, the sanctity of human life is a matter of less concern than it would be to the Western civilised mind.* This so-called Western civilised mind had recently emerged from a world war in which their 'civilised' behaviour had killed more than fifty million people.

These white men were also part of a society in which the N.G. Kerk [Dutch Reformed Church] was seen as the 'establishment at prayer' and in which Dominee D.F.B. de Beer, public morals secretary of this church, could in 1961 pronounce it desirable that *punishments for some crimes should be extreme if certain groups were to be protected from the lawless and violent behaviour of other groups.*[4] Helen Suzman MP can be forgiven for asking in Parliament eight years later who needed to be protected from whom — when *whites commit murder and rape on non-whites at a rate four times greater than non-whites on whites?*[5]

---

[3] Appointed by the South African government in 1947 to investigate penal and prison reform and, at the time, the only official body ever to have investigated capital punishment in the country — even if only in the course of a wider investigation.

[4] SACC pamphlet: 1970.

[5] Ibid.

This was also a society in which no white man had ever been executed for raping a black woman but in which the Minister of Justice C.R. Swart boasted in 1955 that during his office not a single black man who had been sentenced to death for raping a white woman had escaped the gallows. Over twenty-five years later, in the period June 1982 to June 1983, eighty-one blacks were convicted of murdering whites and thirty-eight of them were hanged. During the same period fifty-two whites were convicted of murdering whites and one was hanged, while twenty-one whites were convicted of murdering blacks, but not one was hanged.[6]

Sheena committed herself to the issue for many years in the Black Sash, giving her wholehearted support to other champions in the Society for the Abolition of the Death Penalty — and to younger Sash activists. Beva Runciman, Jacklyn Cock and Laura Pollecutt remember working closely with her, as did Paula McBride who was very active in trying to get a reprieve for her husband Robert. *The abolition of the death penalty issue was not a new one,* remembers Laura, *but Sheena helped revive it in Sash. The group was quite conservative because lots of people were part of it, all with different agendas regarding abolition. For example, there was a view that the issue itself was not crucial but it was important to get the comrades off. The youth also had a death penalty subgroup and there were also some UDF groups, and a general view that the Sash should not have its own position on the issue, but must follow the 'leadership'. Paula had started a group of families and friends of people on death row, and she was instructed by 'the leadership' to dissolve it. Many of our meetings were at Sheena and Neil's house and Sheena was very inspiring. We considered a number of cases, looked at their backgrounds and put together a document — with a title borrowed from Brian Currin,* 'Inside South Africa's Death Factory'.

In the SACC, Sheena was firmly supportive of the stand taken by both Frank Chikane and Brigalia Bam in each of their terms as general secretary. *The execution of Christ on the cross made no sense for some,* Brigalia wrote in a conference paper. *It is therefore no surprise that the execution of people at the South African gallows makes no sense to some. The church has and should always be opposed to the barbaric way in which human life is ended by the South African judiciary: hanging by the neck.*

Brigalia also addressed the doctrine of common purpose: *For many years this doctrine has been part of the South African law, as well as legal systems elsewhere. This doctrine is applied in the case of the 'Sharpeville Six' and the 'Upington 26'. The judge found the accused guilty on the grounds that they had a common purpose with those who killed — although it must not be forgotten that the actual people who caused the death are still unknown, and technically, if at a future date their identity is known they may still be charged, whether the 'Sharpeville Six' or the 'Upington 26' have been*

[6] Report No.23 *The Abolition of the Death Penalty in South Africa:* Raoul Wallenberg Institute of Human Rights and Humanitarian Law: Lund, 1996.

hanged or not. Many more people may be hanged for crimes like murder under the doctrine of common purpose, even if they might not have lifted a finger in the said murder. All Christians who respect human life must take a stand for the abolition of capital punishment.

The SACC played an exemplary humanitarian role as well. In its circular of 23 November 1988 it informed member churches: *The ministry to those prisoners on death row and their dependents has been approved by the SACC executive. This ministry has been funded for 1989.*

The SACC executive have decided that all prisoners on death row and their dependents are eligible for assistance, if there is material deprivation caused by the imprisonment and imposition of the death sentence. This decision was taken in support of the campaign against the death sentence, as a show of solidarity to those awaiting the death penalty, and also because no other agency is at present administering to these prisoners and their families.

The Southern African Catholic Bishops' Conference (SACBC) approached another important humanitarian and practical issue. On 17 July 1989 Brother Jude Pieterse, Secretary General of SACBC, wrote to the Minister of Justice H.J. Coetzee:

It has been brought to my notice that prisoners who have received the death penalty are debarred from pursuing any formal studies.

Given that there are those prisoners who, on appeal, have the death penalty set aside and walk out of the prison free people, given that there are those who have their sentences commuted to a jail sentence and that there are many who spend a considerable length of time awaiting their execution, a request is hereby directed to you that, if for no other reason than that of Christian compassion, the appropriate steps be taken to allow prisoners on death row to pursue formal studies.

On 30 November 1989, the minister replied, refusing to change the policy and closing off further communication with the words: *I am not unsympathetic towards these prisoners but regret that I cannot be of more assistance in this regard.*

Fortunately, this broad alliance of death penalty abolitionists were a resilient and determined lot for it was indeed going to be *miles to go* before they could sleep.

The moratorium announced by F.W. de Klerk in February 1990 did not last. The following year, on 28 February 1991, the Death Penalty Desk of the National Directorate of Lawyers for Human Rights sent out a press release alerting the public that: *At the same time the Minister of Justice was addressing Parliament and informing them of the resumption of executions, Mr Bezuidenhout was given notice that he is to be hanged on 5 March 1991. It is puzzling that the Minister refused to make public the exact date of this first execution since the lifting of the moratorium.*

The day before the scheduled hanging dawned, Frank Chikane added his voice on behalf of SACC, writing to President F.W. de Klerk on 4 March 1991:

We at the South African Council of Churches (SACC) are distressed that the moratorium on the death sentence, which came into force last year, has recently been lifted and that Mr Paul Bezuidenhout is to be hanged Tuesday, 5 March.

We urge you to use your powers as state president to intervene to stay the execution.

We also appeal to you to reinstate the moratorium on the death penalty for this interim period as South Africa moves towards a new constitutional and judicial order.

The SACC opposes the death penalty because we believe in the sanctity of life. We also believe that the death penalty does not serve as a deterrent to others.

The legacy of apartheid is a multitude of socio, political and economic problems. We would ask the authorities to address these problems rather than resorting to punishment by death.

Paul Bezuidenhout was granted a last-minute stay of execution that afternoon, not by the State President but by the Supreme Court (Transvaal Provincial Division).

The 'independent' homelands continued on their independent way. On 15 November 1992, Sheena wrote to the Minister of Foreign Affairs and to the State President on behalf of the Black Sash. She attached to the file copies a note to the Black Sash secretary saying that she hoped she had not been rude but she could not bring herself to address them as 'honourable' anything.

Dear Mr Botha

I urge you to intervene to prevent the hanging of 3 persons in Bophuthatswana on Tuesday.

Should these executions proceed it can only exacerbate tensions in that region, and in the Transvaal as a whole, which will in turn have an adverse effect on the process towards a negotiated future.

I fail to see how killing people by judicial execution can teach other people not to kill. Our country is in dire straits.

We talk about peace and commit violence.

It is time to call a halt to all deliberate killing, including planned killing by the state. You are in a position to prevent these executions should you have the will to do so.

I TRUST you have the will.

Yours sincerely

Sheena Duncan

and to the State President:

Dear Mr de Klerk

I do not know if you will by now be home after watching the rugby in London but I believe that this issue demands your most urgent attention.

The last time I met you was when you received a delegation of church leaders in Cape Town. You urged us not to keep raising things which belonged to the long ago past under a different dispensation when we were in a state of war. I did not agree with your interpretation of past responsibility but the present imminent hangings in Bophuthatswana are not that 'long ago past.'

They are in the here and now for which you are responsible. I make no special pleading for the persons concerned. I know nothing of them or of the crimes for which they have been convicted. I just firmly believe that more killings can only exacerbate our present dire condition.

There needs to be a moratorium, not only on judicial executions, but also on the imposition of the death penalty by the court. We are responsible for what happens in the independent states. They are corrupt creations and your government does have the power to control what they do. I urge you to intervene to prevent the executions on Tuesday.

Yours sincerely

Sheena Duncan

A last-minute stay of execution was granted.

On 6 June 1995, South Africa's first Constitutional Court delivered its first judgement. In the matter of the *State v. T. Makwanyane and M. Mchunu* (Case No CCT /3/94) the court unanimously declared all provisions of legislation sanctioning capital punishment, which were in force in any part of the territory, to be inconsistent with the constitution and accordingly to be invalid. By the order, the state was forbidden — through any of its agencies — to execute any person already sentenced to death under any of the provisions thus declared to be invalid.

Dare we hope that we will never again know that records[7] are being created in an autopsy room in some special prison somewhere in our country, where death tickets hang with details of neck measurement, height, weight, length of fall, length of rope and cause of death: *fractured dislocation of the first and second cervical vertebrae*?

[7] Such as the records in the 'death factory' Gallows museum at Pretoria Central Prison (now known as C-Max Correctional Centre).

CHAPTER 10

Pacifism

War does not only destroy lives and infrastructure. In its blood and dust and flames ideals of justice and democracy are also consumed. War destroys the future as well as the present and always it is the people who suffer.

SHEENA DUNCAN — Presidential address Black Sash National Conference: March 1983

Militarisation and other forms of sanctioned violence in our society have successfully infiltrated the hearts and minds of most South Africans. We permit — even encourage — the creation of 'the other' through various means, including the economy, education, culture, greed, racism and misogyny, all of which also had their place in the apartheid ideology. The media was managed strategically. Real life in South Africa had little to do with what was heard on radio or seen on TV. South Africans were at risk, as Sheena put it, of being 'seduced by the image of an enemy which is so skilfully being presented to us'.

Actions may be supported by theories of 'just' wars — with or without limitation on the types of weapons used — and 'legitimate' executions by hanging, electrocuting, poisoning, stoning, shooting, decapitating or in other ways killing individuals convicted of certain crimes (the nature of which can vary depending on factors such as the culture, religious practices, sex and age of the victim and/or perpetrator, social norms and the laws of a defined geographic area). We thrive (or starve, or somewhere in between) on economies that sanction — indeed, selectively support, reward and boast about — the development of ever more efficient lethal weapons and the degradation of a natural environment on which we rely for our survival.

Sheena abhorred the killing of her fellow human beings, through war or any other means. Her pacifism was an inspiration to young peace activists like Richard Steele and Anita Kromberg: *Sheena didn't support the Just War theory at all. It was the dominant position in the church, so she was against the mainstream. The reason we were so attracted and felt so supported by Sheena was because she was a pacifist and there were few pacifists in our world. She didn't preach 'this is the only way' but very few people understood pacifism the way Sheena did. It's an analysis of power and of society which is extremely radical: seeing how power and violence are associated on the left and the right — pretty much as mirror images. It was really amazing to be able to talk to her about it. We didn't have to defend ourselves, or our point of view. She was not dogmatic about it and nor were we; we supported all ways of working for justice. We were keen on non-violent action and Sheena was too. The way in which we expressed our pacifism was to try and directly undermine the structures that perpetuated apartheid and injustice and violence. Sheena understood perfectly what the logic of non-violence is and what the qualitative aspects of non-violence were — both strategically and also its way of modelling alternative approaches. Sheena saw the importance of linking means and ends but, sadly, many didn't and that is partly why, today, means and ends are coming home to roost in our society.*

Sheena's lack of dogmatism, however, and her unwillingness to lead the Black Sash into a blanket condemnation of violence under any circumstances opened her to considerable criticism for not taking a firm stand either way. For example, in *Sash*[1] in a context of community-based politically motivated violence raging through many parts of the country and also involving the United Democratic Front's resistance to apartheid, she wrote:

> It is exceedingly difficult to comply with the editor's request to write a few words about the debate published in this issue of Sash.
>
> We are engaged in a discussion which has no beginning and no final end. It is a discussion which is always part of the ongoing debate within any human rights organisation and this must be so.
>
> Sometimes the debate is muted and takes second place to other issues because there is no particular event on hand to make it a priority. At other times, and this is one of them, it becomes a matter of urgency to address ourselves to the problem once more.
>
> This is not the kind of discussion which can comprehensively be contained in a few pages of typescript. It requires long hours of verbal communication and argument. It will never be resolved satisfactorily because it always has to be argued out again and again in the light of new circumstances.
>
> It is a debate which challenges the most fundamental principles of justice and democracy. It is a debate about just war and just revolution — is there or is there not such a thing? It is about justification of the use of violence in fighting repression, or judgement upon that violence.
>
> It is about coercion in all its many forms. Coercion to force the opponent to give way is one thing. Coercion to force the compliance of reluctant people in a planned action such as boycott, strike or stay away is another. Both present moral problems. When does persuasion become coercion and is there a point at which it becomes morally unacceptable? It is a debate about strategies and whether the means do shape the ends, about whether the ends do justify the means.

[1] Duncan, Sheena: Editorial, *Sash*, vol.27, no.4, February 1985.

It is about democracy and about the strengths and limitations which need to be placed on leaders, as well as about the ways in which leaders can sometimes shed the shackles which bind them to their followers.

It is a debate which sometimes seems to challenge our loyalty to friends. It makes us feel uncomfortable and often very angry.

Nevertheless it is absolutely essential and very healthy that discussion is taking place and that it will inevitably have to be repeated over and over again.

There will never be any absolute and final answers. The line between right and wrong, guilt and innocence is a fine, faint and wavering one. The search for definition and guidelines on which to base our own actions is an unending one.

My own personal commitment to total pacifism remains unaltered but when the Church and society in general justifies and condones violence as a means to an end personal pacifism only provides guidelines for one's own behaviour. I can preach and teach nonviolence to others but my views do not often prevail so we have to struggle through with everyone else to some kind of accommodation within this violent, coercive and exploitative world without sacrificing the basic values of justice and peace, truth and compassion. We must not be tempted to compromise those things.

I think, suggests Adèle Kirsten, *there might have been an ethical dilemma for Sheena but there were two other factors. She was practical, so at some point it was — 'I'm working with these people, so let's get on with it.' The other was compassion. She was never sentimental, but she was deeply compassionate and I think sometimes we confuse those two. Her compassion wasn't just a matter of feeling sorry for people. It was an astonishing ability to span differences, to be alongside the other person.'*

Throughout her life Sheena sustained a belief that 'guns and tanks, bullets and bombs cannot prevail against the principles of truth and love'.[2] Her life's work during the apartheid period was rooted in a commitment to ending the structural and legal forms of violent oppression perpetrated against black South Africans and the systemic material impoverishment of the majority. This included giving her full attention generously and strategically also to various non-violent campaigns and civil disobedience resistance initiatives.

Characteristically, even as the apartheid system crumbled, Sheena did not shy away from responsibility. Perhaps it is not after all surprising that of all the post-apartheid issues crying out for the quality of attention that Sheena could have given, the final call on her activism — and pacifism — was a passion to rid her country of guns. Since the time the area now known as South Africa was formally colonised in 1652, the exercise of 'power over' has been most compelling through the barrel of a gun.

[2] Sheena's presidential address at the Black Sash national conference, March 1984.

CHAPTER 11

For a Gun Free South Africa

The shocking news of the shooting of an eleven year old child who was pointing a replica toy gun at a security guard is the result of the actions of a number of culpable persons, of whom the security guard is probably the least to blame.

SHEENA DUNCAN, Chairperson Gun Free South Africa —
From press statement to SAPA: 30 December 1998

The campaign for a gun free society and the hunt for hidden weapons were worthy causes in a society that had been ravaged by violence — causes that served the security agendas of 'both sides' — and the work needed dedication and unswerving integrity. Sheena could offer those — and, in both cases, she was asked to. So, being Sheena, she stepped up.

Initially intended as a one-off, twenty-four-hour national amnesty campaign in the run-up to the 1994 election, Gun Free South Africa (GFSA) became a registered non-governmental organisation (NGO) in March 1995. Sheena was a patron, Adèle Kirsten as co-ordinator was the first full-time staff person, and Peter Storey, former president of the Methodist Church of Southern Africa and past president of the SACC, was chairperson. Peter had worked extensively in Soweto and District Six, had been chaplain to Nelson Mandela and other political prisoners on Robben Island and committed much of his energy to non-violence and reconciliation. More or less at the time of founding GFSA, Peter had also co-chaired the regional Peace Accord structures intervening in political violence before South Africa's first democratic elections.

According to Adèle, *Peter was definitely in charge in the first years. From the outside, people assumed that he and Sheena might be close, but I don't think they were. Certainly from my perspective they had quite a difficult relationship, each saw the other one as bossy and they were both strong personalities.*

Peter is an extraordinary orator, a visionary with energy and drive — and he is networked — but Sheena was not only central in conceptualising the campaign, she had a much better strategic sense than Peter and without her the organisation wouldn't have achieved what it did.

Peter would not disagree with this last remark and he admired Sheena enormously. He remembers that when he approached her, despite Sheena's initial hesitancy about serving on yet another organisational governance committee — at a time when she rather wanted to cut down her commitments — there was something about the idea of a gun-free society that sparked a strong and positive response, *something deep inside her.*

Taking firearms out of society was undoubtedly congruent with Sheena's ideal of a non-militarised, egalitarian and peaceful society. But not only must she surely have known that it was a lost cause in her lifetime, she also knew what else lay ahead for the fledgling democracy. Sheena understood better than most what any new government would inherit in terms of maladministration, corruption and morally injured citizens. She also understood the ideologically dangerous territory of compromise facing the government's 'delivery' responsibilities to an expectant electorate.

From the onset, the gun-free enterprise was indeed seen by many as a quixotic 'tilting at windmills' sort of idea. Even Peter, as the founding chairperson of GFSA, acknowledges that it was absurdly optimistic to think that, within a few months, a 1994 gun-free election was a possibility. In the hope of gaining support from as many religious organisations as possible, Peter had pitched the 'hand in all firearms for a gun-free election' idea to the religious leaders with whom he served on the Wits-Vaal Peace Committee. He got a mixed reaction, which included small pockets of encouragement.

I know, says Peter, *that from the time we drew Sheena in as patron, it was wonderful to have somebody on that committee who just had no doubts at all that this was the right thing. It was so strengthening that somebody as down to earth and practical as Sheena was, with such sharp analytical ability and such a grasp of what was possible and not possible, put her weight behind this impossible dream. Sheena was the tower of strength.*

Sheena played a crucial role in several organisational decisions, one of which was changing the deadline for firearm hand-ins from the pre-election date to the first, post-apartheid, Day of Reconciliation on 16 December 1994. Peter remembers that they came to understand that *there was no way a lot of people were going to hand in their firearms before that election had been somehow successfully negotiated. For example, Tokyo Sexwale confirmed this when he said to me, 'You'll get my AK-47 — I'll lead a procession of people with AK-47s, once we know that these people are out of power.'* Still, there were bleak days. *Some of the religious leaders — particularly the Chief Rabbi — were urging us to shift our focus from a gun-free South Africa to something a little less extreme, more in the line of gun control. At the time we were trying to raise a large amount of money (about half a million rand) to organise all the hand-in centres around the country and also to have a prize that we could offer as an incentive. We were battling. The gun lobby had suddenly come alive. I didn't even know there was one until we started this campaign, in fact there wasn't one — they found their identity in resisting us.*

Slowly but surely, even before she became chairperson, Sheena moved GFSA away from a role of embattled outsider with a 'moral high ground' message. Strategic and political, she transformed the organisation into a kind of central reference point for ordinary citizens and for people like the police and politicians; GFSA began to set the norm for what might be reasonable and rational around gun control.

With GFSA in the forefront, the Gun Control Alliance (GCA) was formed and launched in Johannesburg in February 1999. A charter for gun control was developed. The focus was on strict screening of gun license holders, control of guns plus an appeals process, and a total ban on the sale or possession of replica toy guns. The sole purpose of the GCA was to support stricter gun control, and organisations that endorsed the charter were not expected to make any commitment to broader aims and objectives of any of the other organisations which endorsed the charter. Five years after South Africa's first democratic elections, writing in the 'Gun Free Quarterly Newsletter',[1] Sheena recapped as follows:

> The need for stricter gun control has led to the formation of a new South African network called the Gun Control Alliance (GCA), with organisations and individuals clamouring to endorse its Gun Control Charter.
>
> 29,694 firearms were reported stolen last year. Contrary to the frequent claims of the pro-gun lobby, most of these guns were not stolen from the police, whose losses accounted for only 1,775 of the total number.
>
> Considering that many people do not report the loss of a firearm because they could be charged with negligence, there is no doubt that legal guns in the hands of licensed owners are a major source of illegal guns in the hands of criminals.
>
> This is what makes the need for much stricter gun control so urgent, and what is leading large numbers of organisations and individuals to endorse the Charter for Gun Control, and to wish to be part of the Gun Control Alliance.

Firearms control a priority

The proliferation of firearms in South Africa is a matter of great concern to the government, and firearms control is one of the priorities in the National Crime Prevention Strategy. This has to be a multifaceted approach because illegal guns in South Africa arise also from being smuggled into the country. Firearms are smuggled across borders with our neighbouring states, and also enter by sea. There is also an unknown quantity of guns still hidden in arms caches, accumulated by all sides during the apartheid years, and there are large numbers of guns which were distributed by official sources to government departments, local governments, parastatals, traditional leaders and others, prior to 1994.

[1] Gun Free South Africa: April 1999.

Government is taking steps to control this proliferation. Government departments may no longer sell their surplus weapons but must hand them in for destruction. An audit is being conducted to list all firearms in the possession of all government departments, at all three levels. An amendment to the Arms and Ammunition Act is going through Parliament at the time of writing. This will forbid the lending of a gun to anyone who is not in possession of a licence to carry a firearm, and which is not on the property owned by the licensed lender. This will prevent criminals, who are unable to buy their own guns because of previous convictions, from having easy access to legal firearms by 'borrowing' them from relatives and friends who have been able to get firearm licences.

HANDGUNS A GREATER THREAT THAN WEAPONS OF WAR

South Africa is part of the growing international movement towards controlling small arms, and is cooperating with other Southern African Development Community (SADC) countries and the UN in this regard. Handguns are now recognised as being a much greater threat to human security and development than the larger weapons of war. Experts say there is no need to manufacture any more small arms because huge quantities are in circulation. These are available wherever there is money to be made from their sale, and wherever there are people seeking power by confrontational or illegitimate means. This threat is compounded by international criminal syndicates dealing in drugs, guns and motor vehicles.

New gun-control legislation will tackle one part of this enormous problem, and will go some way towards enhancing public safety in our own society and in countries beyond our borders.

Gun dealers would be wise to start to diversify!

According to Adèle, *Sheena was passionate about her commitment to non-violence and her understanding of social justice. Her language was about using the law as a way of reducing access to guns and reducing gun deaths — an incredibly practical approach — and her understanding of the law was extraordinary.*

I'll never forget when the Firearms Control Bill was coming before Parliament. I sent her the 120 pages of the bill. She spent two days looking at it in detail and then we had email interactions and then I sat down with her at her home and we went through what we saw as the key places where both Gun Free and the newly launched Gun Control Alliance needed to intercept. The things we wanted to support, we did through an approach of building and supporting the committee, saying 'This is really good — this is what we want.'

Then we considered stuff like protecting women in the home, one handgun only — new innovations and interventions from our side. Then, the very technical stuff: where the 'mays' and the 'shoulds' should be and how that altered the meaning. Sheena would notice when there were contradictions in the use of words that had potential for finding loopholes in the bill.

It was really important for GFSA to have that kind of expertise and approach to the law. No one else had that kind of eye for detail, coupled with that overview of the law in its entirety. She was brilliant on that.

Once prepared, the bill had a speedy legislative trip: it was tabled and passed at committee level on 8 March 1999, presented for debate in the National Assembly on 17 March, sent to the National Council of Provinces, and ratified on 24 March 1999, completing its passage through Parliament.

In the context of a violent society, where sources quoted by GFSA in its quarterly newsletter in 1999 estimated '11 to 13 million firearms in South Africa, 4 million legally owned, 5 million belonging to the South African National Defence Force (SANDF) and the South African Police Service (SAPS), and 2 to 4 million illegally held', the Firearms Control Act was a welcome piece of legislation. On 22 September 1999 Sheena wrote to her family, 'On the gun front things are suddenly going much better. The new Minister made an excellent statement to Parliament at the beginning of last week and it looks as if we are going to get the kind of new legislation on gun control we have been pushing for. Communities are mobilising around the issue and today I got a fax from one of our rural groups with their press statement, which is headed "Children are not Bullet Proof".'

The act was signed into being in 2000 and the Regulations Governing the Act, in 2004. The GCA saw its part in achieving these measures of control as a first victory. There was indeed cause to celebrate, even though ideological and self-interest arguments, legislative amendments, tardy regulations, amendments to the regulations, amendments to the amendments and problems of implementation dogged its existence. The legislation was not doing much more than 'treading water'; water that was and still is polluted with the economic politics of power, war, arms production and arms trade.

Getting accurate statistics about the number of guns in the country was not an easy task. Sheena, who was already also involved in a Joint Investigation Team (JIT),[2] was well aware of the complexities. Responding to 'official' statistics provided by Senior Superintendent Andrew Lesch of the SAPS, Sheena cautions Adèle and Judy Damon in a confidential memo dated 30 January 1999:

[2] A joint initiative of the South African National Defence Force and the South African Police Services, accountable to Sydney Mufamadi, Minister of Safety and Security at the time. In his letter of appointment to Sheena on 29 July 1997, the minister stated: *The mandate of the Joint Investigation Team is to investigate and recover state owned arms in the possession of private individuals. Your specific mandate will be to facilitate contact and liaise with municipal and government bodies on behalf of the Joint Investigation Team.*

We absolutely must not use the statistics as being definitive or accurate in any way. As Lesch is a communication officer in SAPS support services he must've got his information from Central Firearms Register (CFR).

To my own knowledge the figures he gives for the total of the country for 1996 are quite wrong. The committee of enquiry into the CFR had superior access to the computers at that time and the figures we gave in our report for that year are quite different. I am convinced we were accurate and the CFR did not refute our figures in their reply at the time.

From my own current experience with JIT, I also know his figures for the National statistics have to be totally wrong.

The SANDF has over 700,000 firearms and they and SAPS and correctional services must be excluded from what he refers to as state departments. In the second place the work we are doing toward a state-owned firearms [registry] indicates that departments at national, provincial and local levels have huge numbers of firearms which are not accurately recorded in the central register, if they are there at all. The whole thing is a colossal mess and there is no way anyone can yet give any accurate figures for state-owned firearms. In the third place there are about 5000 security companies in South Africa, some of which are absolutely enormous and most of them employ armed guards.

At the time of the committee of enquiry there were more than 600 legal gun dealers in South Africa and there must be more by now. Most of them have large stocks of firearms in their possession.

There is no way all these, together with manufacturers, can add up to only 802,206.

We have been using that figure of 4.1 million as being the number of licensed guns in the hands of private individuals, nothing to do with dealers or manufacturers or state departments. We must look back where we got that from in the first place and there is now Adèle's new estimate compiled from somewhere, which I have not yet seen.

The problem is that all information originates in CFR, and includes the research ISS [Institute of Security Studies] does as well as figures given by [Minister of Safety and Security] Mufamadi to Parliament. I don't know how we are to handle this at all.

JIT is under threat at the moment because CFR is trying to get our access to their computer system cut off. So far we are winning the battle because at last some very senior officers are taking us seriously but it is precarious and we cannot risk doing anything beyond our mandate unless we are authorised to do so. We will just get chopped altogether and the work is too important to risk that.

> The only thing I can think of is to have a research project on every single licensed gun dealer in the country to find out how many firearms they sold during 1998. As they cannot sell any gun unless there is a licence, that would give us the number of guns legally obtained in the year. They would of course not disclose how many guns they had sold illegally but it would still be helpful to find out about the legal sales and compare these with what the CFR says. Local police stations are also supposed to inspect the registers of all gun dealers every three months, which would enable a crosscheck if the reports could be obtained directly from the police stations rather than from CFR — which is where those reports are supposed to go.
>
> I very much doubt that gun dealers would cooperate with us because we would also need to ask them how many large orders they got from security and other companies.
>
> The Superintendent [Steenkamp, leader of the JIT] is kinder than I am. I think the whole operation is corrupted. He reminds me that most of the staff in CFR do not understand what they are supposed to be doing and that the computer system is totally inadequate. That is true and our committee also reported on it in our report.
>
> We must just let our minds wander around this and pay serious attention to it after we have got over the current rush of the launch of the charter.

Meanwhile, the pro-gun lobby was examining and using statistical research such as that of Antony Altbecker and CIAC/SAPS; statistics which indicated that, in 1999 for example, total murder rates, firearm murder rates and handgun murder rates had all fallen since 1994. Indeed handgun murder rates had fallen by 22% in that period. With such information the pro-gun lobby believed they could quite plausibly dismiss GFSA's positions on gun-related crime and issues of armed self-defence.

Once the Firearms Control Act became a reality, it was blamed for the closure of gun dealerships and massive loss of jobs. GFSA was accused of being soft on the African National Congress (ANC), of exploiting the growing crime rates to wage a propaganda campaign, of encouraging and receiving blatantly biased support from the media and of having been party to the drafting of 'secret' and misinformed firearms control legislation.

Gun Free was also blamed for the increased number of illegal firearms in the hands of criminals. The pro-gun lobby attributed this to poor auditing of firearms voluntarily surrendered at police stations, but subsequently sold, given away or lost by the SAPS, instead of being destroyed.

Many gun owners also believed that, because of bureaucratic processes and the alleged lack of SAPS efficiency in response to legitimate requests for licensing and/or re-registration, they were being criminalised for not surrendering their guns or for possession of guns — that through no fault of theirs were suddenly illegal, unlicensed firearms.

Fundraising was going slowly, says Peter. *We were getting an awful lot of negative press and letters threatening us. I was a bit down. At our meetings, the voice for shifting from a clear clarion call for a gun free South Africa to something more nuanced and less threatening was growing stronger, but Sheena just stood totally firm. She was so formidably clear at what was to be the last such meeting that she turned the meeting and we never looked back after that, nor considered that shift again. I will never forget that moment and how grateful I was to her.*

Then, there was also the time, in 1997, after I retired as Methodist bishop and left GFSA to go overseas to do some teaching. Sheena was the obvious choice to take over as chairperson. She was unwilling and hard to persuade but took it on, I think because of her passion for the cause. Adèle was by then in the driving seat as director and those two had a good relationship and mutual confidence in one another. I was thrilled that Sheena agreed.

It is clear that Sheena offered GFSA wise and principled guidance — based on the scope of her connections, her dedication to accuracy, her strategic insight and her extraordinary capacity to understand and shape the law. In addition, as she did in so many of the other organisations in which she was involved, Sheena also offered her unstinting support — at all levels — to the younger generation of activists who staffed GFSA. Because of her characteristic acceptance of the goodness within each person, Sheena generally inspired those who had contact with her. They knew that she trusted them and they, in turn, trusted her and were able to work creatively and confidently, even in the most challenging circumstances, knowing they had her support.

Sheena was amazing, remembers Adèle. *Our GFSA office was under attack — we were not sure by who — perhaps just by the gun lobby. Our offices were vandalised twice — seriously, a whole lot of really violent stuff, lots of graffiti on the walls. Sheena was completely unfazed. On one occasion, there was glass all over the place and Sheena came at 6 o'clock and helped me clear up the mess. She just had that incredible ability to be calm and to see it as 'a sign that what we are doing is on the side of justice'. As solid as a rock, Sheena was always there, always available, never talking about her own pains or losses or fears.*

I think Sheena trusted me and trusted my judgement strategically. Practically, she trusted those I brought in to support me. She wasn't interfering. She didn't get overly involved in some of the management stuff. On strategic stuff, I worked with her in two ways. The one would be to say — this is what I'm thinking, put my idea forward and then get her feedback. That worked really well. There was never a point of huge differences. Sheena would be clear when she thought it was inappropriate or when she thought I was going ahead of myself. But then, she would often defer back to me and say, 'You're in touch with this much more on a daily basis: if you think that's where we need to go …' She seldom vetoed or used her power to block. The other way would be when I was really uncertain and would say, 'I don't even know where to begin thinking about this, what do you think?' I'd go a little bit with a blank slate and ask for her views. She would say — she seldom talked off the cuff on new or complex issues — 'I need to think about this.' Then she would come back to me in a day or two, sometimes in writing, articulating very clearly in a logical, quite linear sequence, what she thought needed to be done; what she thought the advantages were and the disadvantages. As a director, I couldn't have wished for a better chairperson of the governance structure of GFSA.

Nearly ten years into its life, GFSA started going through a difficult time. Adèle had left, after being director for six years. Sheena — wanting to spend more time with Neil and to visit her children and grandchildren more frequently, and wanting to give more space to younger people in GFSA — gradually withdrew. The pro-gun lobby moved in on the advocacy space, shifting members of parliament, the general public and the police towards its views, and was much more present and interactive on a range of levels.

Rather than legal ownership of guns, the pro-gun lobby cited lack of regard for the law, increasing urbanisation, unemployment, a reduced police service, less effective police investigations, images of great wealth discrepancies, and immigration of international criminals as more compelling reasons for an increase in violent crime. They sealed this line of argument by accusing GFSA pressure organisations of denying women the right to grasp control of their own lives. A legally armed woman, they said, was not going to be a slave to anybody, mentally or physically. By arming themselves, women would be able to demand and acquire their — as yet unobtained — social and Constitutional rights. They called on everyone involved in the debate to consider the statistics and the social realities, and then to look their own consciences straight in the face.

Sheena, on the other hand, had called on everyone to consider the implications of even just toy guns.[3] 'Those who make these toys for profit, the manufacturers, the importers, the retailers, know what it is they are doing, so deliberately, to seduce children into the gun culture that will maintain their profits into the future, when the children graduate to wanting real guns. Those who give such gifts to children also do their part in raising yet another generation of adults whose only moral value is the power they so wrongly think is conferred by possession of a gun.'

The accidental shooting of the eleven-year-old child 'is just the latest in a history of tragic events caused by replica (non-powder) guns. Robberies have been executed with them; children have been injured in eyes and ears by the little yellow pellets

[3] Press statement to Sapa: 30 December 1998.

spat out by the latest model; the toll of damage caused by BB guns with their metal pellets continues to mount.

'How many more tragedies have to happen before the government acts to ban the manufacture, importation, sale and possession of these toy guns.

'They are not toys. They are dangerous weapons. Their promotion and availability can only cause an ever increasing culture of violence that spells death to development and to any hope for a society "committed to human dignity … and the advancement of human rights and freedoms" as we stated in the Constitution we are so proud of, but do so little to defend.'

As we have learned, Sheena's work with guns was not only with GFSA. It had taken on a related but different dimension when she was invited by the post-apartheid Ministry for Safety and Security to work on the Joint Investigation Team (JIT) to recover state-owned weapons in the possession of private individuals. 'The next bit is entirely confidential and you must not mention a word about it,' Sheena wrote to her daughters in November 1996. 'Peter Gastrow (ex-DP MP and now a special advisor to Sydney Mufamadi, the Minister of Safety and Security — i.e. police) phoned me today and said the Minister is considering appointing me to chair an inquiry into possible corruption and/or maladministration in the Central Firearms Registry. They were evidently looking for someone incorruptible and my name was suggested. I am going to meet him in Pretoria next Monday to see if they really want me and if I am really prepared to do it. It would be a challenge and quite interesting but it depends on how much time would be demanded and how many hot trips to Pretoria.' The meeting must have been mutually satisfying. Sheena agreed to her appointment as chairperson of the investigating team of which François Thomas Steenkamp, a South African Police Services superintendent, was the project leader.

Sheena and the Superintendent ended up working well as a team, despite early misgivings from her side. In February 1997 she wrote to her daughters, 'My gun enquiry continues. It is really very difficult because the most important policeman on my committee seems to be suffering from a really bad paranoia — I mean really mentally quite sick.[4] I can't get him to write anything down or to give me solid evidence. I know the evidence is there because I have seen the computer printouts but it is useless unless he gets coherent. We are having a meeting tomorrow and if he does not produce the goods then I am going to have to do the difficult thing and suggest he be put on sick leave to get treatment. He has cause to be afraid but that overlaps with his mental condition, which is decidedly unhelpful.'

Yet, as the Superintendent became more settled, an extraordinary, and to some a seemingly unlikely, relationship did develop between these two — Sheena a seasoned,

[4] Sheena learned later that, in addition to the job stresses, the superintendent had in fact been experiencing family relationship problems when they first started working together and was subject to serious depressions from time to time.

mature and brilliant anti-apartheid human rights champion and the Superintendent a young former security police officer. The kindness, humility and love evident in Sheena's letters to him[5] suggest something of the spirit of South Africa's Truth and Reconciliation Commission (TRC), which was hearing submissions during the first years of Sheena's work with the Superintendent.

I could never work out what was going on there, says Adèle. *I met Steenkamp once; he was in awe of her and she just adored him. Even when things were going a bit awry with the secretariat after JIT was closed down, Sheena would phone Steenkamp and ask for his view on that — though he wasn't involved anymore; he'd been shifted off somewhere. Maybe there was mother-son stuff but I think another thing that attracted her to him was that he had been an army chaplain. So, whenever she talked about their trips a lot of it was about the really interesting theological and quite deep philosophical discussions they had. He had a lot of interesting ideas and despite the fact that she didn't always agree with him, somehow that seemed to be a point of connection, a mutual interest.*

Although he was not prepared to talk further about his relationship with Sheena, or of their work together, the Superintendent confirmed that, *I have two degrees in theology, which I did not use in my work in SAPS and although Mrs Duncan had no such qualifications, we had many meaningful theological discussions. When we differed she would say that she understood what the source of my view might be, but that she learned a lot from me. Because of her phenomenal and unblemished integrity, I was able to take her into my confidence regarding my family and draw her into my small circle of friendship.*

In his 'Ministry for Safety and Security Briefing Paper on 1997 Priorities', dated 20 February 1997, Mufamadi described the context of the project as follows:

When the new democratic government was elected in 1994, our first challenge was to transform a repressive and ineffectual police force into an effective and legitimate police service.

We first had to amalgamate the existing eleven police forces into a single unit. The police in the old homelands were hopelessly incompetent, and badly under-resourced for the size of the territories and populations. Resources were skewed in favour of white areas and components perceived to serve white needs, while crime-fighting units such as the detective unit were undertrained and poorly staffed (even now, only 27% of detectives are trained). We had to amalgamate these old forces within a single command structure.

We also had to undertake a transformation process. The old SAP was good at fighting 'terrorists', not catching crooks. The relationship between police and most communities

[5] The official aspects of these letters are by now a matter of public record. Author's source Cullen Library Historical Papers (University of Witwatersrand): SHEENA DUNCAN personal papers: Item M.14. Collection number A3238.

was so poor that police could not even enter some areas, never mind establish effective community intelligence links. We knew that a major priority was to get communities to accept and trust police. In short, the old SAP and the old homeland police were a force *whereas we needed to create a police* service.

After expressing some cautious optimism about changes in the crime situation, Mufamadi itemised the priorities for 1997, which he named a 'Year of Service Delivery'. In his view, the first of these was to control and reduce firearms — legal and illegal — and the problems and violent consequences related to the *proliferation of fire-arms in SA. This means we must prevent more weapons coming in, and we must mop up the sea of weapons presently in circulation. We also must tighten up the licensing and usage of illegal firearms.*

The priority issue of firearms may be considered in more detail as an example of the scale of the problems we face and the types of solutions we will pursue this year for our 5 top priority issues.

Mufamadi's briefing paper continued with chilling facts, including the issue of firearm licenses to people with previous criminal records and the number of people who possessed between 10 and 648 firearms *each*. Not all these people were bona fide collectors. The paper further itemised the number of gunshops; license applications approved, refused and outstanding; and the number of firearms lost or stolen by civilians, police and army. *In short,* the minister commented, *the preliminary reports have identified an overloaded, clumsy system that demands urgent, comprehensive action.*

Much of Mufamadi's information was based on statistics gathered by Gun Free South Africa and Sheena's report to him as responsible cabinet minister, in her capacity as chairperson of the investigating committee.

Many things were happening as South Africa tried to find its feet as a new democracy. One worth remembering in the story of JIT is that, almost concurrently, Parliament approved the Defence Review in August and on 2 October 1997, Deputy President Thabo Mbeki announced that tenders would reopen for the purchase of arms, setting in motion what was to become a scandalous arms deal.

Knowing nothing yet of the parallel energies at work in the matter of weapons of destruction, Sheena accepted the challenges of appointment and set about her duties with typically prompt and wide-ranging thoroughness. Her networks, efficiency and commitment to the cause were ideal qualities to bring to her role as facilitator of a difficult process.

For example, on 3 November 1997, she wrote in a letter to Dr Charles Villa-Vicencio at the Truth and Reconciliation Commission: 'The other day I saw the announcement of amnesty granted to Riaz Saloojee in respect of the storage and distribution of weaponry to ANC structures between 1991 and 1994. I asked for a copy of his amnesty application but it only gives the most general description of the geographical areas where the firearms were distributed and no idea at all of where they might be now. It also does not specify where they came from.

'It occurred to me that the TRC must have a great deal of factual information about arms caches and about the distribution of weapons during that period so I consulted Mary [Burton], who said you would be the best person to approach about getting information which might assist JIT in its work. I fully understand that you cannot release the information which is still the subject of pending amnesty applications but it would be a great pity if SAPS had to wait for the full and final report of the TRC before following up leads that might be in your hands.'

Typically, Sheena took great care with the accuracy of information she gathered. Not only was it obvious from her first report to the minister that there was indeed evidence of negligence, gross abuse of powers and co-option in the CFR and that in many cases firearm licenses were issued too easily and to the wrong people, but it was also clear that he had full confidence in her capacity.

In spite of this, the first year of the team's work was unsatisfactory all round. In a background report signed by both Sheena and the Superintendent early the following year, Sheena notes that: 'JIT's progress has been much slower than it should have been due to a totally inadequate staff complement. It is only now in February 1998 that sufficient support staff have been appointed. After the initial training period we hope that we can move faster to implement the task given to us.'

The report mentions some of the work done in the provinces and stresses the importance of the 'great political sensitivity required in dealing with the issue of state-owned firearms still in the possession of traditional leaders', and the importance of noting local recommendations and suggestions made in this regard.

Details of her correspondence with him show that in many ways Sheena was like a personal assistant and analyst to François Thomas Steenkamp and he must have been one of the most efficient and well-informed superintendents in the SAPS. For example, in 1998 against a backdrop of tension between Minister Mufamadi and his Police Commissioner George Fivaz, and covert but escalating shenanigans around the arms deal, mixed with pre-election friction and violence between the ANC, the United Democratic Movement and Inkatha, Sheena kept Steenkamp up to date about the politically destabilising violence in Richmond, KwaZulu-Natal. In the form of handwritten reports which she then faxed to him together with her own assessment of each situation, Sheena provided facts and opinions as gathered from her reliable and trusted contacts 'on the spot' including Peter Kerchhoff, Luke Pretorius and violence monitor Mary de Haas. In addition, she kept Steenkamp informed about legislative matters, sent him English press news cuttings, often with her own commentary on the side, and connected him directly to people she trusted, when she thought this would be helpful to him. Sheena often drafted correspondence and reports for Steenkamp — whether for her signature or his, or both.

In the process of identifying weapons under their jurisdiction, Sheena's communication approach with local authorities was 'to start off in a gentle way and then get tough if we need to if they still do not respond. I have tried to keep it short because I think the text should be sent to them in Setswana, Afrikaans and English.' Once Sheena had made contact, she followed up and followed up again — and again. Endlessly willing to provide greater clarity, consistent in courtesy and sensitivity, not only to language but also in a spirit of genuine consultation and respect for local dynamics, Sheena nevertheless persisted until there was some sort of response. She used her contacts and influence across a wide field, national and international — including the Church, the legal fraternity, politicians, ANC members, Gun Free South Africa, Black Sash and other organisations — to gather information, to guide the team, to champion and enhance the quality of the Superintendent's work and, above all, to give her best to curbing the violence and the proliferation of guns in South Africa.

Sheena worked tirelessly to honour her mandate. Accountability to the Superintendent as team leader came first, but she also remained meticulously accountable to the minister — sometimes through Commissioner Fivaz — and to the Civilian Secretariat. This period also required a lot of her energy in terms of Neil's health, demands on her time through church and other organisational responsibilities, work on the Poverty Hearings and the joy of the birth of her granddaughter in Morocco, yet Sheena remained ever willing to give more.

Then suddenly, on 20 September 2000, the whole staff of JIT was summoned to a meeting and abruptly told that JIT was being closed down and its functions transferred to the Central Firearms Registry. According to Sheena in follow-up letters, 'There has been no consultation, and no discussion was allowed at the meeting as to how CFR proposes to take our work forward.' In a letter to the Superintendent the same day, she expresses her feelings more forcefully:

> I have just been erasing all the pencil dates I put in my diary for possible trips to Nelspruit and Pietersburg with some tears for the abrupt end to our work together, and regret for the fact that we have not been allowed to complete it. I am exceedingly angry and no longer wonder why the police are so incapable of addressing the problems that confront the citizens of this country. If this is the kind of dishonest stuff that goes on and the total lack of care and concern for the people who work in SAPS it is not surprising that there is such a lack of morale and such disorganisation that the criminals have the upper hand.
>
> I am completely shocked at the behaviour of de Beer at this morning's meeting. He would not allow the JIT staff to see the document he was referring to and he

> did not even read the whole thing and explain the process it has been through. … He was exceedingly arrogant. … The very least he could have done as chair was to give everyone an opportunity to introduce themselves so that we could all know who we were meeting with.
>
> I don't think [the shutdown] had anything to do with any specific thing we have done. I think it is the culmination of a long process of trying to stop us and, especially, to punish you for being a whistleblower. It has been a very long process and you have always come out on top until now. … As long as Minister Mufumadi and the old strong secretariat were there we were protected. Now the secretariat barely exists and I do not think that either Minister Tshwete or the national commissioner know anything about policing.
>
> The Firearms Control Bill has given the CFR etc. the excuse to say that JIT is no longer necessary. This is quite extraordinary when you think about it because it has not even been passed in the House of Assembly yet and still has to go to the National Council of Provinces. Then there will be the process of making the regulations and putting new systems in place. There are many months to go before it is implemented so all that stuff in the information note that has put an end to us is nonsense.
>
> I can't do anything about it right now but there is one thing that has been very significant this year which is the control Parliament is seeking to exert over the executive. The Arms Control Bill has been thrown back to the Department of Defence and will now not come forward again until it has been reworked and there have been public discussions. … Next year I am going to start stirring to get the Safety and Security Committee to start asking questions about what has happened to the Secretariat and why the White Paper as approved is just being ignored. Now is not the right time to start asking these questions because it is too near the end of the year and the local authority elections and no one will be paying attention but I am not going to let our experiences go to waste. One thing I have learnt in all my long experience is that if one fails in tackling a problem from one side, one just has to find a way of tackling it from the other.
>
> This is the first time in my life that I have had to stop doing something before the task is completed. It annoys me to be thwarted in this way.

Despite the premature shutdown of the team on which Sheena and the Superintendent had worked together, their investigation had surfaced information that, although incomplete, could not be ignored. Two months after the disbanding of Steenkamp's team, in November 2000, a new joint investigation team (JIT) was set up to investigate the notorious arms deal. This JIT comprised the Auditor-General, the Public Protector and the Directorate of Public Prosecutions. It faced hostility and denial from the executive, but after several delays finally tabled its report to

Parliament a year later amidst allegations that the report was criminally 'doctored', apparently by the President's office. Its executive summary exonerated cabinet and government, in stark contradiction to 350 pages of content that indicated significant tender irregularities.

Coupled with the work done by other organisations and groups such as GFSA and the de Caris Committee,[6] the findings of the JIT on which Sheena served had nevertheless made an important contribution, not only to the new legislation but also to uncovering crucial and disturbing facts about weapons in South Africa. Guns remain the ultimate tool in both perpetrating and resisting criminal acts. Trying to establish records of ownership — whether legal or not — and measures of controlling ownership and use of guns is a noble cause, but a complex, controversial and often unpopular one.

In his foreword to *Destroying Surplus Weapons*[7] Mosiuoa 'Terror' Lekota wrote: *It can be said that small arms are the scourge of Africa. They find their way into various parts of the continent raising levels of fear and violence. They move from countries that experience conflict and war into other countries that are at peace but where there is a market for them. One of the key features of these small weapons is the ease with which they can be bought and sold at low cost. The increased levels of firearms-related crime has become untenable for African security forces and requires clear government action.*

It is also of some concern that a culture is developing with the use of guns, glamorized by Hollywood, and associated with what is considered cool and macho.

The new political dispensation in South Africa has had far-reaching effects. The AK-47, once referred to by the South African freedom fighters as 'the liberator', now has to be taken off the streets. The new dispensation is committed to destroying illegal weapons and surplus small arms. Ironic words from a man who was Minister of Defence at the time, when nothing effective was being done about the scandal of the not-so-small arms deal negotiated in the ministry he had taken over.

For Sheena, there were still years of activism ahead, but the timing of the end of her work with JIT was quite opportune. Neil's health was erratic — as she put it to the family, 'his batteries are running down' — and her personal commitment to his wellbeing and that of other family members, young and ageing, became a priority.

Sheena, who stayed involved for as long as her failing health allowed, would be pleased to know that by 2012 GFSA had recovered significantly from the near collapse it experienced in 2010. It received some money and Adèle was once again involved as one of a board of about seven people who shared responsibilities on a

[6] A separate committee set up by the minister to work on proposals for a new policy for the control of firearms in South Africa. The committee was named after its chairperson Rick de Caris.

[7] Meek, Sarah and Stott, Noel: *Destroying Surplus Weapons: An assessment of experience in South Africa and Lesotho,* United Nations Institute for Disarmament Research Geneva, Switzerland and ISS Institute for Security Studies Pretoria, South Africa. United Nations: 2003.

voluntary basis. *It would absolutely have helped if Sheena were still around,* Adèle says. *I think the loss of her experience, her eye, her wisdom, her clear assessment of what you can afford to give up and what you can't is an enormous loss. I don't think even now I have fully realised the extent to which Sheena's voice is inside my head and how much that influenced my thinking. With her not here physically, that diminishes and in a way I'm not even aware of what I'm missing. I don't think there's anyone else who could fill that gap.*

There is a saying among writers of fiction that once a weapon has been introduced into a scene, it must be used. Sheena would have hoped that this was not so in real life. But she claimed the space that GFSA, the new firearms control legislation and the JIT offered and she did her best to ensure that if the weapon could not be removed from the scene altogether without being used, at least its presence there should be known and legitimate, and it should be held there responsibly.

CHAPTER 12

End Conscription Campaign

Sheena was one of the fore-parents. As you know, the entire campaign revolved around the Black Sash conference resolution calling for an end to conscription. It was an incredibly far-sighted and courageous resolution — very risky and dangerous in the circumstances but identifying exactly a poignant and prevalent issue for mobilisation in the white community.

LAURIE NATHAN — Interview

On the planned agenda of the 1983 Black Sash national conference, hosted in Cape Town by its regional membership, was to be a discussion led by the Natal Coastal region on the matter of alternative service options for conscientious objectors. By the time the item came up on 13 March, the third day of conference, Sheena's opening presidential address had already taken members 'face to face with the harsh realities of the National Security State' and its terms 'Total Strategy' and 'Total Onslaught'. Some of her concluding remarks had offered a clear indication of the direction she was suggesting on conscription:

'At this conference we will be considering the question of conscientious objection and the harsh and unreasonable new proposals for alternative service and the punishment of objectors. We will be asking why there should be conscription at all.

'In the Second World War there were deep emotional divisions of opinion in this country about the war and we had no conscription.

'In the war of occupation in Namibia and in the conflict within South Africa there are even greater and more intensely felt divisions.

'If in this conflict, it is considered necessary to have conscription is that not an admission that the war is already lost?

'There is no enemy out there. There are only people who want food and shelter, land and opportunity, security and peace, and who know that their anger will only be assuaged if they have some political power and that there can be no peace unless there is justice.'

It is not at all surprising that, when the time came to consider the agenda item on conscientious objection, the ground had shifted. Conscription itself was the issue and with her usual sharp eye Sheena had also spotted a small but crucial legal distinction: although the apartheid regime had made it illegal to advocate opposition to the *actions* of the South African Defence Force (SADF), *it was not illegal* to oppose the mandatory nature of conscription. The Black Sash passed a resolution that did just that — it called for an end to conscription.

The significance of the Black Sash resolution should not be underestimated, says Mike Evans. *It really was decisive ... I'm not even sure if they realised at the time what the potential impact of that was but it was an unbelievably foresightful move on Sheena's part as the driving force. We suddenly realised that actually this was the stick that we needed to shift the whole movement against the military from a very small, individually focused objectors' support movement to one that had the potential to be a wider campaign. Also by that time there was a heavy prison sentence of up to six years if you persuaded or assisted somebody to refuse to do military service. So that was a risky step even if you weren't objecting yourself, if you were involved in persuading or assisting somebody. The call to end conscription didn't intrude on any of those territories at all and it wasn't threatening to conscripts because it was calling for a policy change. It wasn't saying, 'Object and go to jail.' It was incredibly clever. It was one of those things when you look back in time, you think, well maybe it was obvious. But it wasn't obvious. It wasn't at all.*

The history of the exact nature and timing of the various converging factors that led to the first recognised moment of the End Conscription Campaign (ECC) is, it seems, open to interpretation — with each perspective offered with a persuasive degree of certainty.

Whatever the details of its development and the precise launch date of the ECC may be, however, there is agreement that locally it was preceded by various individual, church and organisational influences that shaped its 'character'.

Also unlikely to be disputed is the recognition that, at the time of the beginnings of the ECC, three of the most significant organisations were: an independent conscientious objectors' support group (COSG), the National Union of South African Students (NUSAS) and the Black Sash.

The aggressive actions by the SADF during the seventies, first by taking over from the South African Police (SAP) as the official occupying army in Namibia (then still South West Africa) and then by its hostile crossing of other borders, alienated a growing number of young white male South Africans, who were the people being called up for military service. The men had different reasons for not wanting to become soldiers — but none had the freedom to choose not to.

COSG was set up in 1979 after Peter Moll, the first conscientious objector (CO) to go public, was imprisoned. The focus was on alternative service possibilities and it was by nature limited to supporting specific individuals who objected to doing armed military training and service. Rooted in South Africa's history of war and in the chronicle of anti-war ideologies that reach far back in time and across the world, COSG was initially essentially identified with some form of — mostly religious — pacifism or anti-militarisation, ideas that had the support of, for example, the SACC, which had by then issued the 1974 Hammanskraal Resolution on Conscientious Objection.

Then, at the 1982 COSG national conference in Cape Town, there was a significant influx of young people from NUSAS. Despite the sometimes debilitating ideological differences that continued within the student body, the white NUSAS members did represent robust anti-apartheid sentiment and activism and, compared to many others who were part of COSG, this influx introduced more politicised views on serving in the SADF — views which incorporated a message of encouragement from the ANC in exile. These young people confronted enormous ideological issues and strategic differences — as well as real practical threats to their well-being — whether at war with people they did not see as the enemy, or in prison.

Emerging from these dynamics came the first specifically political objector, Brett Myrdal, national co-ordinator of the NUSAS labour committee and politically respected. Brett was willing to refuse his call up publicly, travel around the country to clarify his political reasons, garner support for the conscientious objection campaign and then face his initial two years in jail. Thirteen objectors had already been jailed by then and, just before the start of Brett's ideological journey, along came the groundbreaking Black Sash conference.

Among future recorders of the history of the ECC, some will say that it was clearly Sheena Duncan, through the Black Sash, who authored and championed the call for an end to conscription. Others might say her call was ANC influenced, although, according to Gavin Evans who had been an underground member of the ANC since 1980, *I would have heard if there was any ANC input in that regard.* Others will say that the mothers, partners, sisters and friends of the young white men who were being conscripted to fight in apartheid wars collectively formulated the call; still others will claim it was started by the SACC. Some will say the ECC was born when, following discussions about the Black Sash resolution, a group within COSG started meeting and strategising as an 'end conscription' committee and, at its inaugural meeting in November 1983, was supported by signatures from white anti-apartheid luminaries such as Beyers Naudé, Helen Joseph, Kate Philip and David Webster. Others will say it started in

gille de vlieg ©

Sheena speaking on an ECC platform

1984 when the ECC held its first public 'stop the call-up' meeting in the Claremont Civic Centre in Cape Town — with Sheena Duncan and Allan Boesak among the key speakers — or the following year at its big national Peace Festival in Johannesburg.

No matter. What Adèle Kirsten calls *one of those synchronicities* had occurred and the ECC was to become one of the most dynamic and influential anti-apartheid organisations of the eighties and nineties.

The ECC succeeded in avoiding internal disputes, despite the fact that it grew in size to include thousands of young activists, a huge support base from its affiliates and strong leadership. The campaign was quite tightly focused — on the conscription law itself, the war outside of legitimate South African borders, troops in apartheid's black-defined townships and voluntary forms of alternative service. It allowed space for many, including English and Afrikaans speakers, Christians, liberals, lefties, graphic artists and musicians. It was one of the few anti-apartheid movements to be openly gay-friendly and which prized creativity and self-expression without losing sight of South African society as a whole. It was able to produce enjoyably politicised social events as well as media that attracted attention to the campaign issues in poignant yet often delightfully amusing ways — and which infuriated the apartheid regime. Events and demonstrations generally resulted in a violent state response and anti-ECC propaganda — including at schools and universities. When the state of emergency was declared in 1986, repression worsened.

Defence Minister Magnus Malan called the ECC a direct enemy of the SADF and said that it was disgracefully misleading young South Africans with propaganda. Major General Jan van Loggerenberg claimed that the aim of the ECC was to destroy the morale of the youth and ultimately leave South Africa defenceless against its enemies. Police Minister Adriaan Vlok declared it part of the 'revolutionary onslaught against South Africa'.

ECC resistance intensified. In Cape Town, a group of twenty-three conscripts refused to obey their call-ups in 1987, directly challenging state power. The state retaliated with detentions of more than a hundred ECC members, forcing many others into hiding. In 1988 the state banned the ECC in terms of the emergency regulations. In that same year, 143 conscripts had refused to do national service nationally; by 1989 their number had swelled to 771, several of them SADF officers, and soon the number of objectors exceeded 1 000. The state was unable to charge them all, although three previous objectors were jailed during this period.

In 1989 the ECC 'unbanned' itself and re-established its branches and its work. It challenged continued conscription of whites only, claiming this to be illegal now that the Population Registration Act had been scrapped. Soon after this the state reduced the period of conscription from two years to one, and after 1990, when the state also officially unbanned the ECC, conscription was procedurally phased out, officially ending in 1993.

What prompted Sheena to take such an interest in the ECC? In all likelihood, it was her unshakeable pacifism and her committed anti-militarisation standpoint. Not all ECC members shared these values with Sheena, but they did all appreciate her ability to span differences. The older generation found her respectability reassuring. Sheena was able to get parents to understand their sons' choices and she herself was able to understand a young white conscript and his dilemma. Sheena strongly believed that it was wrong to go into the military, yet she also supported young men who chose to go in, if they made their choice on conscience. She offered no judgement, despite the fact that it was in direct contrast to what she believed.

According to Laurie, *Sheena was a rock, she had an uncommonly sound sense of strategy. Strategy meaning — we are not just going to complain about apartheid and we are not going to just say, 'Well something must be done,' we are going to target our intervention. In other words, we are going to cut where it hurts.*

Sheena also had an acute sense of politics and where the vulnerabilities of the state lay. All of us in the anti-apartheid community were idealistic, but in a sense one also had to be pragmatic and hard-headed and she was that. Sheena was no bullshit: clear, forthright, open, open minded, and her leadership presence was always there and always strongly felt and always respected.

Sheena wasn't a controversial leader. We had leaders that we respected but who were controversial. Sheena wasn't. We knew where she was coming from and she didn't meddle in factional politics. We were fighting apartheid but sometimes we were fighting within the student movement as well or in the broad white left or in the anti-apartheid movement as a whole. I never saw or heard of Sheena being involved in that kind of politics. She had enormous integrity.

Sheena was a radical in the positive sense. She was on the cutting edge of progressive thinking and she had the guts to take a bold stand and to do so in a constructive way and there is no doubt that this is needed in many of today's issues. In other words, to be able to take a stand against government — not in a way that is partisan or indulging in partisan politics but from a position of righteousness — without chest thumping, without wearing a halo — as we say, speaking truth to power.

Within the Black Sash itself, Sheena held things steady. Beva Runciman recalls how at the organisation's 1985 national conference, when some members were not easily convinced that their organisation should be associated with this rather radical ECC and its activities, *I looked at Sheena with new eyes. I'd been a bit wary of her. She was a big woman physically and mentally and I was a lot younger than all of them and a passionately committed ECC member. I was getting quite agitated by what seemed like resistance and at some stage of the debates Sheena told me to 'keep quiet Beva — sit*

gille de vlieg ©

Sheena with Peter Harris and Anton Lubowski at an ECC meeting on Namibia

down and be quiet!' I remember feeling absolutely fine about it. It was done in such a way that it made me laugh. It was beautifully direct. Simply, 'Don't worry about it — sit down now.'

Sheena supported the ECC *in every way she could: she would fly down to talk at meetings; she would talk with us before she went back. Although we didn't have those in the ECC, she acted just like a patron.*

Mike agrees: *Sheena was significant to ECC in another role — she was a strong forceful person and she was a bridge builder. That was quite crucial to the way the campaign developed because you had UDF and UDF area committees being formed at that time, but they were more exclusive and more overtly anti-parliament in every way. So there was no potential meeting point with the wider white community that at the time supported the Progressive Federal Party, which later became the Democratic Alliance, and certainly in Cape Town you often had a very hard line position being articulated. In Johannesburg it was a little bit more flexible. So it was people like Sheena who became that bridge between the extra-parliamentary movement gravitating around the UDF and the white opposition within Parliament that gravitated around the PFP and also included a lot of Black Sash members who came out of that tradition of white parliamentary opposition. People like Sheena in Johannesburg and Mary Burton in Cape Town were quite crucial in that bridging role.*

There was one short period of conflict between Sheena and some of the ECC activists, on the matter of the security police spy, Joy Harnden. The background is complicated, but, says Gavin, *in summary, Joy Harnden, a former Rhodes student, joined a number of organisations, including Jodac*[1] *and ECC in 1984, without having had any political background, and she managed to get herself elected to the Jodac executive. She was employed, I think, by the Black Sash's Transvaal Rural Action Committee and had access to Sheena through that. Several of us were immediately suspicious of her. I sent a report on my suspicions to the ANC in Harare and I know that Aninka Claassens was also suspicious. Then we received concrete information from sources at Rhodes that she had been connected to the exposed security police spy, Lloyd Edwards, and that she had told someone else that she was working for the police. This was immediately reported to the ANC in Harare, who encouraged us to get her out of the country. At the time she was living with Sheila Weinberg, having tried and failed to get a place in Mike Roussos's house. Sheila, who had not been informed Joy was a spy, went to visit her family in Maputo and took Joy with her. The ANC in Harare were tipped off. They passed the message on to their people in Maputo with the instruction to detain Joy. However, because of rivalries within the ANC, the message was never delivered. So, instead, Joy was recruited to the ANC and placed in an underground unit headed by Iggy Mathebula. Joy returned to Johannesburg, linked up with Iggy, who disappeared soon after. This placed the ANC in a quandary. They did not want us to expel her because they were worried this might compromise Iggy's position (although he was never seen again), so they asked us to encourage Joy to travel to Harare. But, by then, the security police had got wind of the suspicions around Joy (through another spy, Olivia Forsyth), so Joy always made excuses. Eventually, Valli Moosa said, 'Enough!' and informed Sheila Weinberg that Joy was a spy, after which Jodac expelled her. ECC then had no alternative but to act, and also expelled her. Joy then went to Sheena in tears, saying that she was innocent and that a cabal had ousted her and so on. Sheena supported Joy and was very angry with Jodac and also ECC. She called us Stalinists and so on, and relations were very frosty for a while — until, after Forsyth's escape from ANC detention, the security police revealed that both Forsyth and Harnden were security police lieutenants.*[2]

Like Gavin, several other people active in the ECC were also underground members of the ANC, and in supporting Joy — while at the same time keeping up to date with the ECC and other resistance activities — Sheena might have unintentionally put these and other anti-apartheid activists at risk. *I imagine Sheena might have been a bit embarrassed about it*, says Gavin, *but no one mentioned it. It was best forgotten.* Sheena herself, in a letter to her daughters on 22 February 1989, in which she tells them how she is responding to one of their friends who had recently

[1] The Johannesburg Democratic Action Committee, formed as an affiliate of the United Democratic Front in 1983.

[2] There was extensive media coverage. See, for example, *The Sydney Morning Herald* of 9 February 1989.

crashed Sheena's car, concedes that Joy 'is another person to whom I feel motherly. Woe is me!'

Sheena's open heart and home were mostly used to good purpose, however. Peter Storey remembers *so vividly when Sheena opened her home to the 'infantry company' of the conscientious objectors. These youngsters made their way there in dribs and drabs and then we made an announcement [to the press] that we had robbed the defence force of an entire infantry — here they were, a group of young white males, two of them my sons, who are not members of the SADF. It was a dramatic moment and Sheena's presence was incredible.*

In the campaign to end conscription Sheena had indeed once again blazed a new path. Typically, she sustained the delicate balance between stepping back and stepping forward. She accompanied these brave young white people — when they needed her — on a route that undoubtedly made a difference to the policy of apartheid and that undermined the acceptance, by large numbers of white South Africans, of apartheid's brutal — and brutalizing — implications.

In 2009, huge numbers of former ECC supporters gathered once more, for a vibrant twenty-five-year celebration at Spier in the Western Cape. Some had not seen each other for more than twenty years. *What struck me there,* remembers Mike, *was that every single person who had been in ECC — even if they were now in conventional jobs in health, education, philanthropy, law, conservation or whatever — was playing a positive and progressive role in South Africa. All of them said that the period in the eighties was crucial to their value system and their morality and their whole approach to life. Their time in ECC wasn't a sort of student phase that they went through and then ditched. In other areas I've seen that happen. I have seen lots of ex-NUSAS people, for example, who've abandoned completely what they stood for in those days in every single way. Not the ECC people. That was the legacy.*

Sheena was part of this legacy — part of something these people, no longer young, can remember and pass on to future generations with pride.

CHAPTER 13

Last Years

I thought Sheena would live forever and there Sheena runs off and leaves me in this world. May she rest in peace, together with her beloved husband again. I still do miss her so much.

EMMA MASHININI — Interview

Sheena lived fully, dedicating more than half her life to a public and articulate struggle for justice and human rights. She demanded of her spirit and her intellect all there was to give, and although she reserved a privacy of self, she gave her heart and her trust and her respect to others freely and warmly. Whenever she could, she rested her sometimes troublesome body in the cool water of her dark walled swimming pool, she released her feet from the confines of shoes, and she welcomed to her senses the sounds and smells of the wild and of her own tranquil garden landscape.

It can't have been easy for such a powerful force to feel herself fading out. But by all accounts, Sheena faced this steady decline in the last two years of her life, including the months, weeks and days before her death, in the same way she had faced other challenges in her life — with faith, fortitude, a fair amount of frustration, laughter and a stiff brandy, or two.

Sheena's body had not ever had an easy time of it. Starting with a first operation at the age of about four, for an abscess in her ear that had to be lanced in hospital, 'because there were no antibiotics in those days', her body endured miscarriage after miscarriage, difficult pregnancies, a burst appendix, a gall bladder operation that left the gallstones behind, failing and then replaced and then dislocated hips, broken ribs, carpal tunnel syndrome, osteoporosis, frequently recurring skin irritations and high blood pressure. She comforted and distracted it with seemingly addictive appetites for work, alcohol, cigarettes and good food and, when she couldn't ignore them, accepted all physical challenges with her typical courage and good humour.

Before her first hip replacement operation in August 1988, for example, she wrote cheerfully to her family, 'You should not all worry so much. I am exceedingly healthy and all they need to do is make a cut in my thigh to extract a few crumbling bones and replace them with some ceramic/acrylic joints. It is merely a physical procedure like having the car serviced and the oil replaced. I shall have the next hip done next year and will probably follow that with my knees. I still have my tonsils!' To hospital she took a suitcase full of books and papers, with nighties and toiletries crammed in a small corner, and two days after the operation demanded that Neil bring up a small bottle of Scotch. *We took it up last night on our way out to dinner,* wrote Neil. *She apparently offered some to everyone else in the ward, who eagerly accepted, so now I have had to take a full bottle.*

Ma is in great form, he wrote two weeks later, *galloping around on her crutches at twice the speed she could walk before the op. She can't go out, so every meeting — and there are plenty, specifically as a result of the bomb*[1] *but also lots of others — is here. There is a constant stream of people in and out of the house with a resulting pile up of cups, saucers, glasses, etc. waiting to be fed into the dishwasher. Quite apart from the 'business' side, every Tom Dick and Harry or Sally and Sue as the case may be, whom we don't see from one year to another has felt impelled to pay us a visit. More tea or coffee, more drinks, more washing up. Ma is getting quite desperate as she had envisaged her recuperation as a quiet time to catch up on work. The house looks rather like a funeral parlour with so many flowers and there are masses of cards too. One said, 'Lucky you are not a horse, or else we would have had to shoot you' and another, 'Do you know that in hospitals they use water to drink and alcohol to rub your back — no wonder there are so many sick people!'*

'There's nothing like a bomb for instant convalescence' was Sheena's reason for getting immediately back to work after that particular health challenge. Through all the ones that followed in years to come, as her heart ached at the injustices of the world and then with the loss of her beloved Neil in 2003, she reciprocated stoically, with her seemingly limitless capacity for mental concentration, late nights, long days, unshakeable faith, love, compassion and arms wide open to all life had to offer.

Twenty years after that first hip operation, Sheena, a widow now, was no longer galloping around anywhere, with or without crutches. Some people might have said she lived 'alone' in her home, her husband dead and her daughters and all close family members living far away in other countries. But she was not alone, really. There were visits from Lindsay and Carey or other family every few months, temporarily homeless friends stayed over for however long they needed to, other friends dropped by frequently to discuss with Sheena the politics of the day or get her help in making difficult decisions, Alina Dlamini was still keeping house for her and she and several members of her family lived on the premises.

Sheena's physical strength was fading, but not her capacity to appreciate life's blessings. 'We have our baby at last!' she wrote in a family letter in March 2008. 'After several weeks of me lying alert at night in case I was called upon, in the end Nthabeleng[2] went into labour in a civilised fashion on Thursday morning. I called

[1] Khotso House, home to the headquarters of both the Black Sash and the South African Council of Churches, was bombed on 31 August 1988, a week after Sheena's operation, by the security forces of the government.

[2] Alina Dlamini's young niece, living at the Parkhurst home with her aunt. The course of her pregnancy had been followed with much interest by all of the family.

Sheena on her stoep with Bernard Spong

the ambulance at 1.30 pm. It eventually arrived at 5 pm while I worried in case I would have to cope in circumstances I have long forgotten.

'The baby is sweet. I had forgotten too, how very tiny newborns are. Alina has put a mattress on the floor in their room and is sleeping there for a few days to make sure all is well. She regards herself as the grandmother — very proud that the milk has come in and the baby is sucking.' Rethabile[3] Victoria was to become a vibrant presence in Sheena's life for the rest of her days, a period that was soon to be defined as startlingly finite. By the time Rethabile was two months old, Sheena had been told she had cancer and had fallen down the stairs and suffered a compression fracture in her lumbar spine, diagnosed only much later. She was in a great deal of pain, but remained stoic and cheerful.

'Dearest family,' she wrote on 3 May 2008, 'I am very grateful to Carey for telling you that I have cancer and will probably have to have a mastectomy. You do not need to be shy to comment. I would have told you anyway but we were away in the Pilanesberg[4] with no computer contact. You really do not need to worry about me. I am not worried except about you worrying. It is just one of those things that happen

[3] Happiness.

[4] A favorite Duncan family destination, the Pilanesberg National Park in North West Province is set within the crater of an ancient volcano and exists in an ecological transition zone between the dryness of the Kalahari and the wet Lowveld vegetation. It is a comfortable three-hour drive from Johannesburg, and in addition to exquisite natural landscape and rock formations, most of the animal species native to southern Africa can be found there. It is also a malaria-free zone.

to one. The surgeon is a very nice man who said he would not do anything until I had had full diagnostic tests which have now been done. Lindsay insists on coming with me on Tuesday when he wants to discuss next steps. It is good to have her here for that but I do not want to disrupt her holiday. It is too short for that and it would be ridiculous for her to stay here to watch me dopey on pre-op sedative and even more dopey coming round from an anaesthetic.

'We had a lovely time in the Pilanesberg — they have had good rains and the grass is long and the water courses are all flowing so the game is scattered and not congregating around dams but the peace and quiet was wonderful.'

Sheena did not have the operation because the cancer had spread and, in November, after six months on medication, Carey wrote to update the family about her check-up. *Briefly, it went brilliantly; we took the wheelchair but Mum didn't need it — she walked with her frame all the way. The oncologist is a bit of a strange person — as you know — but apart from that, the brilliant news is that the lump on her breast has DISAPPEARED and the lymph node lumps have reduced to one small lump. The oncologist says that if the treatment is working in these areas, it is also working on her liver. Mum is so much more mobile, cheerful and generally 'en forme'.*

Clare[5] *and I got a lecture [from the oncologist] about why we didn't take Mum to the orthopaedic man she had recommended. As Clare said, if a patient doesn't go, one should delve to find out why, not read the riot act at her. Then when Clare was helping Mum onto the table for the examination, I got it in the ear again, 'Your mother should be in care — she is an accident waiting to happen — she could fall at any time,' to which I replied that she could also fall in care and at least she was where she wanted to be, that she did have 24 hour care where she was, and her improved condition was proof that she was being well looked after.* The oncologist couldn't disagree with that and became more conciliatory, although pain management remained contentious.

The next appointment was scheduled for three months later, in February 2009, and in the meantime, morphine patches dealt effectively with the pain. Carey's short-term goal was *to get Mum in and out of the workroom to the TV and her computer for a little bit* and indeed, on January 2009 Sheena wrote what was to be her last email to the family, 'Hurrah. I'm at my computer — first time in months. Another milestone! Thanks to Clare and Alina. Fondest love mum.'

From then on, however, Sheena seldom moved away from her bed. Visiting friends found her there, settled in among piles of books, newspapers, the radio and her phone, with tea or a drink at hand.

When Sheena told me via email that she had liver cancer, recalls her lifetime friend Liz Hagen, *I immediately flew out [from New Jersey] and foisted myself upon her, arriving just after she had fallen and fractured her coccyx. I spent a week with her,*

[5] Sheena's physiotherapist and a close and important member of her caregiving team.

cooking and trying to make myself useful. She was in great pain, but, of course, not complaining.

Kathy Satchwell lived around the corner in Parkhurst. *After she became ill,* says Kathy, *I would pop in often — I would phone first and she would always say, 'Oh, that would be so nice.' It was easy going and we would always find something to talk about.*

Sheena's dear friend Ethel Walt took special care of her, visiting almost daily, as did Judy Bassingthwaighte. Judy had taken over as director of Gun Free South Africa some years previously and she and Sheena had developed a close relationship when they were working together, and when Judy had lived at Sheena's house for a while during a difficult period of her own life.

Many other friends visited — often at first — but then less frequently. This was partly because, although Sheena was happy and grateful for their attention, she seemed equally happy if they didn't come. Several of her friends, especially the younger ones, were actively continuing with their work in the new democracy, either in government, civil society or the corporate sector and did not have much spare time. Ishmael Mkhabela, on his own or with his wife Bongi, was one of those who popped in from time to time. *We continued to see her until the year she died,* remembers Ishmael. *If there's something I miss it's talking with her. Even the last conversation I had with her — I was talking to her on the phone, driving to Pretoria, and I said, 'Sheena, I'll come and see you — I feel a delinquent, I haven't been in your space for a long time.' Well, I never saw her again.*

The lay minister at St George's church, Harold Gregory, regularly brought communion and his dignified conversation and support. But as much as she appreciated this, Sheena would not have berated the church if no one had come.

Sheena's daughters, Lindsay and Carey, both lived many thousands of kilometres away, with their own families and professional responsibilities. But, in that last year they made sure that for much of the time at least one of them was with Sheena.

Sheena kind of settled back into this bed, says Kathy. *I was surprised at that — and we talked about the* Mail and Guardian, *we talked about a book she'd read, Sheena talked a lot about her children. She showed me a whole photo album of all the gardens Carey had done. I'd never really seen Sheena before as a proud mother.*

There was a little baby toddling around and I used to chat to this little person and Sheena would say, 'Oh, she gives me so much pleasure.'

The little person was, of course, Rethabile Victoria. Alina was devoted in her care, both for the child and for the ailing woman who had once been so strong and so caring. As Aninka Claassens observed, *In the end Sheena's philosophy won out — this woman really loved her.*

Sadly, Kathy herself was diagnosed with cancer a short while later, *and in September 2009 I started chemo. I was feeling shit when Sheena phoned and said, 'My cancer is back and I've been told I must have chemo but I don't want to, and I hear that you are having a terrible time.' So, I lied! 'Sheena, it's not that terrible. Listen I'll go with you. I'll come and visit you now and show you it's really not that awful. You can survive anything.' So, off I went to see Sheena and I said, 'Look here I am and, yes, I'm bald and I go round bald all the time and when I'm in court I put a wig on and the rest of the time I wear a hat because of sun. You can manage it and you make a plan and then the cancer goes to silent.' In fact, why I did that was because somebody had told me that Sheena had said no to chemo, but that her daughters had persuaded her to give it a try.*

Chemotherapy did not work well for Sheena and in spite of all the professional and personal care and support she got from her 'home team', she found all aspects of the process extremely uncomfortable, particularly because of her injured back.

In January 2010, Liz Hagen flew out again, bringing her twenty-one-year-old granddaughter Sophie with her. *We stayed with Sheena for a few days, during which Sheena told Sophie a lot about South African politics and Sophie cooked vegetarian dishes and hung out with Alina. Sheena and I both knew it was time to say goodbye, and our parting was sad but, of course, not tearful.*

Sheena died in her bed in her home, in the early hours of Tuesday morning, 4 May 2010. Never one to feel sorry for herself, the last words she had whispered to Carey over the phone the day before were, 'I'm fine.'

The last few weeks of Sheena's life tore the heart out of me, wrote Ethel to her sister, *and then her actual death — I was with her the day before (almost every day in fact) and then when she died, they phoned me and I went straight there. I had to see for myself, had to hold that hand and stroke the hair. The actual funeral was heart-breaking. It was SO hard for me to get up there and speak. I really loved that woman. She has been the single most important influence in my whole life.*

We have been informed that Sheena 'died ***peacefully****',* said Bongi Mkhabela at the Regina Mundi memorial service in Soweto on 17 May 2010.

Yes that might be so, Bongi cautioned, ***IF*** *we remain firmly on the side of the poor and the marginalised .... and boldly speak truth to power.*

May the legacy of our beloved be entrusted to our next generations, from whom we have borrowed the future.

Black Sash members at Regina Mundi memorial service

* * *

APPENDIX

Selected Writings

This small selection from Sheena's written work cannot possibly do credit to the range of her writing, but it offers some of her thoughts — for often she was 'thinking on the page'. It gives her more of an opportunity to speak for herself. Many of these words provide further insight into issues touched on elsewhere in the book. All illuminate aspects of Sheena's distinct capacity for analysis, inspiration and practical intervention, or her warmth and compassion. Isolated from its context, the writing is sometimes harshly naked, but it remains relevant in contemporary South Africa.

Drawn from Sheena's speeches, articles and correspondence, unedited except for minor cuts to shorten some of the pieces, her writing is loosely organised under topic headings. Each topic illuminates a particular interest of hers.

Statistics may seem academic, but Sheena recognised that in order to address issues of human rights — eradicating prejudices, poverty and inequality in the process — it is essential to track social realities and all aspects of the performance of government. Although much of her writing provided facts presented statistically, Sheena did not ever lose sight of the human beings that inhabit each statistic.

The six topics, Migrant Labour, Writing to Sister Members, Preparing to Speak, In Response to Proclamation R133, Change, and Civil Disobedience, are arranged in no known order of importance to Sheena, but roughly chronologically, based on the first text offered under each topic heading.

It is significant that years before her death, when South Africa was finally free of the system of apartheid and in a fragile period of euphoria, Sheena predicted with sadness that it would take several generations of recovery before much could change. Her writing gives us a glimpse of how well she understood the politics of her time, as well as the enormous and enduring impact of friendship, compassion and solidarity.

Migrant labour

For those who are too young to remember or those who choose to forget, it might be useful to consider this particular legacy of apartheid in the light of contemporary controversies surrounding labour brokers — brokers which the Congress of South African Trade Unions (COSATU) bravely continues to condemn in the face of much opposition, twenty years after South Africa's first democratic elections and almost forty years after Sheena wrote these words.

The original full text of Sheena's first article on migrant labour included detailed and extensive consideration of the expenses related to the average amount a migrant worker could expect to send home to his family in 1974. It outlined facts on the state of education — including drop-out figures which showed that, of an enrolled total of 13,990 in fifty primary schools in the area, 1,160 studied further at the four post-primary schools and 110 children at the one high school. It noted the impact on the women who were left 'at home' by the migrant worker and concluded by describing the many facets of family life, social cohesion and supportive cultural practices that disintegrated in the context of forced migrant labour — and the inevitable, tragic and repetitive cycle of unstable relationships, for the adults and the children.

HARD FACTS AT NQUTU

Sheena Duncan, 1974[1]

The statistics of life at Nqutu reveal the harsh realities of existence for thousands of South Africans living in overcrowded homelands with no employment opportunities and where to survive at all is an achievement. The land is badly eroded and grossly overpopulated. The Tomlinson Commission estimated that Nqutu, if fully developed, could support 13,000 people. 86,000 live there now and it is estimated that by 1980, 120,000 people will be living there. This population explosion is not due to natural increase. People have been resettled into the area from 'Black Spots' and white farms and others have moved in 'voluntarily' because they have been forced off farms in the common area and have had nowhere else to go.

Yet, with the population this size there are only 1500 jobs in the district so the men are forced to leave to work. They must, of course, register at the labour bureau and wait to be recruited. They are also compelled to have paid the annual poll tax of R2,50 before they are registered as work-seekers and to raise this amount often means getting into debt before having any hope of being offered work.

Once a man has found work he may expect to be paid between R30 and R60 per month if he is lucky enough to be sent to a large urban centre such as Johannesburg but much less if he is sent to a small town or is recruited for farm work. Of such

[1] Duncan, Sheena: 'The hard facts', *Sash*, vol.17, no.1, May 1974.

wage, an average of R9,90 is what a migrant worker can send home to his family after he has paid his own expenses in the city where he works. Even in 'rural' areas, one third of the families have no livestock of any kind because most of them have been 'resettled' into the area.

For people living in such poverty, expenditure on food, fuel and transport in that order has priority. If there is anything left over it will be spent on clothing and schooling for the children.

THE LEGAL BACKGROUND

Sheena Duncan, 1974[2]

South Africa's migrant labour system has been much analysed and discussed in recent months, but the full weight of the legal controls which supply labour units to the white economy is not generally understood.

Migrant workers in the bantustans are processed through labour bureaux which are more like cattle markets than anything else. Men register there as work-seekers then hang around to await recruitment. They wait for days, weeks, months. Then comes the great day. The recruiting agent is expected. He arrives. Two hundred and fifty men line up. He wants 184 labour units for the companies he represents. He walks along the line and beckons forward those he chooses. This one looks strong, this one looks young and teachable, this one is too old, that one looks too thin. This one says he doesn't want to work at R8 per week because he was paid R11 in his last job. He must be too cheeky. '*Get back in the line. I don't want cheeky boys*.' Those who are not picked must wait, maybe weeks, maybe months, until the next recruiting agent comes. The 'cheeky' one won't argue next time. He will be ready to accept whatever wage is offered. His children are starving and a little is better than nothing.

These men do not come to the labour bureau to undergo this degrading process of their own free will. Every man who lives in the bantustans *must*, by law, register as a work-seeker at his tribal labour bureau within one month of becoming 15 years of age and must continue to register as a work-seeker within one month of becoming unemployed throughout his life until he is 65, unless he is exempted by the labour officer because he is a bona fides scholar or farmer, or has been allowed to be self-employed or is, *in the opinion of the labour officer*, physically or mentally incapable of being employed.

When a man registers at his labour bureau his reference book is stamped that he is registered as a work-seeker, but this does not mean that he is actually permitted to seek work. He is not allowed to leave the area of jurisdiction of the labour bureau to sell his labour. He must wait to be requisitioned for. He cannot choose which area he wishes to work in. If he wishes to work in Pretoria for example, he cannot do so

[2] Duncan, Sheena: 'The legal background', *Sash*, vol.17, no.1, May 1974.

unless an agent from Pretoria chooses to and is allowed to recruit at that particular bureau. If a directive has been issued that agents from Pretoria may not recruit labour at that specific bureau there is no way that he can go to work in Pretoria.

Mr S serves as example. He is registered as a work-seeker in Hammanskraal. His wife and children are lawful residents of Johannesburg [more than 100km away] but he cannot be employed in that city because agents from Johannesburg are not allowed to recruit labour at 'his' bureau. Nor is he allowed to move to live in the area of any other labour bureau, which might be open to recruitment from Johannesburg.

If employers in one area are short of labour then a certain labour bureau may be closed to recruitment by all but agents from that one area. Mr N for example, is registered as a work-seeker at a labour bureau which is closed to recruitment from all areas except the nearby border industrial growth point. He is earning R16 per month in a factory and is forbidden by law from selling his labour for what it is worth in any other place. Mr T is in a similar but worse position. He is an experienced steelworker with a wife and four children to support but his labour bureau has been closed to all recruitment except by white farmers in the district. He is therefore prevented by law from using his skills and must work as a farm labourer for a wage which in no way compares with what he was earning three years ago.

White farmers are, of course, a privileged group of employees in South Africa and some of the provisions of the 1968 Regulations appear to be designed to keep them happy, with a ready supply of workers.

When a man registers as a work-seeker for the first time he is classified by the labour office in a specific category of employment. The labour officer is supposed to take into account the man's own wishes and qualifications '*as far as practicable*' but there is no law which prevents the labour officer from placing a man in a category of labour to which he has the strongest objections. His wishes do not, in practice, count for much. Once a man has been classified he may not be employed in any other category of labour unless he is signing a contract for mine or farm work. This means that the type of work he is classified for when he is 15 is the only type of work he may do for the rest of his working life. If he begins as a domestic worker he will have to remain one whatever skills he may acquire, or however he may hate his work in 'the kitchens.'

All migrant workers must now work on annual contracts. When the one-year period expires the employee *must* discharge the worker and return him to his home area. This system was devised to prevent workers from qualifying for permanent residence in the urban areas. Even if the worker returns to the same employer each year for ten years this is not deemed to be the ten years of continuous employment required by Section 10(1)(*b*) of the Urban Areas Act. It is not continuous because it must be terminated and renewed every year.

When a worker accepts employment a written contract is entered into. Everyone has a copy of the contract — *except the worker himself.* The employer or his agent has one, the tribal labour officer and the labour officer in the work area have one each and the attesting office has one. If a worker wants to dispute any of the conditions of his employment he has no copy of his contract to produce as proof that the employer is not fulfilling the contract. Workers often seem to have misunderstood the terms of the contract because deductions are not explained. For example, advances made to the worker for fares or food may be deducted from his pay packet provided that he is left with R1 after 30 days work.

It is axiomatic that a man should be the owner of his own labour. In South Africa this is an accepted principle for white workers, but African men do not own their own labour. It is controlled, directed, used and abused by the State according to a master plan over which the worker has no control. Migrant workers have no choice whatsoever as to whether they will work, how, where, for whom or for what reward. Slave labour? At least a slave owner had a financial interest in the health and strength of his slaves. He paid good money for them.

Writing to sister members

Sheena's leadership and membership of the Black Sash was characterised by her warmth and intelligence — and her inclusivity. She understood the value of regularly involving sister members with updates of her activities and her analytic observations, to which she welcomed feedback. In addition to her more formal annual presidential and Advice Office Trust reports and addresses to members, she wrote regular letters from the Black Sash headquarters when these were in Johannesburg — although she did not limit her communication to Gauteng issues only. Sheena made a point of staying closely in touch with all the advice offices and regional offices, and including their work and challenges in her writing.

When she accepted invitations to travel and engage with audiences internationally, Sheena recognised both the honour and the responsibility. She accounted for her time and her actions, providing accurate and politically stimulating information, but also affectionately shared her more personal observations and enjoyment. Signing off on a circular to all regions[3] she closed, 'With my love to you all, from she who Rosie van Wyk Smith refers to as your buxom blonde earth mother. Your security blanket, which is another of her descriptions, looks forward to seeing you all in Durban on 13 March.' Sheena's letters not only made Black Sash members understand more of what was happening in their society and in others — she made members feel like family.

[3] Number 3/1986.

LETTER FROM AMERICA

Sheena Duncan, 1974

From the first of six weeks in the USA on an International Visitors' Programme grant: US State Department 1974[4]

Here I am, like Eloise, in the DuPont Plaza hotel. Yesterday was a very long day starting when I left the hotel in London at 8 am and ending at 9 pm Washington time, but actually 2 am in London.

At about 5 o'clock I walked down Connecticut Avenue, to the White House. I really couldn't believe it was me standing in Lafayette Square with grey squirrels and starlings in the trees growing at the White House. I felt like Edith Evans and 'imagine me sitting here drinking port with a man who's going to Ceylon.'

When I get into my hotel bedroom I can't take my eyes off the TV news. There are a lot of rows going on at the moment especially the row over pardoning of President Nixon. People are angry — not because of the mercy shown to Nixon but because they feel it subverts the due process of law. They say you cannot pardon a man before he has been tried and found guilty and it raises questions about the other Watergate accused and convicted.

One thing which has hit me at once is the importance of organisations independent of government.

For instance 75,000 telegrams have been sent to the President in the last 36 hours over his pardon. This figure is made public because Western Union which handles all telegrams is an independent company. Also my trip which is paid for by the American government is programmed by the Governmental Affairs Institute which is an independent non-profit making organisation, so there is no question of government controlling what visitors should see or not see.

Today Washington is having the primaries for the first city council elections. Up to now the city has been administered by a committee of Congress. Both Democrat candidates for Mayor are Negroes.

It is strange coming from SA to see on TV how interviewers and announcers and commentators are black and white and also a great many women — not just announcing women's programs and advertisements but also interviewing politicians etc. There are also women traffic cops directing traffic at intersections.

I walked for three hours this afternoon. First I went from the State Department down to the Lincoln Memorial, then walked across the tidal basin which is a big lake fringed with flowering Japanese cherry. I can't quite fathom what makes the whole city so impressive but I think it is the space. All these monuments are simple, enormous, and have vast acreages of green space around them so in a way it all seems unreal. Of course one of the things is that any city built on a big river has a tremendous initial advantage.

[4] Duncan, Sheena: 'American diary', *Sash*, vol.17, no.3, November 1974.

Then I walked up to the Washington Monument and from there across the Ellipse to the other side of the White House. It really is absolutely white and quite exposed to the public gaze with the most beautifully planted trees running down from the house to the road on each side of a very green lawn.

I have had two very fascinating days and have learned a great deal which will help us in the office. Yesterday I had an appointment at the Paralegal Institute. This organisation trains people to assist lawyers and to handle administrative legal work before tribunals of various kinds.

They give them an intensive five-day training session and the rest they learn on the job. They then go and work in a thousand different poverty law and community law offices. The director of training went through the whole training programme with me and then showed me two of the videotapes they use to teach people interviewing techniques.

I have lots of ideas to improve our efficiency, although the big difference is that most of the people they train are going to work full-time and get paid because legal aid in this country is recognised as being crucial to the provision of justice and government pays extensively to provide it.

Most of the people I have met so far are young and most could be earning far more if they went into the normal professional or commercial fields. I was there the whole morning and only left when I had to do so to get to see Mr Boggs of the Lawyers Committee for Civil Rights under Law. After that I was free so I took another long walk through the streets.

Washington is in many ways a rather unreal place because it has no industry and its only reason for existence is the government being here. It is full of nonprofitmaking organisations and the national headquarters of hundreds of institutions.

It has a building height ruling. Nothing can be built higher than the Capitol which is not very high so there are no skyscrapers and eight floors seem to be the maximum. It's difficult to get an impression of what the downtown area normally looks like because the subway building works have everything in a mess. It is all very complicated finding your way around because there are a series of squares and circles each going diagonally, then numbered streets go horizontally and lettered streets cross them at right angles. Added to this the whole city is divided into quadrants radiating from the Capitol and these are North West, South West, North East and South East and the numbers do not go consecutively. You can see why I keep getting lost.

I was asked to lunch by the legal adviser on human rights to the State Department. There is tremendous security to get into the building so your host has to come down to the entrance to get you. When we walked into his office what should I see but our poster, *Ban tyranny not people*, on his safe door in this, an otherwise very conventional senior executive-type office.

20 DAYS, 29 SPEECHES, 21 INTERVIEWS, FOUR RADIO AND TWO TV BROADCASTS

Sheena Duncan, 1982

CIRCULAR TO ALL REGIONS: 11/1982: 16 NOVEMBER 1982

The YWCA conference at Hoddeston, about an hour's drive north of London, was most restful compared to what followed. It was a conference on human rights in preparation for the international Y conference in Singapore next year. They had chosen three areas to concentrate on — sexism, racism and economic injustice.

I had been invited to speak in the racism section where, of course, South Africa loomed large but where I learnt a good deal about racism in other parts of the world.

There were two most interesting women from Palestine — one a fiery individual from Jordan and the other a charming person from Jerusalem who composes and sings beautiful songs to express all the tragedy in the Middle East. There are many similarities between the emotions and frustrations of the Palestinians and those of Black South Africans and the language of dispossession is the same but we were unfortunate in that there were no Israeli women there so felt pressurised sometimes by one side of the story only. The Y is having a consultation in Jerusalem early next year at which they are hoping to achieve a complete across-the-board representation.

Incidentally, I had never realised before that the YWCA is the largest women's organisation in the world with approximately 6 million members in 84 different countries. Women from all over the world were there. We had a party in which we had to come in ethnic dress — we two South Africans were part of the African group from Tanzanian, Nigeria and Zambia all glorious in African prints and Xhosa weaves — but I had to make do with a doek and a blanket.

Holland

I went to Holland properly for the three-week lecture tour on October 14 and didn't draw breath again until I fell onto the plane in Edinburgh on November 4. The women's church organisation which organised the program is VKW — Vrouw, Kerk, 2/3 Wereld — and they did a fantastic job — 29 public meetings, group meetings and lectures; 10 interviews with various individuals; 11 newspaper and magazine interviews; four radio and two television broadcasts — in 20 days. I talked and talked and talked and met some very interesting people. The two most terrifying meetings were the Moderature of the Dutch Reformed Church and the Foreign Affairs committee of the First Chamber (i.e. the Senate) of the Dutch parliament but both were very much easier than I had expected. I had meetings with Catholic and Protestant church groups, the women members of the Dutch parliament, the Dutch member of the European Parliament, a member of the Belgian parliament, the Dutch lawyers for Human Rights, two trade union groupings, the general secretary of the Dutch Council of churches, students at three different universities and lots of women's groups just like us, as well as various groups which work only on the South African issues.

The 'dwaze moeders'

One newspaper headlined its interview with me, 'Blanke Dwaze Moeder Uit Zuid-Afrika.' The 'dwaze moeders' are the foolish mothers of the Place Di Mayo in Argentina who demonstrate, demanding the release of the disappeared ones.

In Holland the women's groups demonstrate every month at The Hague in support of the foolish mothers. It was a comparison I was proud to be associated with. It is good to feel oneself part of the worldwide struggle for the security and survival of ordinary people against the dark powers of States. I felt very at home with all the women's groups in Holland who are working on a multitude of facets of the fight for simple justice both in Europe and further afield. They are just like us and experience the same internal debates about 'lifestyle', group rights versus individual rights, guilt about wealth and being placed among the 'haves' of the world, etc; also share the same ideals as we do and work in the same way to achieve them.

The only difference is that they have freedom to express dissent. I think Holland is the most democratic country I have ever been in.

I was astonished by the level of interest in South Africa and the sound factual information which so many groups circulate, and by the way in which so many people work with commitment on South African issues. I think I probably gained a distorted impression because I was not meeting the big business interests and the more conservative politicians (although some of them were present at some of the meetings). Our government information service does a most efficient job.

However, the re-imposition of the ban on Beyers Naudé undid all their efforts. He is very well known in Holland and greatly admired and respected. I was overwhelmed with kindness the whole time I was there and came back laden with messages of love and support to all of you. Our concerns are their concerns and they really do care about the people here which is most strengthening. I don't really understand why they should care so much. It seems to have something to do with 1652 and a lot to do with the Reformed Church connections. There are echoes of the Second World War and the Nazi occupation — the resistance and the oppression — and the liberation.

I expect I shall be writing again soon once I have got my feet on the ground. Everything is still rather unreal to me just now and I'm sure there is a whole lot you are waiting to hear about conference etc. Jill and Joyce have been overburdened and I feel guilty about going away at all but I do think it was useful and work that should be done.

LETTER TO ALL MEMBERS OF THE BLACK SASH FROM THE NATIONAL PRESIDENT

Sheena Duncan, 1985

November 1985

Dear member,

In all the regions of the Black Sash there is anxiety, uncertainty and unhappiness about the terrible violence in our country at the present time. We find ourselves withdrawing from words like 'comrades', 'progressive' and even 'democratic' because there is a new jargon in current use which reflects a new kind of ideology. Like the misuse of words by the National Party government for so many years it leads us to wonder whether words mean anything at all any more or whether words just mean what the user wants them to mean.

Here in the Transvaal we had our first Regional Conference this month and of course, much of the meeting was taken up with discussion of these things. It was all rather inconclusive and some members who were there felt that I should have spoken up and given a strong lead. Perhaps they are right but I have been listening hard to what everyone is saying and sharing the anxiety, uncertainty and unhappiness which we all feel.

I have not wanted to smother the debate because it is not an easy one and we need to learn from each other. There are no simplistic solutions and we have to think about everything that is said most carefully. I do not think it is helpful for me to lay down the law and silence everyone else.

However there are certain definite statements we can make.

1. The Black Sash is itself totally dedicated to the use only of non-violent means. This is written into our constitution and there is no debate about it. There is no member of the Black Sash anywhere who has expressed any disagreement with this.
2. Black Sash members deeply regret violence of all kinds where ever, when ever and by whomsoever it is used. I have not heard any Black Sash member in any region supporting or encouraging the use of violence.
   (The question of *excusing* the use of violence is dealt with below.)
3. There is unanimity about our reaction to the structural violence of the apartheid system and to the armed violence of the state against the people of this country. We have no disagreements about our attitude to torture of detainees, assaults on persons by officials of the state, the violent means used to crush all black opposition to apartheid, the excessive use of force against protesters, the provocative actions of government which fire the anger of black people etc., etc.

We have worked for thirty years against apartheid, against the abolition of the rule of law, against punishment by arbitrary decree, against all the manifestations of violence by the forces of the state, against the violence of pass laws, migrant labour, forced removals, denationalisation, against economic policies which make the rich richer and the poor poorer.

We all know about these things and we have consistently and publicly opposed them. I do not intend to repeat all the arguments about structural violence. We agree with all of them and have often in the past been the first to oppose aspects of this structural violence. We will continue to do so.

We have always, as a mainly white organisation, acknowledged our particular responsibility for the violence of the state. We are voters and we are part of the white minority in South Africa which has imposed this violence on black South Africans. We have known that we have a duty as white people, to vehemently, resolutely and publicly, condemn this violence and we have done it.

The debate is not about these things.

Now I come to the difficult things and as I write I am really thinking it out and trying to get some sort of order into the current confusion in the hope that it will be helpful in the ongoing discussion within the Black Sash.

There are no absolute answers although sometimes people on both sides of the argument present absolute solutions which they want us to conform to. This debate is *not* going to bring us to absolute conclusions. We have entered into a period of very violent confrontation and I do not think that we are going to come out of it very soon. I think the horror of violence is going to become worse and worse in the years ahead of us and we are going to have to think about it and debate it over and over again. *Nothing* will be worse than pretending it is not a problem and trying to sweep it under the carpet. We have to wrestle with it and we have to do our best to decide how we as Black Sash must react. We are all fearful about the future but we have to live through it and we will have to find the courage to live according to our convictions.

There are things I want to get out of the way first before trying to get to grips with the real problem.

1. The first is the *credibility* argument. Some people are saying that the Black Sash will lose its credibility with black people if we do or do not say certain things.

   I don't know whether we have credibility with black people or not. If we do it is because we have never claimed to have and if we do have it it is with some, not all, black people.

   But whether we have it or not it is *not* an argument we should be using.

   We do not base what we say or do on whether or not it will gain us credibility. We base what we do and say on whether it is the truth and whether or not it should be said and done irrespective of whether people will like it or not. The Black Sash existed without credibility for a long time and those of you who joined the Black Sash in the early days and who continued to work and to stand on principle through the long sterile years of the nineteen sixties without any 'credibility' to speak of will remember clearly the loneliness you experienced when you were raising small voices proclaiming words about justice and democracy in the wilderness.

It may be that we will have to live through another time like that in the future. It doesn't matter at all whether or not we have credibility with one group or another. What matters is that those words should go on being spoken and that we remain true to our own consciences.

2. Secondly I had better explain my own personal position so that you can measure what follows in the light of what you may regard as my own prejudices.

   I am a total, committed pacifist which in my case is based on my religious belief although I think I would still be a pacifist if I had no religion.

   This has been rather a long personal journey and I don't suppose I am at the end of it yet. I am constantly tormented by doubts and confusion but you had better know about it because it also makes me reluctant to trample over people's honestly held and expressed views.

3. Thirdly, I do not believe there is a conspiracy within the Black Sash membership seeking to take us over or to use us for its own revolutionary ends. The Black Sash does not want revolution. We are firmly committed to the principle of negotiation but we reject many of the processes which are currently being described as 'negotiation' in this country.

   I have not yet come across any member of the Black Sash who is working for revolution. If there were to be such people I am confident that they would not prevail over the sound common sense and commitment of our members.

   We in the Black Sash try to debate openly all our different perceptions of events and our differing opinions about strategies. We have had in the past, and will continue to have, arguments with one another but I hope we can continue to deal with them by working through them without manipulation from any group on either end of the debate, and without rancour towards one another.

   One thing that is worrying some of our members is that some people on both sides of the debate (and I mean *both* sides) have strong convictions and speak them out with such assurance that other people feel stupid and unable to speak for fear of being slapped down. Because of the nature of the Black Sash we are a bunch of rather strong minded people and we need to be careful that our procedures at meetings enable anyone who wants to talk to do so. Some of us should perhaps talk less and others should talk much more.

Violence

We have now entered into a period when all the violence in our society can no longer be attributed almost entirely to the state and its agents. People are being killed and tortured every day. Homes are being burnt down every day and children are sometimes killed or injured in the attacks. Most of the time we do not know who is committing these atrocities. Sometimes we think we know but we have no evidence to support our interpretation.

We don't know how to respond to all this. We have warned for years about the inevitability of violent conflict and now that it is upon us we don't know what to do about it.

Earlier this year a white church leader in Johannesburg delivered a most moving, well-reasoned and honest speech pleading for peace and nonviolence, and condemning violence. It was excellent and one agreed wholeheartedly with everything he said. But a black clergyman, who is himself working 24-hours a day at the interface against violence and for non-violent strategies, said to me, "how can he talk like that when he has two sons in the army?"

That really sums up our whole agony as white women whose sons, lovers, brothers, husbands are faced with the terrible choice between permanent exile, or six years imprisonment, or military service in an army which is pitted against the sons, lovers, brothers and husbands of our fellow citizens. Only total pacifists whose objection to military service is based on religious grounds are granted alternative service.

According to Mr Le Grange 500 houses belonging to black policemen have been burnt down countrywide. We know that policemen in many townships have left their homes and are living in tents and compounds at police stations. We know that in some areas councillors of local authorities have been killed and that in other places they have had to abandon their homes and retire to a well guarded compounds, or taken refuge in secret hideouts. Their wives and children have been at grave risk of being killed and some have died in petrol bomb attacks.

We all know why these people have been targets for violent attack. Knowing why and understanding all the reasons for the attacks does not however resolve our problem as to what we are to say about it, or about the attacks on police or military installations and vehicles. We are at war in Namibia and Angola and our government has admitted to gross interference in Mozambique and armed raids into our neighbouring countries, Lesotho and Botswana. Now that warlike conflict is going on in the townships in many different parts of the country perhaps the traditional teaching of the Church on just (justifiable) war and justifiable rebellion can be of some help to us although we are not actually at war in the formal declared sense. This teaching has its roots in pre-Christian Greek philosophy and Roman law so it is not only applicable to those who adhere to the Christian faith.

The criteria for justifiable war are:

1. It must have a just cause.
2. It must have a just intention.
3. There must be careful weighing of means in relation to ends.
4. It must be a last resort.
5. It must be declared by a legitimate authority.

The criteria for justifiable rebellion are the same except for the last, because rebellion occurs where the nature of the legitimate authority is brought into question.

The criteria for conduct in war include:

1. There must be a careful weighing of means in relation to ends. This concerns the use of weapons and methods of waging war, and the avoiding of wanton violence and atrocities.
2. There must be discrimination in terms of targets. This concerns the need to avoid injury being done to innocent non-combatants wherever possible.

The Jewish teaching is similar. War must be the last resort and violence can be used only in self-defence, which includes the defence of children. There are strict rules about the waging of war, which include a prohibition on the destruction of fruit trees. There is also an obligation to provide cities of refuge to the victims of war.

I do not find that either side in the present conflict fulfils all of the above criteria and I have argued about this often and openly, not just in the security of my northern suburbs home but on many occasions in both formal and informal meetings with black and white people who do not agree with me.

Other kinds of violence

There are so many other kinds of violence going on that I shall probably leave some out inadvertently. It seems to me that there are five main categories.

1. The spontaneous violence which is unplanned and which erupts in the heat of the moment in response to provocation. These tragic happenings and the deaths which result are a consequence of the high level of tension, hostility and anger in our society and I don't know how much can be said or done about them. They are literally too sad for words.
2. Attacks on the persons and homes of members of one political group by members of another. This category includes the UDF/Azapo conflict in the Eastern Cape (whatever we think were its origins); the Inkatha/UDF conflict in Natal; attacks from the right on those active in the opposition to apartheid; attacks on followers

of one squatter leader on another, for example in Crossroads etc., etc. There are bestial killings which fall into this category.

3. Assassinations of political leaders and the mysterious disappearance of political leaders. Rumours abound about those things. So far there is no evidence to say who killed Griffiths and Victoria Mxenge, Matthew Goniwe and three other leaders from Cradock, among others. We can only hope that the rewards currently being offered by the Civil Rights League will bring evidence to light which will lead to full exposure. This is the 'dirty tricks' syndrome and I think we will experience much more of it.
4. The violence being used in some places to enforce boycotts of various kinds. There is considerable violence and intimidation being used in many areas to enforce the school boycott and the consumer boycott. We reported extensively in the Johannesburg advice office report which was published in March this year about violence used to enforce the November 1984 stay away from work.

   This is not to say that all the boycotts are being enforced by violence but we do all know that many are. The degree of violence has a direct relationship to the amount of organisational work done in communities beforehand. The less work the more violence.
5. The terrible killings of people pointed out as informers or traitors who are kicked and beaten to death or subjected to the cruel and inhuman necklace treatment.

I unequivocally condemn all the kinds of violence listed above except for the first, and I think that the overwhelming majority of members of the Black Sash do so too.

This then leads us to the next question and that is what we do and say about it and how do we react.

This is an exceedingly long letter and I hope that you are still persevering with me through all the arguments. The length of it is a measure of the complexity of the problem. More than 800 people have died in the unrest in the past year and the Minister of Law and Order has said that two thirds of them died as a result of action by police.

We have to be very clear about one thing. We do not have any idea about who is responsible for 99% of the violence perpetrated in categories 2 to 5 above. We have no evidence whatsoever as to who is doing what. Sometimes we have our own suspicions and opinions but that is very different to having proof.

I am working very hard at the moment on a project with the South African Council of Churches which takes me all over this country to assist people who want to set up advice offices and/or crisis centres in black communities. Almost all the people I work with are black. Most of them are local leaders in UDF affiliated civic associations and residents organisations. Some are in church groups or self-help projects. Some have political affiliations other that the UDF.

In no case has the initiative been taken by me. I only go to meet with people at their invitation. These people are without exception wanting to establish advice/information/resource centres in their own communities in order to try to establish or maintain a process of orderly non-violent opposition to apartheid. Many of them are faced with the threat of violent retaliation against themselves and their families because of the peace-making work they are involved in and the threat posed to them is from both extremes of the political spectrum.

In the course of my work I also come across church fieldworkers who persevere sacrificially with long hours of unrewarded overtime seeking to prevent violence and to act as agents of reconciliation and healing in conflict situations.

These people do their work widely and are not seeking public recognition. In fact they shun the high profile approach because it hampers them in what they try to do. Many of them are exceedingly worried by the fact that violence has gained a momentum among some young groups that is uncontrollable and irrational.

Some of the peace-making efforts by such people have been reported in the press. In Pretoria parents and student leaders were attempting to cope with the violent elements. Consultations were underway and success was imminent when the police detained the woman who was the leading figure in those efforts.

In Port Elizabeth the consumer boycott has been negotiating with the Chamber of Commerce. A 14-day suspension of the boycott was announced. Two members of the boycott committee were attacked and nearly subjected to the necklace treatment. They were rescued by the police.

In Langa township at Uitenhage over 400 households were disturbed between midnight and 3 am when police delivered notices to them telling them application is being made to the Supreme Court for their eviction. The whole of Langa is scheduled for removal to Kwanobuhle. City Press reported that the Langa Co-ordinating Committee which has succeeded in controlling violence in this township now fears that it will be unable to do so if the removals begin and the demolition of the shacks continues.

I do not know who is behind the violence but I am absolutely certain that the UDF both at national and local level and every place I have been to is as concerned as we are and is doing a great deal to try to contain and prevent it.

I say this from my own experience and from the experience of Black Sash members while working in advice offices and crisis centres in different parts of the country.

So what are WE doing?

Every one of you is in some way involved in the work of peace-making. We all know the truth of Pope John's dictum "If you want peace work for justice". Whatever you do to further the work of the Black Sash, be it moral support, financial support, fundraising efforts, work in the advice offices, on committees against removals, protest meetings, writing letters to the press, work in church and women's groups — all of it is done for justice.

We are engaged on many fronts.

We work for the Rule of Law and uphold the idea of law in almost everything we do because we seek legal redress wherever that possibility exists.

Where it does not we have sometimes entered into civil disobedience in the full understanding of what this means accepting the awesome responsibility involved. Civil disobedience is *not* a denial of the importance of law but an affirmation of what just law is all about.

In all our advice offices and in the crisis centres and monitoring committees we have been involved in we seek to teach, inform and to promote the ideas of democracy and orderliness. We faithfully record *all* that is reported to us and publish what the law allows us to publish. We support the victims of violence in whatever ways we can and *no one* is turned away from our doors.

We protest injustice. We lobby for justice we work hard on all aspects of the injustices of apartheid.

We work in the End Conscription Campaign because we believe that the individual conscience must be allowed to be free to decide what to do in the South African conflicts and that no one should be forced to take up arms.

In a whole variety of ways we are now involved in wider movements for peace which are springing up in the white community.

We look all the time for effective strategies which can be used to pressurise government to move towards real change — towards the radical transformation of this society.

I and other Black Sash office bearers have spoken on public platforms here and overseas about violence and have tried to report truthfully about what is happening. I have and will continue to make clear my condemnation of atrocities whomsoever they are committed against and by whomever.

Excusing violence

I think we do sometimes excuse violence and I do understand why we do this. The people who come to our advice offices tend to be the victims of the violence of the agents of the state and of structural violence. We also received requests for help from the victims of the violence outlined in 2, 3 and 4 under 'other kinds of violence' outlined above.

Of course we are emotionally involved with the people who seek our help and tell us their terrible stories. Many of them do not wish to make statements and do not want their names revealed. We cannot in these circumstances release their stories to the press. We are absolutely bound by confidentiality. It has to be their decision and not ours.

Nevertheless we must be prepared to speak out against violence when we do have evidence and when we are free to publish, however much we understand the causes.

This 'speaking out' however is also a problem. The press does not want unsolicited statements being thrust upon them all the time and they make an awful mess of statements one does make by chopping them short. I much prefer to prepare our own memoranda when we do have factual information which we are free to publish.

We must not be afraid to speak the truth. We need to support and strengthen those who are right in the middle of the daily violence and be sensitive to their position in whatever we say and do, whenever we know them to be seeking to control violence and to direct anger along orderly channels of opposition and resistance.

I do not think it is possible to lay down rules for ourselves that will cover all eventualities but we do need to be as diligent in recording and exposing the violence of opposition as we are about the violence of the state.

If we condemn violence we have an absolute obligation to work in nonviolent ways and to demonstrate that there are other ways of forcing change.

What else should we be doing?

I don't really know the answer to this but will be grateful for any suggestions from members which could be considered at our next National Conference in March 1986.

The first Regional Conferences to suggest resolutions for National Conference and items for discussion are going on now.

The second round of Regional Conferences when we discuss items which have been put on the agenda for National Conference will take place in January/February 1986.

I urge you to attend these meetings and to speak out if you have criticisms, suggestions for action or anxieties you want to share.

These are most difficult and depressing times. I went to America for the second time this year on 26 September feeling quite optimistic because the State President had announced on 11 September the restoration of citizenship to the 9 million people from whom it had been taken away. On 12 September the President's Council disclosed its recommendations for the repeal of Pass Laws and the removal of Influx Control.

I returned to South Africa on 18 October and was totally depressed. I had spent 3 weeks telling Americans that these two announcements really did mean reversals of aspects of the apartheid policy. I was misguided and naive I think. Nothing has been done which convinces me that there is any intention of the government side to dismantle apartheid and our daily experience in the advice offices and removals committees shows us that apartheid is being enforced as rigidly as it ever was.

We have much work to do and we will go on doing it. It is not easy but we never expected it to be easy. We just know that it is worth doing. That is sufficient.

THE FRUIT TREES ARE BEING DESTROYED AND WE MUST BUILD THE CITIES OF REFUGE.

May all those of you who celebrate have a most blessed Christmas and may all of us find strength and courage to face 1986 with commitment and determination. I know we will.

THE 'DISINVESTMENT' CAMPAIGN

Sheena Duncan, 1986[5]

I visited the United States twice in 1985, at the invitation of American churches and most of my time was spent talking to church groups although there were also meetings at universities and with secular groups of various kinds. I was not in the States on any kind of campaign of my own but to respond to requests for factual information about South Africa.

Inevitably at all meetings I was asked what I thought about disinvestment and economic sanctions because this is at the forefront of the campaigns against apartheid wherever these are centred.

I did not find these questions easy. It is a complicated subject and difficult to think through. There are no glib answers and there are most serious consequences to be weighed in the balance. It is also a question to which the answers may change according to the developments at different times.

It is necessary to clarify the different terms which were used.

Economic sanctions are those sanctions which may be legislated by governments, such as the oil and arms embargoes and embargoes on new bank loans to the South African government. There are sanctions which may be imposed by private institutions such as the refusal of international banks to roll over South African loans following the state of emergency and the disastrous Rubicon speech made by President Botha in August.

There are also economic sanctions which can be effected by ordinary people such as consumer boycotts of South African private use. Trade unions which refuse

[5] Duncan, Sheena: 'Some personal observations on the "disinvestment" campaign', *Sash*, vol.28, no.4, February 1986.

to unload South African goods in foreign ports are imposing a form of economic sanction. There are many different examples.

Divestment is a call on American shareholders, particularly the large investors such as pension funds, city and state governments, and churches to divest themselves of their stock holdings in companies which do business in South Africa.

This campaign has a twofold purpose. It is designed to raise awareness about apartheid and the situation in South Africa and it puts considerable pressure on companies to exert political pressure towards the dismantling of apartheid.

Disinvestment calls on companies which have operations in South Africa to withdraw by selling off their South African interests and by cutting their ties with South Africa. Shareholder divestment is of course one of the pressures which might lead a particular company to disinvest.

Motivation

There is a whole variety of different motivations behind these campaigns. The most evident are, *firstly* a very strong feeling of moral revulsion about apartheid. This is deeply felt and is all the stronger because South Africa claims to be a civilised Christian member of the community of Western democracies.

Terrible crimes are committed against human beings by governments all over the world but apartheid is seen as being a legislated, deliberate and evil racism defended with lies and hypocrisy by South African spokesmen and apologists.

Many Americans do not wish to profit from apartheid and see their financial involvement in the South African economy as strengthening and perpetuating the apartheid regime.

Secondly, there is a real concern for the people of South Africa which shows itself most clearly in the work American churches have done on South African issues. Many people are convinced civil war is inevitable in this country unless sufficient nonviolent pressure can be brought to bear on our government to face change.

This concern for South Africans usually (but not always) extends to encompass concern for the white minority which is seen to be tragically bringing about its own destruction through its intransigence.

Thirdly, there is a certain amount of guilt for the racism which held sway in the States for so long and which still rears its ugly head too often and most painfully.

Strategies

It is in this area that I found myself embroiled in the most argument. In the churches there is a clearly thought-out purpose behind the pressure they are seeking to exert. They want to put sufficient pressure on American companies doing business in South Africa to force businessman to put pressure on the administrations in

Washington and Pretoria for real change. This is why the churches have singled out certain important companies as primary targets for the divestment campaign.

The same cannot be said for all the different organisations involved. Too many people are calling for total disinvestment without thinking through their strategies. They have no answer to the question 'what then?'

The South African arguments

South African businessmen and lobbyists are doing themselves a disservice. They argue that black people will suffer most from economic sanctions and that change can only come through economic growth. They claim that the benefits of economic prosperity will break down the walls of apartheid and will inevitably be distributed among the whole population. They claim that economic recession slows political change. This is demonstrably untrue. It is in times of economic growth and prosperity that apartheid has been entrenched. In periods when the profits are rolling in, white businessmen switch off their interest in political developments. It is only in times of recession that there is a sudden concern for human rights and political 'power-sharing.'

The apartheid structures are built on the needs and the plans of big business interests; the pass laws, migratory labour, the reserves/homelands policy were all designed to satisfy the demands of profit-making and the need for cheap labour.

It is only the threat of economic sanctions which has led to a new concern about black unemployment. We did not hear those voices raised as South Africa's pattern of industrial development created a structural unemployment problem. Until recently we never heard them complain about the removals programme which exacerbated unemployment by taking people's land from them.

Those South African companies which are now investing their money in other countries have no right to talk about black unemployment. Their concern for job creation falls short of actually creating new jobs with their own money in their own country.

It must also be noted not all sanctions cause unemployment. The oil and arms embargoes created thousands of jobs in this country. Bans on the sales of some kinds of technology to South Africa might prevent the destruction of jobs which so often goes hand-in-hand with mechanisation.

The structure of apartheid ensures that unemployment and poverty are concentrated in the homeland areas — out of sight and out of mind. We had not noticed white anxiety about the plight of that 54% of the black population which was officially resident within homeland borders by the year 1980 until economic recession made unemployment, retrenchment and redundancy a possibility for everyone, including white people, in workplace and management.

The Black Sash has for years criticised businessmen for doing nothing whatsoever to resist apartheid policies and programmes. Businessmen have sometimes lifted up their heads to say that they do not approve of apartheid but they have not taken action to oppose it or to prevent its excesses.

It is most welcome that the unholy alliance between business and government has at last been broken and that the private sector is now doing its best to find ways of pressurising the government for real change. It is welcome that some businessmen are seeking to negotiate with those in whose hands future government will lie.

On past evidence I do not believe that this would have happened had pressure not been exerted on them. And will it last if the pressure is removed?

It is for these reasons that I am in favour of strategic, selective, economic pressures carefully thought out, carefully monitored, and adjusted according to observed effects.

It seems to me that these economic pressures may be our last hope for avoiding a long drawn out civil war, which would result in total economic collapse.

MESSAGE FROM SHEENA

Sheena Duncan, 1993

For the 'launch' of Sash, East Cape Focus: Grahamstown: 22 January 1993

I am truly sorry that I cannot be in Grahamstown tonight because I love your city and its people. My absence is unavoidable due to all sorts of family problems. Neil, my husband, who has been a faithful supporter of the Black Sash and who has done all sorts of things like the cooking for many years, has some kind of unexplained problem which means he cannot drive and cannot walk very well (he can still cook thank goodness) and my mother fell out of bed and broke her leg.

I was going to say something about her indomitable spirit because she was the driving force behind the Black Sash from 1955 to 1975, and for some years after that is a very vocal backseat driver. She fell out of bed because she refuses to wait until someone comes to help her to get up in the morning. She is fine and giving the physiotherapist a hard time because she does not see why she should try to walk if she does not want to do so. It is an infringement of her human rights! Many of you here tonight know her, or know of her, and if she could she would want to send you messages of exhortation and encouragement.

As I thought about her I got hung up on that word 'indomitable.'

According to my dictionary it means 'incapable of being subdued' and 'unconquerable.' All through this special issue of Sash this is what insists on our attention — the indomitability of the people of the Eastern Cape.

The magazine is a litany of the impossible statistics of poverty, unemployment, drought, neglect, a history of conflict and exploitation. Yet in every article the shining sign of hope is what the people are doing about it.

You in the East Cape are not alone in your condition. It is the common experience of people in most parts of this country, in the whole of Africa, and in the rest of the two-thirds world.

I expect there are many ordinary people in Iraq who are mourning tonight for their dead (who are never shown on CNN). People in Cambodia, Mozambique, Angola, India, Bosnia, on the streets of New York or London, are cold, hungry, homeless, and feeling ill. Many of them are terrified

Whatever became of the concept of 'ubuntu'?

Sometimes one feels there is nothing to be done but to draw up the sheets over one's head and ignore it all.

As I write this I am listening to the news reports of the inauguration of the new president of the United States. I think I hear that he has promised to maintain the 'new world order … by force if necessary.'

Our new world order is not like that. It is something which the language of the powerful cannot encompass.

It is something which happens in the neighbourhoods and in community and we can build it here where we are.

Is there anywhere you would rather be than here in the Eastern Cape?

The answer is, of course, NO. There is nowhere else where this richness of belonging and being can happen for us because this is *our* place of belonging.

I just wish I could be with you tonight to talk about this. It is impossible to write it all down because my thoughts rush ahead of my fingers and anyway it needs to be developed in discussion.

I used to think that the one word I would use to describe the people of this country through the long years of apartheid was 'endurance — the ability to withstand hardship, adversity, or stress.'

Now I have a new word — 'indomitable' — incapable of being subdued.

Note the curious construction. We are INCAPABLE OF BEING SUBDUED.

It is very much more than the ability to withstand hardship. It means that no one can subdue us because we are *incapable* of being oppressed by them. They cannot touch us and nor can war, pestilence or persecution.

WE ARE INDOMITABLE

(Please note that this also applies to us in Johannesburg.)

Preparing to speak

When Sheena spoke on public platforms, she rarely referred to notes. She looked her listeners straight in the eye and every word seemed to come straight from her heart. It did, and she spoke with memorable power and presence, but she also prepared meticulously, mostly on index cards[6] in her own clear neat handwriting and always with her facts correct and with her audience in mind. Four diverse examples of Sheena's written notes are offered below.

THE RIGHT TO LIVE FREE

Sheena Duncan, 1974

NATIONAL CONFERENCE OF THE WORLD AFFILIATED YWCA, THABA 'NCHU: DECEMBER 1974[7]

In this country women, and especially black women, share in the deprivation of rights with which all black people in South Africa must live. It is a significant fact that in the United States of America the women's liberation movement grew out of the civil rights struggle and only really got going after recognition of the rights of blacks had been achieved. Women who worked in the South came to a new understanding of human freedom as a total concept.

Since then much has been achieved in the States and in Europe and, although much remains to be done, it is a heady experience for a woman from South Africa to live free. To be recognised for what one is — a person — without preconceived ideas of femininity, to be taken seriously in discussions and consultations, to be free to move where one will without the restraints which arise from male-orientated social sanctions, this is wonderful. It is inspiring to know when looking at the realities of our situation here that the battle can and will be won and we, too, will one day take our place alongside women all over the world in accepting responsibility, sharing influence and enjoying freedoms we now only dream of and which some of us do not even recognise we are without.

Four years ago the Black Sash drew up a charter for women. The preamble says "The rights enumerated in this charter might appear to be so fundamental as not to need stating at all. All women should have them but in South Africa the majority of women do not. In fact, African women do not enjoy any of them, because the whole policy of apartheid, which entrenches discrimination on the basis of colour, has caused the denial of these rights to be written into the law of the land."

[6] Many of which are preserved in her personal papers at the Cullen Library Historical Papers.

[7] See also: Duncan, Sheena: 'The right to live free', *Sash*, vol.17, no.4, February 1975.

Deprivations shared by all South African women

There are certain disadvantages which we all share. A woman in this country cannot share in joint guardianship with the father of her legitimate children. This means that the father can always overrule the mother in disputes which arise regarding the upbringing and care of the children. Only in exceptional circumstances will a court of law uphold the mother's decisions against the father.

If a woman is married in community of property, immovable property such as a house cannot be registered in her name even if she has paid for it. She cannot deal on the stock exchange or make hire-purchase agreements without her husband's consent. If she wishes to open a bank account she must have her husband's written consent. If she is married out of community of property she has no statutory rights to receive a portion of her husband's estate. In other words he can make a will leaving her nothing and she has no legal redress.

Into this area in which we all share falls also the social discrimination against women which is not legislated for, which is often disguised as masculine protection of the 'weaker sex.' This discrimination is so deeply rooted and so very basic to our society, that we must not underestimate the difficulties which lie in our path as we seek to eliminate it. That it can be done is being proved in other places and every one of us can do something, however small.

Do you ever say, 'I must *ask* my husband'? If you do, change the word 'ask' to 'consult with.' Do you ever say, 'My husband doesn't allow me to do this'? Why?

Perpetual minors

Then there is discrimination which applies only to black women in South Africa. We have the scandal of the perpetual minority of African women in Natal, a scandal which was partially extended to women in the Transvaal in 1972 when it became compulsory for an African woman in that province to produce the written consent of her father or legal guardian before her marriage could take place. This has long been the case in Natal and means that many young adult women have to suffer the indignity of asking a guardian who may be unknown to them, younger than them, have less education than them, for permission to marry. The only way in which a woman can get around this if she cannot find her guardian, or if he refuses his consent, is to ask the Minister of Bantu Administration or a judge of the Supreme Court.

It is a matter of concern that millions of women therefore have no right to choose their own marriage partners. It is a matter of urgency that both the Natal code and the 1972 legislation be abolished and that all marriages be regulated by the Marriage Act of 1961 which rules that the consent of the father or guardian must only be obtained if the woman is under 21.

The Natal Code

African women in Natal are governed not only by the laws which rule the rest of us but by the provisions of the Natal Code. Very briefly, the Natal Code means that all African women in Natal are legal minors however old they may be and however respected by the community. These women always remain subordinate to a male guardian, to their fathers or to other relatives when unmarried and to their husbands if they are married. A woman may not enter into any contract such as a hire purchase agreement, nor may she seek employment without the consent of her guardian. She cannot sue or be sued in a court of law if the action falls under customary law without the assistance of her guardian. She can own property but the law is unclear as to whether she can sell it without his consent. She cannot ever be regarded as the guardian of her children. If she is married whatever she earns belongs to her husband. If her customary union marriage is dissolved her guardianship reverts to her father or other male relative and she cannot start divorce proceedings without his consent. She may be given temporary custody of her young children but must have the father's consent to anything she may wish to do on their behalf.

If she is married, widowed or divorced she can apply for emancipation from the state of servitude but she must have her guardian's consent to do so. The Bantu Affairs Commissioner can overrule him if he refuses consent but he must go with her to the Commissioner to make the application and if he will not do so there is little she can do about it. She must also be 'thrifty' and 'of good character' and must own property. If an emancipated woman marries she becomes a minor again unless she and her husband have an antenuptial contract.

In all provinces of the Republic a woman who is married by customary union has very little protection if her husband contracts a civil marriage with another woman. Her union with him is, in effect, dissolved. He is not obliged to give her any of the joint property and retains guardianship and custody of the children unless the children are very young when the mother might be allowed to keep them for a while … She may only use such of their property as was allotted to her by her husband if she lives in the place he tells her to. She can only get maintenance from him for herself and the children if she can show that she is without means of support.

The Pass Laws

These laws totally deprive all African women of the most basic human rights, to live with their husbands and children and to move with their husbands to live with them where work is offered. Women have to have a permit to do these things, a permit which is usually refused. They are also prevented by law from seeking employment where they wish to do so. A woman who lives in a small town may find herself compelled to work as a domestic worker or cleaner because there are absolutely no other openings in the only place where she is legally entitled to be. She will not be permitted to move to a place where the work of her choice is to be found. In the homelands women are in an even worse position. A woman may not move out of her home area to seek work and the work that is offered to her by the local labour officer is likely to be of a very badly paid, unsatisfactory kind. Job opportunities in the homelands and border industrial areas are extremely limited. She has a chance of employment carrying some job satisfaction if she is qualified in one of the professions where her skills may be required by her homeland government but this is hardly free choice of employment if there is only one possible employer offering openings suited to her abilities. If she has limited skills or no training at all she will most likely have to remain unemployed or, as she cannot afford to earn nothing, be forced to accept very badly paid work as a seasonal farm labourer or domestic worker in a rural area, if even this kind of employment is available.

In those towns which do allow women in from outside to work on one-year contracts unacceptable conditions are imposed. In Randburg, for example, women who come from Bophuthatswana to work on contract must sign an undertaking that they will not 'introduce' their children into the area and if they do so the contract is rendered null and void.

The housing regulations which control urban African townships also severely prejudice women. Only a man may become the registered tenant of a house. Women who are the heads of families, such as widows, divorcees and single women with children are no longer allowed to rent a house. They can only live as lodgers in a room in someone else's house, irrespective of their age, income or permanent residence rights in the area concerned. A woman who has been living in a house with her husband may be evicted if he dies or deserts her.

Employment

South Africa is so far behind the Western world in her employment policies that it is difficult to select those areas of the greatest concern. There is legalised discrimination and discrimination which is not imposed by law but which arises out of the attitudes of white men to women and to blacks.

If one looks at the display advertisements offering vacancies in any edition of a daily newspaper a trend is immediately apparent which is universal in this country. An employer with the vacancy rarely just advertises the position, the conditions of employment and the skills he requires. He has a preconceived idea of whom he wants. If it is a senior position he thinks in terms of men only and white at that. If it is a junior or clerical position he thinks of 'young ladies.' He also decides what colour he wants, and — a less obvious discrimination — what age he wants. It seems that if you are not between 18 and 25 you have a very limited choice of employment offered and if you happen to be black, female and 40 you don't stand a chance.

There are also clear indications that employers think that if they fill a vacancy with a woman they can pay her less.

These stereotypes affect us all and lay down a limited category of jobs in which we as women can hope to earn a living. The boundaries of our ambition are defined for us at birth. The result of this kind of attitude being inculcated in childhood is that we fail to fight for our rightful place in society when we become adult. We accept opposition too readily and come to doubt our own abilities.

Discrimination in pay scales

Much has been written about the scandalous racial discrimination in pay scales when whites are paid more than blacks for doing the same jobs requiring exactly the same training and skills, but we hear less about the sexual discrimination in pay which pervades our society.

In all wage determinations and in all sectors of the economy women are paid less than men for doing the same job.

All this leaves one with the feeling of despair. There is so much to be done and so many crucial deprivations that one does not know where to begin. Legalised discrimination is the hardest to tackle. The Pass Laws are the cornerstone of the whole edifice of apartheid and any attack on them is an attack on the very foundations of our so-called 'traditional way of life.' Discrimination which occurs as a result of custom and attitude may seem easier to change but in a society which is rooted and grounded in a false presumption that certain people are superior to others because of the colour of their skins, this presumption is extended to an assumed superiority because of sex which becomes as deeply entrenched as if it were legislated for.

But women are moving all over the world and are throwing off one restraint after another. I do believe that we can find a way through all of this, that women do have the power to change our society. Here in South Africa it is impossible to separate the liberation of women from the liberation of all people.

One day perhaps historians will say of all of us that it was the women who won freedom for all South Africans.

HOW MUCH WOULD WE SACRIFICE?

Sheena Duncan, 1975

FROM ADDRESS: WOODMEAD SCHOOL FOUNDATION DAY, JOHANNESBURG: JUNE 1975

I have been unsure as to what to speak about today. The things that I wish to share with you may seem to be impossibly repetitive of speeches you have heard over and over again before because much of what I intend to say is contained in the principles upon which the school is founded, but I have become increasingly concerned about the role of the individual in our present situation.

I feel it is of the utmost importance that we should learn to relate what we say we believe in to the way we act, so I make no apology for trying to think it through again with you. There are several threads which I want to pull together. All of them lead to the same place and that is the responsibility and duty of the individual.

The first of these threads is the current talk of detente. Over and over again we are told in newspaper editorials and by opposition politicians that detente between South Africa and Black Africa and between South Africa and the rest of the world cannot succeed unless we bring about change within our borders first.

When we read these articles or listen to these speeches we cheer and agree wholeheartedly. We feel good because we can feel part of a liberal, progressive movement. It is nice to feel that we are in agreement with lots of other people, and it's even nicer to hope for a while that our generous feelings may somehow or other be big enough to defuse the tensions which are building up to intolerable levels in the rapidly deteriorating relationships between those of us who are white and those of us who are black.

We call for dialogue. We say, 'open the theatres, open the hotels, talk to blacks, give blacks a better education, allow blacks freehold title in the urban areas.'

We seek complicated formulae to allow people political rights without disturbing the status quo because we do not really want to contemplate other political philosophies as alternates to our own.

We talk of a shared society but cling to the capitalist, free enterprise model, which has provided for us here, so well. Can it provide for everyone else on the same scale? I do not know the answer but I would like to know that we were asking the question. We have not asked it yet.

We visualise change as being an end in itself, a Utopia where we lose nothing but everyone else is raised, however slowly, to our position of power and privilege. Merely saying it out loud makes us realise what a nonsensical premise it is.

However change comes about in this country and whatever political philosophies and systems are tried and adopted it is going to mean fundamental and continuing change in the lives of everyone of us and we must not speak of it lightly.

We have wealth — or we would not be here in this place at this moment in time. How much is each one of us personally prepared to sacrifice in the interests of the change we declare we want to see?

We will have to pay more in taxes. We may no longer be able to afford frequent trips to Europe, five-star hotels, fast and luxurious motorcars, clothes bought for fun rather than for warmth and modesty.

Perhaps you are saying now: 'We know all this; we are prepared to do without these things, or with less of them.' But, we may be called upon to do without many things we regard now as necessities — to eat meat every day, two bathrooms, hot water, more than one winter coat, service.

Are we still going to fight for change understanding of the implications or are we going to go into reverse when it looks as if real change could come about?

Most of us here have been able to purchase more space (that most wonderful of all the privileges of the rich) than can even be imagined by the vast majority of the world's people. Sharing our space means sacrificing some of our privacy. Can the world afford people who own acres of precious land merely for the satisfaction of ownership?

The West Rand Administration Board says there is no more land to provide housing for Soweto's 100,000 homeless people. When the change we say we want comes about and Soweto's people have the political means of satisfying their reasonable demands, they will see that the land they need is lying at hand uncultivated, unproductive and sterile.

We can expect to be expropriated, to have subdivision into realistic urban plots enforced, to have high density housing schemes across the road, at the bottom of the garden, next door.

And that farm we bought as a tax evasion dodge and a retreat from the noise and tension of city life — when that is taken from us because the new regime makes it compulsory for all agricultural land to be worked on a full-time basis by the owner — will we still gladly accept change?

When we have to share the facilities we now have provided for us on a ridiculously exclusive basis will we gladly accept change? When our queue for the bus is everyone's queue and stretches round the corner; when the platform for a commuter train is everyone's platform and we have to push and shove for a place as is taken for granted by the majority of city people in the world; when we can no longer get what we want by a combination of pulling rank, bluster and knowing the right people will we still gladly accept change?

The challenge in all this is to each one of us, irrespective of whether our families, our friends, our contemporaries, our political parties are able to meet it. The reward and the joy of it is in knowing that even were we to be entirely alone, what I do and what you do is of vital importance.

It can be a hard thing to learn that, however repressive the society in which we live may be, we as individuals can live free. Whites in South Africa do not always understand how unfree we are, more particularly those of us who find it difficult to identify the chains which bind us.

Some of us are bound by the necessity we feel to maintain a position of privilege; some of us by our feeling of guilt that we enjoy that power and privilege.

Some of us are bound by fear of change and of the future. This is the worst prison of all and to understand just how it confines us, contrast our position with those who can only run to meet the future with hope and joy because nothing could be worse than their present situation.

Whatever it is that imprisons different societies and groups there are always among them the ones who are free, who walk tall. When you meet people like those you will recognise them at once.

I have been taught about this by people whose sufferings are unimaginable to us; black people here in Johannesburg who live under the oppression we visit on all blacks — the permit system; subjection to police raids on their homes at night and on their persons in the streets; exclusion of everything which gives quality of life; some of them in real danger of arrest and of indefinite detention by the Security Police.

Yet every now and again there is one who is not afraid, whose integrity of spirit cannot be touched or damaged by anyone or anything, who is free in the truest sense of that word.

What are the qualities which can enable us to learn this freedom? To me it seems that there must always be self discipline, an orderliness of thought and behaviour which provides the framework for freedom as much for the individual as for a society.

I do not think it is just because I am middle aged that I have come to think like this. One cannot be free if one's life and thought and behaviour are a chaos of anxieties, good intentions, uncompleted plans or uncontrolled emotions.

Then with this orderliness must come tolerance and courtesy, and humour. Without exception all the free people I have met can always laugh at the ridiculous in themselves and can see the absurdity of those who would enslave them.

But most important of all they have a deep faith in something. For me as a Christian it is faith in the God of love and in the promise that His grace will be sufficient for whatever I may be called upon to do, but others have other faiths — in goodness, in humanity, in the future, in God by other names.

Here at Woodmead you are presented with the opportunity of learning all these things. When the time comes for you to leave this community, go out and live free in the new communities in which you will be called upon to serve.

TRIBUTE TO MOLLY BLACKBURN

Sheena Duncan, 1986

At the funeral service: St John's Methodist Church, Port Elizabeth: January 1986

When Gavin phoned me last night to ask me to speak briefly this morning my mind went totally blank.

There are some things which are too deeply felt for any words and such is my sorrow. There are no words to say what we have all felt over the last days and what we are feeling now.

I went back to share with other Black Sash people who have come to Port Elizabeth from all over South Africa my feelings of inadequacy. One of them handed me an old envelope on which she had scribbled some words.

She says she writes things down when she hears them. She doesn't remember when she heard it but she has given me the words I needed.

This is what it says:

A warrior for justice had walked briefly in a troubled land, seeded the minds of men and women with new visions of themselves and changed the course of history.

Molly was such a one.

I have not known her for very long and I wish there had been more time for us. But there are some people whom one instantly recognises as great from the moment one meets them.

Molly was such a one — a truly great person.

Yesterday I opened the Black Sash magazine of May 1985 which reports on our national conference held here in Port Elizabeth last March.

There is a photograph of Brian Bishop taken in Namibia.

There is a photograph of Matthew Goniwe and one of Molly. All of them — *Warriors for justice who walked briefly in a troubled land.*

They are all dead.

We weep today but we know that they have changed the course of history and their work will continue.

This is the tribute we pay to them — our commitment to go on trying to follow them as 'warriors for justice' — our dedication to the cause they served.

We will not forget them and we will not be turned back from the path they trod.

Molly's death is a national as well as a bitterly felt personal tragedy.

All of us today reach out to comfort her husband, her children, her sister, her whole family, her friends, especially Di, and all the thousands of people who mourn her now.

There is a verse from the first psalm which is for our consolation:

And she shall be like a tree planted by the rivers of water, that bringeth forth her fruit in season; her leaf shall also not wither; and whatsoever she doeth shall prosper.

In the shade of her tree we shall bring forth our fruit in due season and we will always seek to prosper the work she has begun.

HEAL, RECONCILE, BUILD

Sheena Duncan, 1991

FROM GOOD FRIDAY SERMON: CENTRAL METHODIST CHURCH, DURBAN

Diakonia's theme for this year is 'Heal, reconcile, build'.

We are overwhelmed by the task before us. Everywhere we look we are confronted by destruction and suffering, death and woundedness. As I wrote this, news came of 15 more people brutally killed at a funeral vigil in Alexandra. There are so many thousands of people who mourn their dead and whose sorrow has to be borne somehow. Each death now seems to lead to other deaths. Each day brings new tragic events which we cannot begin to understand. There are so many thousands of people who are consumed with hatred and anger, whose souls and spirits are deeply wounded by these destructive emotions. Families, communities, the whole society is broken and disordered.

So, here we are, people in exile from the kingdom of God, seeking to find our way home to where justice and peace are to be found. We are a people who are afraid. We know that our adversary, the devil, *as a roaring lion walketh about seeking whom he may devour.* We know in our inmost being the despair which led Jesus on the cross to cry: *My God, my God, why did you abandon me?* But yet we also know that God is the Lord of history. We too, like the people of Judah in exile in Babylon, ask in wonder and incomprehension: *Who could have seen God's hand in this*? Which of us can see God's hand in all this?

In our short time on earth, we, homo sapiens made in the image of God, have almost managed to destroy God's creation, plundering the earth, polluting the waters, blotting out the sun, killing children from hunger and disease. God made us in God's image, but we have so distorted the image and misused the creation that we are indeed in danger of being cast into outer darkness. But yet, Jesus Christ was born. We are lost in wonder, love and praise as we contemplate this incredible purpose which has created and redeemed us; which makes us meaningful in the whole vast universe which God created. We can indeed see God's hand in this.

As we carry this cross through the streets of Durban today, we do so in anguish and sorrow for our sins. For our responsibility for the exiles, the beaten, the poor, the oppressed. But with them we know that we are God's co-creators. That we are given the power to heal, reconcile and build. We know that God has a purpose for us. We know that our peace is only to be found in doing that purpose. We know that the joy of the resurrection is upon us. We know that we too will one day sing and shout for joy in the streets of Jerusalem. We know that we will go out from this place in the power of the Holy Spirit to live and work to God's praise and glory.

So be it.

In response to Proclamation R133

This particular letter to Black Sash members is not included with the collection of others. There are two reasons for this. It is a long letter in its own right, but the second reason is that it provoked a storm of protest from the apartheid regime, much of which was covered in the press.

To illustrate the effect it had at the time, a small selection from the follow-up correspondence is provided at the end of Sheena's critical communication to Black Sash members.

LETTER TO BLACK SASH MEMBERS 17 JULY 1975

Sheena Duncan, 1975

The inmates of an institution shall be detained therein for the purpose of improving their physical, mental and moral condition by:

a) *training them in habits of industry and work;*
b) *reorienting them through the traditions, culture, custom and system of government of the national unit to which they belong;*
c) *generally cultivating in them habits of social adaptation in the community and of good citizenship including the fostering of an awareness in regard to the observance of, and the necessity for, the laws of the country.*

The above is not a quotation from the statutes of communist Russia nor of the Third Reich. It is not even a quotation from prison regulations. It is section 5 of the Proclamation for Rehabilitation Institutions in the Bantu Homelands published as proclamation R133 in a Government Gazette of June 6, 1975 here in the Republic of South Africa.

The regulations allow for the establishment of institutions in the homelands for the reception, *treatment* and training of persons committed thereto under the Bantu Urban Areas Consolidation Act or the Bantu Labour Act, such institutions to be maintained and conducted by the Secretary for Bantu Administration and Development. In other words, the responsibility for running these institutions lies with the central government.

Who are the people who are so in need of 'treatment' and training that they should be admitted to one of these institutions in terms of the two acts mentioned?

They are not habitual criminals, nor are they criminally insane or mentally or physically disabled. They have not been convicted of criminal offences. They *are* pass offenders.

They are ordinary men and women, South African citizens (only black citizens are affected of course) who have the misfortune to be without the proper permits and papers which would enable them to live and work in that part of their own country where they wish to be.

Section 14 of the Bantu Urban Areas Consolidation Act (25:1945) says that any African person who has been convicted of remaining in a prescribed area illegally or who has been introduced into a prescribed area without permission may, *with due regard to his family ties or other obligations or commitments*, be removed together with his dependents, under a warrant issued by the court convicting him, or by any Bantu Affairs Commissioner, to his home or his last place of residence or to a rural village, settlement, *rehabilitation scheme*, institution or other place.

Section 25 of the Bantu Labour Act (67: 1964) says that any African who is arrested for or convicted of contravening or not complying with the provisions of the Urban Areas Act or the Labour Act or the Abolition of Passes and Coordination of Documents Act may be referred to an aid centre.

The officer in charge of an aid centre may, *whether or not he (i.e. the arrested person) has been convicted of such an offence*, make such order as may appear to him to be just in regard to the repatriation of such Bantu and his dependents to his home or last place of residence or any other place indicated by such officer.

Section 29 of the Urban Areas Act provides that whenever the authorised officer has reason to believe that a Bantu outside the homelands is '*an idle or undesirable person*' he may without warrant arrest that person who will then be brought before a Bantu Affairs Commissioner.

The Commissioner may then declare him to be idle or undesirable and order him to, *be sent to any rural village, settlement, rehabilitation scheme, institution .... and be detained thereat for such period and perform thereat such labour as may be prescribed ...*

If a person is declared to be idle or undesirable the onus of proof is on him or her to prove that he or she is not.

The definition of idle as laid down in section 29 is very wide indeed and includes someone who has been required to leave the area concerned and has failed to do so or has returned to the area without permission.

Undesirable people include those who have been convicted of various offences and section 29 imposes a kind of administrative punishment in addition to that already handed down by the courts.

People ordered to rehabilitation scheme in terms of section 29 have a right of appeal but the noting of an appeal does not suspend the operation of the order.

In terms of the new regulations the person sent to a rehabilitation institution is to be detained there for 3 years subject to the terms of the order committing him although the board of management of the institution may discharge an inmate before the period has elapsed.

A person who is serving a prison sentence may be transferred to one of these institutions for the unexpired portion of his sentence but not for longer than 3 years.

The proclamation lays down rules and regulations of the running of a rehabilitation institution among which are the following:

Section 6. There shall be a board of management for each institution which shall be appointed by the Minister of Bantu administration and development.

Section 7. The Minister shall appoint a superintendent as head of the institution. He is to be subject to the control of the board and among his duties are to:

- Determine the duties to be performed by each inmate.
- Have the right to search or cause to be searched an inmate on admission or at any time thereafter provided that the search is carried out by someone of the same sex as the inmate in a seemly manner without offence to his dignity and 'an inmate shall, as far as practicable, not be stripped and searched in the presence and sight of other inmates'.
- Receive and keep in his custody all money, personal effects, clothing or other article which an inmate has in his possession on admission and which, in the opinion of the superintendent, he should not be allowed to retain or receive while in the institution.

Section 11

Inmates shall be classified in different groups with due regard to conduct, educational qualifications, mental and physical condition 'and the provisions of section 5.' Once classified they can be moved by the superintendent from one group to another, subject to the confirmation of the board.

The general treatment, training and care of the inmates shall be so organised as to obtain the purposes set out in section 5.

The physical fitness of inmates shall be improved in such manner as may be prescribed by the superintendent in consultation with the medical officer. Provision shall be made for such leisure activities and hobbies of inmates as may be prescribed by the superintendent.

Section 12

Every inmate shall, unless prevented by illness, be employed in such work as the superintendent may determine.

The assignment of work in an institution shall as far as practicable be so organised as to meet the particular needs and circumstances of each individual inmate and shall constitute an integral part of the programme of treatment contemplated in section 5. Inmates may be required or allowed to work outside the institution but not for any person or body other than the state, or the Bantu authority or for the institution.

Section 13
Inmates *may* be paid allowances for work done by them while they are detained, the rates and conditions of such payments to be decided by the secretary for Bantu administration.

The payment of allowances to an inmate shall be a privilege to be earned by work and the amount of such allowance shall depend upon the conduct of the inmate.

Section 16
Inmates can have visitors only with the authority of the superintendent and subject to rules prescribed by the board. The superintendent shall keep a record of the name, identity number and address of any visitor together with the object of his visit and his relationship to the inmate concerned.

Visitors can be searched and can be refused admission without being given the reasons for the refusal.

The superintendent may open and read any letter or parcel addressed to an inmate or written or sent off by an inmate and investigate the contents thereof, and may withhold any letter or parcel, the further transmission or dispatch of which is in his opinion undesirable by reason of the nature of its contents or of the personality of the writer or addressee or of any relevant circumstances.

Section 18
The board and the superintendent may, with the approval of the secretary of Bantu administration, make rules for the maintenance of good order and discipline.

An inmate will be guilty of an offence if he disobeys these rules, refuses to allow himself to be photographed, measured, weighed, vaccinated or medically examined, if he gives false replies to any question put to him about his antecedents or, *any other matter upon which information is required for records or statistical purposes*, or if he refuses to reply to such questions.

Among other things it is an offence for him to refuse to obey an order or instruction of the superintendent; to be indecent in word, deed or gesture; to use abusive, insolent, threatening or other improper language; to cause discontent among the inmates; to refuse or evade work by any means; to malinger by feigning illness.

If a man is reported to have committed an offence and the superintendent intends to punish him the superintendent must cause the inmate to be brought before him for interrogation. The inmate is allowed to call witnesses or make any statement or explanation.

If he is convicted the superintendent may impose various punishments ranging from reprimand through forfeiture of allowances, privileges or three meals a day on any one day to, *separation from other inmates in a place set aside for the purpose at the institution for a period not exceeding six days.*

Section 21 deals with offences and penalties under the regulations.

Offences include inducing or aiding an inmate to escape; harbouring or concealing him; meddling with an inmate or group of inmates; loitering on the premises of an institution or on any property or at any place where inmates may be for labour purposes; and any person who *publishes any false information in respect of an inmate or concerning the management of an institution knowing the information to be false or without taking reasonable steps to ascertain that such information is correct (the onus of proving that reasonable steps were taken to verify such information being upon the accused).* Any person who, *without the authority in writing of the secretary sketches or photographs any institution, portion of an institution, inmate or group of inmates, whether within or outside any institution; publishes or causes to be published in any manner whatsoever any sketch or photograph of any inmate or group of inmates, whether such sketch or photograph was made or taken before or after the detention of the inmate or group of inmates .... shall be guilty of an offence.*

The penalties are a fine or imprisonment for a period not exceeding six months.

People who have been committed to one of these institutions for a period of three years need not have been convicted of any offence. Nor are they necessarily people who suffer from alcohol and/or drug addiction or some disability.

Sufficient material has been quoted directly from the regulations to indicate the similarity to the prison regulations.

The inmates are not only subjected to detention and forced labour but to the almost unbridled power of the Superintendent.

There is nothing in the regulations which lays down any minimum qualifications for the men to be appointed as superintendents. No standards of education, integrity or plain humanity are specified and this leaves the way open for sadistic perversions and malpractices.

One shudders to think what methods might be used on the inmates for, *re-orientating them to the traditions, culture, custom and system of government of the national unit to which they belong.*

The Black Sash has had much experience in its advice offices of people who have absolutely no contact with their *national unit* and have been repeatedly ordered to leave the place where they were born simply because they are unable to prove that they belong in the city and have no other place to go to.

The combination of the wording of this section with the word *treatment* smacks of nothing so much as brainwashing.

Nothing is laid down in the regulations to ensure that people incarcerated in these institutions are to be given the opportunity to acquire skills or education to assist them to find rewarding employment in an open labour market.

What is the purpose of these regulations? What do they aim to achieve and who are they directed against?

It seems to us that the answer to these questions may be even more sinister than appears at first sight. In effect any Black person can be confined to a rehabilitation centre under prison conditions for three years for minor pass law 'offences' which, after 'normal' court proceedings, usually result in small fines or terms of imprisonment measured in weeks.

Are we in South Africa establishing our own Gulag Archipelago?

* * *

Sheena's response to Proclamation R133 was covered in the *Rand Daily Mail* and provoked a strong media reaction,[8] not only from readers and listeners but also from the Minister of Bantu Administration and Development and of Bantu Education, M.C. Botha.[9] Sheena sent him a copy of the Memorandum on 24 July, noted his comment in the *Rand Daily Mail* that the articles were distorted and badly written and went on to say:

> These regulations are so loosely worded and so wide in their interpretation that no black person in the common area of the Republic whose permit to be there is not in order can be secured against arbitrary committal to one of these institutions for three years without necessarily having been convicted of any offence.
>
> The regulations lay down conditions of confinement which have a close similarity to prison regulations and have practically nothing in common with welfare or rehabilitation institutions.
>
> If, as has been stated by one of your Deputy Ministers, these centres are to make a sincere effort to rehabilitate derelicts then it is essential that the present regulations be withdrawn and new regulations published which will incorporate the following principles:

[8] Including all the major newspapers and SABC's newsroom weekend of 26–27 July 1975.

[9] This was the same Minister M.C. Botha who earlier that year implemented the policy that Afrikaans (for mathematics, arithmetic, geography and history) must be used on an equal basis with English (for general science and practical subjects like homecraft, needlework, wood and metal work, art and agricultural science) as one of the languages of instruction in the department's secondary schools — a move that precipitated the June 1976 student rebellion.

> 1. If people are to be confined to any institution and deprived of their freedom for any length of time very detailed judicial procedures must be prescribed whereby no such committal could take place unless ordered by a court of law after thorough enquiry by social workers and, if necessary, psychiatrists. A person whose circumstances are to be so investigated should have the right to appear in open court and to be defended by a qualified attorney.
> 2. The training to be provided must be specified.
> 3. Provision in law must be made for members of staff of such institutions to be suitably qualified to teach and counsel the inmates.
> 4. Such institutions should be open at all reasonable times to inspection by the press and members of the public.
> 5. Such institution should be established only on the same terms as are acceptable for members of the white population group. They should be removed altogether from the orbit of the Urban Areas Consolidation Act, the Bantu Labour Act or the Abolition of Passes and Coordination of Documents Act.
>
> It has been our experience that many of the people who are warned of intended action to be taken against them in terms of section 29 of the urban areas act are 'idle' only because the pass laws have prevented them from obtaining lawful employment. At this time, when your government has declared its firm intention to move away from discrimination, it seems extraordinary that you should proceed with this clearly discriminatory planning.
>
> We therefore ask you whether you will not agree to withdraw Proclamation R133 and turn the attention of your department towards the positive planning of steps to dismantle the discriminatory system of influx control and migrant labour which make the black person's life a burden to him and which are largely responsible for the increasing frustration, alienation and anger of the African people of the Republic.

Botha referred the letter to his deputy Punt Janson, who wrote to Sheena on 5 August:

> *I have said on numerous occasions that I regard it as my duty to discuss with people of all political affiliations and all organisations taking an interest in the portfolio with which I have been entrusted, matters which they want to discuss with me, especially if they are not happy with the measures or decisions taken by my department. I tried to keep my word in the past and I intend doing so in future.*
>
> *However, if a person sees fit to label an institution of our country or the people being served by my department as follows: 'this is Solzhenitsyn's Gulag Archipelago transplanted to South Africa' and, if in another edition of the newspaper a person compares an Act of our country with the 'statutes of Communist Russia and the*

Third Reich', then I think you will agree with me that an interview or prolonged correspondence conducted in such an emotional atmosphere, would be futile.

The words quoted above have been attributed to you as President of the Black Sash and until such time as these obnoxious comparisons are withdrawn, I am not willing to discuss the rehabilitation centres and proclamation R133 with you personally, or with the organisation which you represent. Your Executive could, of course, through a resolution disassociate itself from your remarks, as reported, in which case I would deem it a privilege and an honour to explain the views of the department and to discuss fully, with an open mind, the objections and suggestions contained in your Memorandum.

Sheena thanked Janson on 21 August, but didn't let up. She wrote:

We are disappointed that the Honourable Minister did not see fit to reply to us himself. We addressed our representations to him because Proclamation R133 is published in his name.

We know that you have always been very willing to meet with people of all political affiliations to discuss with them matters that would fall under the jurisdiction of your department and we have been courteously received by you in the past. However, we confess to having been disappointed in the result of representations we have made directly to you, notably on the issue of wives who are prevented by law from living with their husbands. On that occasion we stood by our undertaking not to disclose to the press what had been said at our meeting but the disastrous breakup of family life proceeds unabated.

As a political pressure group it is our duty to express injustice and bad legislation by whatever means we can discover. If one method proves ineffective then we must try other channels. This is the reason why, on this occasion we chose to go first to the press.

May we point out to you that we have been misquoted in some degree. I refer you to our Memorandum as it was released to the press. The correct quotations are as follows:

Page 1. 'The above is not a quotation from the statutes of Communist Russia nor of the Third Reich. It is not even a quotation from prison regulations ...'

Page 8. 'Are we in South Africa establishing our own Gulag Archipelago?'

My Executive approved the memorandum before it was released for publication and declines your invitation to them to disassociate themselves from what I have said. We all regret, however, that in some newspaper reports we are not quoted entirely accurately.

We welcome your statement as published in the *Rand Daily Mail* of 8 August that your department would modify its proposals for rehabilitation centres and ask you whether the principles we set out in our letter to Mr Botha will be accepted.

We regret that you should see fit to refuse to meet us because of statements which you consider to be emotional and exaggerated. If we are emotional then we defend ourselves by saying that we would be less than human were we to remain unmoved by the tragic circumstances of the lives of hundreds of people with whom we come into personal contact each month who suffer because of the requirements of the pass laws.

Change

In her capacity as president of the Black Sash, Sheena was called on from time to time to appear at various formal commissions, of which the Cillie Commission of Inquiry into the riots at Soweto and other places in June 1976 was one. The previous year, Sheena's mother Jean Sinclair had written, as the last sentence of her final Black Sash presidential address: 'We are called upon to share political and economic power and with no further procrastination; if we do not, our future will be too ghastly to contemplate.' Sheena echoes these words in her memorandum to the Commission, honouring her mother at the same time.

Sheena's vision of a changed South Africa was ideological but she also understood the practicalities of the process of preparation for meaningful change. Sheena agreed that the idea of a national convention was intrinsic to the democratic development of a constitution and the possibility of authentic power-sharing. Within the Black Sash during Sheena's first term as president, Joyce Harris, in her role as vice president, hosted an inaugural discussion on a national convention in her home in July 1977. However, Sheena would not have claimed that the idea belonged to the Black Sash; as she pointed out as witness for the defence in the Delmas Trial,[10] when Advocate Jacobs put it to her that it emanated from the ANC and was taken over by the Black Sash on behalf of the ANC, 'I deny that that idea emanated from the ANC. I think that idea is much older in history in this country and in other countries.' The 1977 call was in response to the government's proposals that eventually led to the constitution act of 1983 and the establishment of the tricameral parliament. The 1985 paper, included here, was in recognition of the urgent need for an inclusive process to change South Africa.

The third paper simply illustrates the likely administrative nightmare of dismantling apartheid.

[10] Page 22831 Volume 392: and on earlier pages, 22658–22622, the text of Joyce's introductory speech is logged as exhibit DA129. The call for a National Convention at that time was in response to government's proposals to introduce the new constitution that led to the Constitution Act of 1983.

'TOO GHASTLY TO CONTEMPLATE'

Sheena Duncan, 1977

FROM PREAMBLE AND CONCLUSION TO THE MEMORANDUM TO CILLIE COMMISSION OF INQUIRY: JUNE 1976[11]

We believe that many black people see the pass laws as being sufficient cause for revolution, whatever other factors may occur to spark off or aggravate this anger.

Whatever the immediate causes of the June riots in Soweto and elsewhere, the Black Sash believes that much of the underlying cause is the great anger and frustration in the urban African communities and the growing hatred of white people by black people.

In 1975, 218,982 men and 50,003 women were arrested for offences relating to identity documents and influx control. In 1974 a total of 214,368 men and 60,273 women were arrested.[12]

It is clear that a significant percentage of the urban African population has been arrested at least once at some time of their lives and that there must be thousands more who have cause to fear arrest but have managed to avoid it by one means or another.

We believe that these are very largely caused by what are commonly referred to as 'the pass laws', and the restraints which these laws impose on every African person in the Republic of South Africa, restraints which are not imposed on any other group.

The term 'pass laws' is usually applied to the statutes which require Africans to carry reference books, which restrict and control their movements to and in the cities and which govern their daily lives.

It is inevitable when the law causes so many people, who are not guilty of any criminal offence applicable to other races, to be liable to arrest and punishment for technical infringements, that people will lose all respect for the law and for the forces of law and order …

Black people are increasingly aware that, were they to have effective political representation in the central government, such laws could not be kept on the statute book. Further, they are aware that until they enjoy political rights such laws are unlikely to be removed.

Hopes were raised by the promises of intent to move away from discrimination made in the United Nations by South Africa's ambassador, promises which led the older, stable section of the black community to think that, after all, change might be brought about by peaceful means.

[11] Duncan, Sheena, 'Too ghastly to contemplate', *Sash*, vol.19, no.1, May 1977.

[12] Hansard 31.3.76, 11.2.75.

These hopes have been frustrated by the lack of government action in any area which affects the life of the average black South African. Conditions have worsened considerably in all important aspects of life for working people and their families.

In addition great anxiety among the older people and great rage among the younger members of the community have been caused by the repressive security measures adopted by the South African government.

The repression of political trade unions, cultural and social organisations by constant security police surveillance together with the imposition of banning orders and detentions of potential leaders for long periods without trial has made it appear, even to the most moderate people, that no change in the social, economic or political ordering of South African society is likely to be brought about by consultation or peaceful means.

We have been brought to a situation where the force used by government to control the whole black community is seen by that community to be so powerful that only violence and an equal degree of force can bring about change.

Where there are large numbers of young people deprived of all opportunity to fulfil their legitimate aspirations, large numbers of men who are prevented from providing food, shelter and security for their families, women who are prevented from holding their families together in stable conditions; and where these grievances exist in a wealthy country where a small minority of the population lives in conditions of extraordinary privilege and prosperity; there are the classic ingredients for upheavals of the kind the Commission is investigating.

What will happen if nothing is done to make changes of a meaningful kind is 'too ghastly to contemplate.'

A NATIONAL CONVENTION

Sheena Duncan, 1985[13]

A National Convention in South Africa must be a meeting of representatives of *all* the people in the country, gathering together on an equal basis to thrash out a mutually acceptable constitution for the future.

It would not be a *National* Convention were representatives of any group or any political conviction or policy to be excluded.

Therefore in South Africa a necessary preliminary to a National Convention would be the unbanning of all banned organisations, the release of political prisoners and detainees, and the free return of exiles.

The Black Sash would not support any attempt to bring together groups in the 'moderate centre' in a pretence of meeting as a National Convention.

[13] Duncan, Sheena: 'A National Convention, negotiation, the Convention Alliance', *Sash*, vol.28, no.3, November 1985.

Nor would we support any Convention at which the representatives were chosen and invited to be present by the Government. Representatives must be chosen by the people in their various constituencies. The present ruling party would be only one of the many constituents of a National Convention, not in control of it. (It seems likely that in the bitterly divided South African society an outside moderator would have to be invited to preside over the meetings of the Convention).

The very nature of a National Convention is essentially a coming together of people with diametrically opposed views and policies to hammer out through hard bargaining, from positions of strength, some constitutional framework broadly acceptable to all of them within which public affairs can be conducted in the future.

Mechanisms for constitutional change

We have to find a mechanism for moving from where we are now to a just and democratic future.

Now that the government has accepted the principle of South African citizenship for all black people including those living within the independent homelands, political rights are an inevitable corollary. Minister Heunis and the South African ambassador designate to Washington have stated this.

The present South African Constitution offers no mechanisms for transformation to democracy. Based as it is on race classification, group areas and the exclusion of the black majority it is not open to real change or to any kind of acceptable reform. No possible permutations and combinations of those parties represented in the tricameral Parliament with the legislative and administrative structures set up for black people could be acceptable to the majority of the people.

It is possible that an attempt will be made by the present Government through the President's Council, in consultation with government-selected black leaders, to introduce yet another new constitution. It is impossible that such a process could bring us to an acceptable democracy. Whatever its details such a constitution would be imposed on the people from above.

Mr Smith tried in Rhodesia with Bishop Muzorewa. The attempt could only prolong our agony and worsen conflict in this country.

Some political leaders have rejected all negotiation and say there is nothing to be discussed but the handover of power. It is unrealistic to think that change in South Africa can, in the foreseeable future, be brought about by the violent overthrow of the government or by coup by armed liberation forces. The power of the state is enormous and the current dreadful repression is only a fraction of the armed force which could and would be unleashed in response to such a challenge. We are in grave danger of moving into a kind of Lebanon conflict which could go on and on for many decades and which would offer little hope of justice and democracy at the end of the misery of killing and wounding, burning and disintegration.

If one sits down and tries to analyse in practical terms what mechanism can move us into that just and democratic future for which we have worked it is difficult to visualise any other way but some kind of meeting together of all the interest groups who are in conflict with each other now.

Whether that meeting is called National Convention or Lancaster House or whatever, is immaterial. It will not be an easy process and it will inevitably be a lengthy one. No one will get everything they want but it has to be attempted.

The Convention Alliance

Dr van Zyl Slabbert has proposed the formation of a Convention Alliance to pressurise for and promote the idea of a National Convention. He has specifically rejected the idea that any convention could take place under conditions of the state of emergency. He said *I am simply saying that those who are in favour of it (a national convention) should come together and demonstrate their commitment to getting rid of apartheid completely and substituting it with one constitution with one citizenship in one individual country.*

On this basis I have supported the idea of a Convention Alliance. I would not be in favour of it were the alliance to make any attempt to set up a mini convention or to try to weld the constituents in the alliance into a power block seeking to impose solutions on the wider majority. I do not believe that this is what Dr Slabbert has in mind.

He has said, *a Convention Alliance does not mean that all who participate in it share the same policy, or belong to the same party, or necessarily have the same detailed plan for South Africa. In other words, it does not seek to compromise its members, or its supporters in terms of policy, support, programme of action, or personalities and leaders of their individual organisations and movements.*

There is considerable opposition to entering into the Convention Alliance.

From conversations I have had it seems that this opposition is *not* an opposition to the idea of the National Convention. There is a very small minority of people who seem to hold to the 'overthrow or nothing' theory.

The majority of those who do not wish to enter the Convention Alliance are certainly not rejecting it because they believe in violent solutions. Many of them agree that a National Convention is the way forward and are prepared to work hard for it in their own constituencies but they do not wish to be part of any 'alliance' with people to whose policies and principles and actions they are diametrically opposed.

This is a major difficulty for some. I myself believe that the alliance has a specific task and that it will inevitably be composed of antagonistic interest groups just as will a National Convention. I do not experience problems with the idea of an alliance but if it is going to be a major problem within the Black Sash we will have to debate it at our next conference. With that in mind all regions should have discussions with their members so that delegates come well-prepared to Durban in March.

One person one vote

My opinion on this is constantly being asked at the moment. I stand firmly behind our long ago conference resolution declaring that we are unequivocally in favour of a universal franchise.

I don't myself think this is really a point of conflict in South Africa. Even the national party has said the vote is essential for everyone. Mr Vorster used to claim that the ruling party recognised the principle of one-man-one-vote and that everyone in South Africa has a vote!

What the conflict is about is what kind of constitutional structure we will build upon the foundation of the universal franchise.

I don't think it is necessary for the Black Sash to produce constitutional blueprints. We would not be represented at a National Convention anyway. Our constituency is too small and insignificant. Our task will be to measure other people's proposals against the yardsticks of justice and democracy and to nag and push from the sidelines a system which guarantees the Rule of Law and the democratic rights of the poor and marginalised people.

I expect we shall have to go on fighting for that to the end of our lives.

DISMANTLING APARTHEID: FROM 'OWN AFFAIRS' TO ALL OUR AFFAIRS

Sheena Duncan, 1990[14]

The proposition that apartheid must be dismantled is more or less accepted by most South Africans, as it is by the international community in the various declarations by the Organisation of African Unity, the United Nations, the European Community, the United States, the Commonwealth, and numerous other bodies.

But the size of the task is not recognised. Dismantling apartheid is not just a question of repealing racist laws.

Apartheid is the whole structure and organisation of the South African society in all its aspects. It has been put into place over many decades predating the access and the power of the National Party in 1948. It is a way of life for all South Africans and it will take many years before we can shed the effects of our indoctrination in racial group thinking and group organisation.

This article deals only with the administrative aspects of the dismantling of apartheid and suggests a way forward which need not be dependent on the progress of political negotiations. We do not have to wait until the eventual gathering of a constituent assembly or a national convention to start preparing for a more just society.

[14] Duncan, Sheena: 'Dismantling apartheid: From "own affairs" to all our affairs', *Sash*, vol.33, no.2, September 1990.

Own affairs government

The extraordinary verbalisation of the concept of own affairs was put into constitutional law only with the passing of the Republic of South Africa Constitution act in 1983 but it was already a fact of life for African people who were all separated out into the various ethnic citizenships in terms of the Bantu Homeland Citizenship Act of 1970. It is a long and boring history which need not be detailed here, except to point out that black people living within the bantustans have been subjected to own affairs government for much longer than the coloured, Indian and white people who are affected by the new constitution which came into effect in 1984.

The present position is that South Africa has 13 separate race-based legislative 'parliaments' in four 'independent states', 6 'self-governing national states' and in the 3 houses of the tri-cameral parliament which legislate for, as well as separately administer, the 'own affairs' of the coloured, Indian and white race groups.

In addition, there is the 'general affairs' government which is in fact, if not in theory, the same thing as the white house of assembly which legislates for such matters deemed to be of general importance such as finance, foreign affairs, defence — and the affairs of African people who live outside the bantustans. The 'general affairs' government has given responsibility for the administration of the affairs of these people to the 4 provincial administrations under the general control of the Minister of provincial affairs and planning.

In case readers are now beginning to think that this article is written as a piece of satire, I need to explain how the system works. Take the payment of social pensions as an example. It is one form of administration we know best from our experience in the advice offices.

- Pensions for white people are administered by the white house of assembly
- Pensions for coloured people are administered by the coloured house of representatives
- Pensions for Indian people are administered by the Indian house of delegates
- Pensions for black people living in the six 'self-governing' states are administered by the governments of those places
- Pensions for black people living in the four 'independent' states are administered by those 'governments'
- Pensions for black people living outside the bantustans are administered by the provincial administration of the OFS, Cape Province, Natal and the Transvaal, subject to the control of the general affairs minister of provincial affairs and planning.

This adds up to 17 different administrations. 13 of them have the power to make laws relating to social pensions, but in fact all of them are subject to the 'general affairs' decisions of the Minister of Finance who decides how much money will be made available to each administration for pensions. In the case of the 'independent' states it is called 'foreign aid.'

The same 'own affairs' provisions apply to health, education, cultural and religious affairs, water supply, welfare, community development and housing, rent control and squatter removal, and agriculture. The effort of imagining the implications of this web of bureaucracy can result in extreme dizziness.

Some of the above functions have been developed by the 'own affairs' Administration's two local authorities. 'General affairs' is anything which is not an 'own affair.'

Race classification

The whole of this incredible structure is built upon the race classification provisions of the population registration act of 1950. This act requires that all citizens of South Africa and all permanently resident aliens must be classified according to their race.

That classification dictates which of the many legislatures and administrations will control a person's life. Take one woman only; it dictates where she may live, where she may go to school, by which church minister she may be married, in which hospital she may give birth, which old age home will accept her, in which cemetery she may be buried, and for which Parliament or local authority she may vote.

Of course, recent reform measures mean that, if she is rich enough, she can beat the system and more or less choose to do what she thinks is best for herself and her family. Most people are not rich enough.

Preparing for the future

The demand for the abolition of race classification is more than justified. Almost all South Africans are agreed that it must go and that it is the basic apartheid law which underpins all the other structures.

On 14 May 1990, the Minister of Home Affairs, Gene Louw, told parliament that South Africa's race classification law was unacceptable, totally inflexible and undoubtedly discriminatory (Citizen 15.05.1990). He went on to say that a moratorium on the act was impractical, and that it could not be scrapped immediately as it formed part of the ongoing constitutional debate.

He is quite right. It is not so much that it is part of the constitutional debate but that it is the very basis of the present constitutional system of government. If it is repealed now there will be total chaos because no one will know who is responsible for paying teachers salaries, maintaining hospitals, paying pensions, running schools.

But we cannot wait for the conclusion of constitutional negotiations. If a democratically elected government comes to power in South Africa it will be totally unable to put its policies into effect if it has to cope with the present multiplicity of administrative structures. It will be a disaster, given the expectations of the soon to be enfranchised majority, if nothing has been done to re-organise the present race based bureaucracy. We have to begin to do it now and this is possible within the terms of the present constitution.

What has to be worked for is the repeal of schedule 1 of the Republic of South Africa Constitution act of 1983.

This is a legislatively simple process.

If whatever is not an 'own affair' is a 'general affair' the removal of the schedule will allow the government to move rapidly towards the establishment of single government departments for health, education, welfare, housing, pensions, etc.

This would greatly facilitate the creation of orderly government in the future. We have not experienced 'orderly government' in our understanding of the term but we can at least make a beginning.

On 28 February this year Peter Soal of the Democratic Party moved a private members motion in the House of Assembly that education and health should be removed from the 'own affairs' schedule of the Constitution Act. The Minister of Health services, Welfare and Housing, Sam de Beer said, *surely it is quite silly for them to advance such a solution to our problems today.*

The Minister of Education and Culture challenged the Democratic Party to *just mention one example of a place in the world where education is dealt with as a general affair ... In the United Kingdom one finds special provision for the English, the Scots, the Irish and the Welsh ...* (Hansard 28 February 1990).

Ah well, by May 1990 the Deputy Minister of Education and Training was saying he foresaw the future in which there would be a single education department (The Citizen, 16.05.1990). Hospitals were opened to all. It was no longer 'silly.'

The process is underway but even when all legislative and administrative barriers have been removed and we have a new government it will be decades before we move out of the separate little boxes in which apartheid has placed us.

Civil disobedience

There is a prayer for responsible citizenship in the *Anglican Prayer Book*,[15] and Sheena's life and work fulfilled all its hopes; she epitomised active, responsible citizenship. She knew that change was not possible without action. When Advocate P.B. Jacobs asked her during cross-examination for the state in the Delmas Treason Trial,[16] *is it not so that the only way it [change] can happen is by violent revolution?*

[15] Church of the Province of Southern Africa: Prayers and Thanksgivings for Various Occasions; Number 13 pg 86 [1989 version].

[16] Vol. 394: pg 22842/3

Sheena replied firmly, 'Oh, I do not believe that for one minute. I believe that the greatest power on earth is non-violent direct action in any situation. I think it is very sad that people all over the world have lost their understanding on the whole and taken to arms. I think it is an obligation of citizens to organise and mobilise and politicise people to bring about change, or to take over the government, or to win power, or however you like to put it. It is the duty of citizens to organise around issues.' Sheena did not falter in her commitment to non-violence, or in putting her beliefs into practice. Typically, she did not ignore the implications of certain choices and the consequences if they were thwarted. Through articles such as this one, in a context of escalating violence, she made sure that members of the Black Sash understood what was meant by their commitment to non-violence.

A STRATEGY FOR NON-VIOLENT DIRECT ACTION

Sheena Duncan, 1987[17]

In South Africa the debate about civil disobedience is ongoing and it becomes more and more pertinent as the state introduces ever more repressive measures which deny the due process of law, which destroy all basic human rights, and which remove the protection of civil liberties from the jurisdiction of the courts.

This is not a new process. Over many decades laws have been passed by the South African Parliament which cannot be obeyed. Disobedience has become a compulsion for many because there is no other way to secure survival. For others disobedience has become a compulsion because some laws cannot in conscience be obeyed. The pass laws are just one example. The Group Areas Act is another. Tens of thousands of people are currently living in violation of this Act.

All of us in South Africa break the law all the time. This is inevitable when a country has a plethora of laws which do not have the consent of the governed and which cannot be complied with.

An act of civil disobedience may be undertaken purely as an act arising from the dictates of the individual conscience. The individual conscience defies guidelines and other people's opinions. Conscience is an internal and very personal thing but sometimes the dilemma of conscience is experienced by so many people that it becomes a matter of public concern. One example of this would be the opposition to compulsory military conscription of white men into the South African Defence Force.

That began when a few individuals refused to obey the order to serve and went to prison or into detention barracks as a consequence. Their action enabled many others to give expression to a conscientious objection to military service and to the militarisation of South African society. Thus the Conscientious Objectors Support

[17] Duncan, Sheena: 'Civil disobedience: A strategy for non violent direct action', *Sash*, vol.30, no.2, August 1987.

Groups and the End Conscription Campaign came into being. It must be stressed that both COSG and ECC work within the law. They will support wholeheartedly those who disobey — but their work is lawful.

This example is of critical importance to any discussion of civil disobedience.

Law is the essential framework for the maintenance of a just society. The law is not to be broken lightly, because without law human community becomes a chaotic, disastrous and competitive battleground on which wars of survival are fought, in which the weak and the poor are destroyed and the strong and wealthy become all-powerful and entirely ruthless.

The South African government has destroyed the essential framework embodied in the idea of the rule of law. The history of the legislation which allows indefinite detention without trial and which denies people redress against the depredations of the state is well known. It does not only relate to 'security' legislation but to the whole fabric of society — removal of land rights and ownership, freedom of movement, freedom of speech and association, and so on. But there is also an administrative disregard for the law, a bureaucratic lawlessness, which is the mark of this country's present social order.

On 16 April 1987 *The Star* reported a statement from the Department of Home Affairs summarising the current position on the issue of identity documents to black people. Among other things, the department said that the figure for applications from blacks includes 253,986 held back pending negotiations with the Bophuthatswana government on the reinstatement of South African citizenship.

This is totally unlawful. The Restoration of South African Citizenship Act lays down certain conditions which entitle people to regain the South African citizenship which was taken away from them when their putative homeland became independent. The desires and opinions of the Bophuthatswana government have nothing whatsoever to do with it. Yet in an act of civil disobedience this state is refusing to obey its own laws for its own political purposes.

There are many other examples of such lawlessness on the part of the state, notably the way in which court interdicts are often impossible to enforce because the enforcement agencies refuse to obey the courts' injunctions.

Herein lies the dilemma for those who wish to use civil disobedience as a *strategy* for opposition to unjust laws and for forcing change. The justification has to be carefully thought through. If one wishes to preserve the idea of law one has to be most cautious in strategies which can lead to its destruction. The means do shape the ends and wanton disregard of the law may mean government lawlessness perpetuated into a new future.

I therefore prefer to discuss civil disobedience in the context of strategies of non-violent direct action. I believe that for those who will not take up arms and who will not use violence, civil disobedience must be the last resort as a strategy. It is not to be entered into lightly but it has to be considered seriously when it is the last resort in relation to the present oppression in South Africa.

The Lusaka statement released by the conference called by the World Council of Churches in Zambia from 4 to 8 May 1987 reads in part:

> It is our belief that civil authority is instituted of God to do good, and that under biblical imperative all people are obliged to do justice and to show special care for the oppressed and the poor. It is this understanding that leaves us with no alternative but to conclude that the South African regime and its colonial domination of Namibia is illegitimate.

There can be no obligation to obey an illegitimate government but nevertheless we want to preserve the idea of Law for the future so how can we proceed? In the following discussion I am not concerned with individual acts of conscience. These are something apart and will continue to be undertaken according to conscience by individuals. We are here concerned with civil disobedience as a political strategy of opposition.

We first have an obligation to test the limits of the law. This is not civil disobedience. Laws in this country are often obscure in their language and are interpreted by the administration to mean much more than is justified by the actual wording and punctuation. Administrative decree often goes far beyond what the law allows and this has been shown over and over again by successful challenges in the courts to emergency regulations promulgated in defiance of what the law actually says, as well as cases such as Komani and Rikhoto that showed how officials had used technicalities to deprive people of their urban residence rights.

Many aspects of the law need to be searched and tested in this way. If we fail to do this we are surrendering to authoritarian decree.

Secondly, we must seek the lawful non-violent strategies which may bring us nearer to achieving our ends. Non-violent direct action is not by any means always unlawful. Indeed it is often more effective and more strategic to work within the law. When the emergency regulations made it effectively impossible for the press to report any incident of unrest, the definition of unrest including any prohibited gathering, it became strategically worthless to plan a campaign of civil disobedience involving unlawful gatherings because these could not be reported and would therefore never be known beyond those who participated and those members of the security forces who took action against them.

Thirdly, if we take a deliberate decision to be disobedient we must accept the consequences. This is essential. Civil disobedience must be based on the preparedness to sacrifice and to accept punishment for breaking the law. In deliberate acts of civil disobedience there must be no expectation that others should rush to the rescue with expensive legal defences and technical let-outs to release one from the obligation to suffer the consequences of a decision to disobey. This is quite different from taking a decision to test the limits of the law, when the whole purpose is to have the courts interpret the law.

It is clear that the government and its security apparatus is well aware of the power of non-violent resistance. There is nothing guns, quirts, Casspirs and teargas can do to overcome concerted widespread non-co-operation. The emergency regulations seek to prevent the organisation of all the non-violent strategies of boycott and stay-away which have proved so effective. The costs of calling for civil disobedience are now a possible ten years' imprisonment or a fine of R20,000.

There will always be brave people who undertake symbolic acts of disobedience without encouraging or expecting others to join them. There will always be the refusal of the Church to allow the state to dictate what may be said and done and prayed for within the worshipping community. But what are the prospects for any widespread, general public campaigns involving disobedience?

It is interesting to note that one of NUM's demands in the current round of negotiations with the Chamber of Mines is that chamber members cease to deduct income tax from workers' wages with immediate effect. There can be no doubt of the justice of this demand. 'No taxation without representation' is a principle accepted in all democracies and its denial was one of the prime causes of the American Revolution. If other unions include this demand on their agendas how will employer bodies respond? It is a challenge to all of us.

Civil disobedience is bound to be in the forefront of opposition strategies in the months to come. Contrary to what we are told by the state's propaganda machine, the overwhelming majority of South Africans who are opposed to the present government and its policies, including the ANC, are anxious to limit and, where possible, prevent violence. When nonviolent strategies of resistance have been made unlawful, then civil disobedience becomes not only inevitable but, wherever there is no other effective means, obligatory.

Data Sources

Interviews

Several interviews were preceded and/or followed up by correspondence, others followed up on previous interviews with Charlene Smith. All interviews with the author were conducted with a commitment to discretion on the part of the author and with permission from the interviewee to record and to quote.

As well as noting the date(s) of interview(s), a few additional details are provided for readers who may be interested. Many of the people interviewed are luminaries in their own right, some already at the time they knew Sheena and others in post-apartheid contemporary South Africa and international communities. Others are not so well known and some may be known to only a few people outside of their circle of family, friends, colleagues or community. Sadly, a few are now deceased. The detail given about each person is brief and relates only to his or her relationship with Sheena.

Adèle Kirsten
12 January 2012 (also Charlene Smith: no date available)
A younger generation and more 'left' activist than Sheena, Adèle was the first employee of Gun Free South Africa (GFSA), of which Sheena was first a patron and then chairperson of the board. With Adèle as coordinator of GFSA, the two women worked closely in this context over a period of almost ten years and also, earlier, in the End Conscription Campaign (ECC), in which Adèle was a leading activist. They developed a mutually respectful, affectionate and supportive relationship and shared a commitment to non-violence.

Adelina Pholosi
23 November 2012
Adelina interpreted for Sheena (and other Black Sash volunteers including Jean Sinclair) in the Johannesburg advice office from 1971 until she retired — a period of more than twenty years. Adelina, with affection and respect for Sheena, remembers times when the office was so full that there were still people waiting for advice at closing time. Sheena would stay until the last one had been seen and then walk alone through almost deserted streets to her car. Adelina felt that Sheena respected her too. Sheena would ask Adelina for her thoughts about how a problem could be solved and they would discuss it together before suggesting options to the advice seeker. Although their relationship was one of work colleagues, Adelina remembers visiting — with all the advice office staff — Sheena's home, which the employees found particularly welcoming and warm.

Alan Maker
17 April 2013
Sheena knew Alan mostly as the spiritual leader most supportive to her father and mother, but also as someone with whom she and the family interacted socially from time to time, usually through Jean Sinclair. Sheena and Alan's relationship was sometimes argumentative as they were both strong personalities with clear, but often different, opinions about how best to resist apartheid.

Alec Walt
(Charlene Smith: no date available)
Alec was the husband of the late Ethel Walt, one of Sheena's closest friends.

Alison Somerville
21 March 2012 (telephone interview)
Alison was a few years ahead of Sheena at Roedean, but their families knew each other well as part of the Scottish community in Johannesburg, which included Neil's family. As children they all spent time together when their parents socialised at places like the Johannesburg Country Club. Sheena and Neil continued to socialise with Alison and her husband in the years that followed, although Alison experienced Sheena as a firebrand, difficult to keep up with. But, she says, *It's nice to think of Sheena also having had to wear those dreadful big Roedean bloomers.*

Alison Tilley
14 February 2012
Alison was a young lawyer and worked closely with Sheena as part of a group that monitored legislation, from inception through to its passage in Parliament. Alison worked for a period as a member of the Black Sash national staff in Cape Town and the women worked particularly closely in the post-1994 period when much of the legislation, including South Africa's new constitution, was created in a process of transformation. As well as developing mutual respect through their collaborative work, they got to know each other personally and Alison was a house-guest at Neil and Sheena's home when she needed to be in the Johannesburg/Pretoria area.

Allister Sparks
22 January 2013
Allister and his wife Sue were friends who shared Sheena's political interests, Sue as an active member of the Black Sash in Johannesburg and Allister as a progressive journalist — one-time editor of the *Rand Daily Mail* — and political analyst. Sue was the Black Sash monitor of the Delmas Treason Trial in which Sheena was a witness for the defence and testified over several days. In a society in which deliberate misinformation was the norm, Allister and Sheena were able to enhance each other's understanding of some of the hidden realities of apartheid. The two couples also entertained each other at home and often socialised in the same circles.

Aninka Claassens
15 November 2011 (also Charlene Smith: 8 October 2010)
A younger generation Black Sash member with political perspectives more to the 'left', Aninka worked closely with Sheena for many years as the first employee of the Black Sash's Transvaal Rural Action Committee (TRAC) and they developed a fond and deeply respectful relationship. Aninka was one of the few Black Sash members fluent in at least one indigenous African language, and Sheena gained unique insights because of Aninka's ability to engage more intimately with many of the rural women facing forced removal and other forms of state oppression. Sheena also placed great value on Aninka's ability to ensure that the situation of such women was integrated with the Black Sash's work and policies.

Anita Kromberg
18 June 2012
A Black Sash member of a generation younger than Sheena but with a shared and profound commitment to genuine pacifism, Anita forged a strong and enduring ideological bond with Sheena. Anita was the first employee of the International Fellowship for Reconciliation (IFOR), with a mandate to support the *practical* strategies of non-violent action and civil disobedience in the South African Council of Churches (SACC) and in other organisations in which Sheena was active. Anita asked IFOR to allow her to choose Sheena and Rob Robertson as her 'support' and reference group as she set about coordinating the training of as many people as possible in the art of non-violent action as a method of struggle.

Arch (Desmond) Tutu
11 January 2012 (also Charlene Smith: 5 October 2010)
Desmond already knew Jean Sinclair when Sheena returned to South Africa from Zimbabwe. He and Sheena then worked particularly closely on the South African Council of Churches (SACC) and the diocese of Johannesburg. From time to time they shared public platforms both nationally and internationally. Both were willing to travel to small rural communities in South Africa as well as to prestigious international events. They shared many important ideological perspectives, an unwavering but open-minded faith, a warm-hearted sense of humour and a commitment to improving the status of women in the Church, including campaigning for the ordination of women. They trusted each other implicitly and each knew that the other would not waver in loyalty to their commitment to transforming South Africa. Desmond and Leah were welcome guests in the Duncan home and even though they didn't see much of each other after their 'retirements', Desmond and Sheena had a warm and affectionate relationship that endured until Sheena's death.

Ashnie Padarath
22 June 2012
As a senior advice office employee of the younger professional generation and based in KwaZulu-Natal, Ashnie worked closely with Sheena on advice office issues. They sometimes had vigorous debates at Black Sash national advice office workshops — but always engaged with mutual respect. Ashnie admired Sheena immensely, particularly her developmental approach, her fearlessness and her sense of humour.

Audrey Coleman
14 November 2011 (Skype) (also Charlene Smith: no date available)
As a Black Sash member, trustee of the Advice Office Trust and regular volunteer in the advice office, Audrey worked closely with Sheena. Audrey and her husband Max were founder members of the Detainees' Parents Support Committee. It was through this work, as well as through her involvement in the United Democratic Front (UDF), that Audrey felt herself becoming more radical and politicised than Sheena. Although the two women often differed widely in strategic perspective, their respect for each other did not waver.

Bernard Spong
22 November 2012 (with Rykie Woite present for some of the interview)
Sheena and Bernard were friends, and Bernard and his partner Rykie spent many sociable hours with Sheena — and Neil, during his lifetime. Bernard was active in the South African Council of Churches (SACC) and, as well as serving as the key communications person, he was asked by Desmond Tutu to be chaplain to Khotso House. This meant that morning prayers became his responsibility and the societal problems of Khotso House were very much on his shoulders. According to Bernard, the building was filled with 'people who had strong views and strong political views — all the way from absolute Black Consciousness to liberal wishy-washiness. There would therefore be a lot of arguments.' Bernard was well known in the community of Khotso House, of which the Black Sash and particularly Sheena were an intrinsic part. Sheena mainly went about her advice office work but participated in the fellowship regularly. Outside of Khotso House, Bernard and Sheena also spent hours together talking on her stoep, acting as sounding boards for one another's ideas and opinions, rather than as critics.

Beth Still
28 January 2012
School friends at Roedean, Beth and Sheena and their husbands continued to socialise from time to time for most of Sheena's life.

Beulah Rollnick
(Charlene Smith: no date available)
Both as a Black Sash member and through her service to the Johannesburg advice office, first as a volunteer and subsequently an employee, Beulah worked closely with Sheena for many years. Despite their mutual respect and commitment to justice, the two women sometimes differed in management principles. When Beulah's employment was terminated for what the Black Sash leadership saw as resource constraints, it caused considerable resentment and distress and Sheena and Beulah's relationship was badly affected.

Beva Runciman
19 October 2011
A Black Sash member of a younger generation, Beva lived in Cape Town, where she was not only an active protesting member but also part of the regional leadership structures. Beva was involved in various other organisations and campaigns in which she also worked alongside Sheena, most notably the campaign to abolish the death penalty and the End Conscription Campaign (ECC).

Bobby Melunsky
24 February 2012
Bobby was one of the key members of the Port Elizabeth branch of the Black Sash. Bobby and Sheena did not know each other well but had a close long-distance relationship, through which Bobby found strength in keeping the membership motivated and the advice office functional in its early days and in the face of much harassment from the apartheid regime. Sheena, in turn, learned from Bobby many of the realities that faced people in the Port Elizabeth area of the Eastern Cape.

Bongi Mkhabela
29 November 2011
A radical younger generation liberation activist, Bongi met Sheena shortly before Bongi married Ish Mkhabela, who already knew Sheena quite well. Bongi, one of the student leaders in Soweto, was at the time newly out of prison after the 1976 student protests and was looking at work possibilities that offered time for her to finish her studies. Ish introduced the idea of working with the South African Council of Churches, and on Sheena's recommendation, Bongi trained at the Black Sash advice office. They came to know each other even better when Bongi became a trustee on the Black Sash Trust many years later and subsequently, again on Sheena's recommendation, took over the role of chairperson.

Brigalia Hlope Bam
25 January 2012
Brigalia and Sheena were contemporaries and worked closely in service to the South African Council of Churches (SACC), Sheena as vice president and Brigalia first as deputy to Frank Chikane and then as general secretary herself. Sheena was an active member of the small group that lobbied successfully for Brigalia to become general secretary of the SACC — a most unusual appointment at the time, for a woman and for an unordained person. These two principled women admired each other a great deal and shared many values and perspectives, particularly in terms of the role of women in society and the church, as well as a deep understanding of development issues.

Carey Haouach (Duncan)
20 November 2012
Sheena and Neil's younger daughter Carey is the mother of their two grandchildren, Samir and Kenza. Carey studied and lived outside South Africa for most of her adult life but both daughters were close friends of Sheena and Neil and visited South Africa often. Neil and Sheena also visited Carey and her husband and family several times in Morocco, where Carey lives. They corresponded regularly, often on a weekly basis.

Charles Villa-Vicencio
8 February 2013
Charles and Sheena knew each other personally and as anti-apartheid activists with a shared understanding of and commitment to civil disobedience as a form of radical resistance to oppression. Charles had interviewed Sheena in depth, and with exceptional insight, for his chapter 'Surprised by Joy' in the publication *The Spirit of Freedom* (see bibliography below) and they were often together as spiritual leadership activists, particularly through the South African Council of Churches. Charles and Sheena also had frequent discussions when he was with the Truth and Reconciliation Commission (TRC) and Sheena with the Joint Investigation Team (JIT).

Clare Cresswell
(Charlene Smith: no date available)
Clare was at Roedean with Sheena and Neil's daughters, Lindsay and Carey. Sheena had some contact with her through St George's Church and Clare became Sheena's physiotherapist in later years. Clare was intimately involved in caring for Sheena after her cancer diagnosis, right up to the night Sheena died. Clare, with great sensitivity, took care of many arrangements for Sheena's wellbeing, medical treatments and household matters on behalf of Lindsay and Carey when they were not able to visit from Lausanne and Rabat respectively.

Clive Jearey
(Charlene Smith: no date available)
A younger generation architect and later a partner in Neil's firm, Clive was mentored by Neil and became a family friend.

David and Elizabeth Jenkins
4 November 2011 (Skype)
David and Neil attended St John's College together and the friendship was enriched during years living in Zimbabwe, where David was Neil's parish priest, and they socialised frequently with a circle of friends as young couples with babies and young children. David and his wife Elizabeth were a great comfort to Sheena and Neil when their toddler son died. David conducted the funeral service, was enormously influential in Sheena's conversion to Anglicanism, and feels pride in having contributed to her spiritual growth. On returning to South Africa, the families lived in different provinces but stayed in touch and visited occasionally.

David Ngxale
20 February 2012
David started work as an interpreter at the Black Sash advice office that was opened by the small group of members in Knysna, became a case-worker, did some outreach fieldwork in the area from time to time, and was then a senior case-worker until the office was closed by the Black Sash shortly after Sheena's death in 2010. David frequently sought paralegal advice from Sheena, interacted with her at some of the annual advice office workshops, and admired and respected her immensely.

David Russell
(Charlene Smith: no date available)
Although for most of their lives they lived in different provinces of South Africa, David and Sheena knew each other as contemporary fellow Anglicans and were frequently in contact through their activities in leadership positions. They interacted in various structures of the South African Council of Churches as well as the Border Council of Churches in the Eastern Cape. Both championed the ordination of women priests and David was the bishop who ordained the first three Anglican women priests. David and Sheena were both unequivocally outraged by apartheid and committed to ending its injustices. Sheena was much inspired by David's solidarity fasting to draw attention to the dire situation of deliberately impoverished Africans, as well as his courageous stand against forced removals. Sheena's mother Jean fasted for some time in solidarity with David. David is the brother of Diana Russell who included a chapter on Sheena in her book, *Women of Courage* (see bibliography below).

Denise Ackermann
8 February 2012
As well their active membership in the Black Sash and their social interactions, Denise and Sheena shared a deep spiritual connection. They had a mutual commitment to non-violent defiance of injustice, with acts of civil disobedience as a legitimate option when oppression became otherwise unstoppable. Although they did not always agree on all matters during their many years of solidarity, friendship and discussions, Denise significantly influenced Sheena's growing understanding of feminism and feminist theology. They both identified with a radical notion of personal freedom despite religious, political, social or other restrictions. In spite of their middle-class white privilege and their high standing in society and the Church, they also shared a particular quality of humility that was largely based on their concept of Jesus — as Denise puts it, *Our Jesus is the man who had to borrow a donkey.*

Di Oliver (Bishop)
(Charlene Smith: 9 October 2010) and the author also had several discussions with Di
As a younger generation member of the Black Sash, Di's relationship with Sheena developed into a gentle and deeply respectful friendship over a period of more than twenty years, enhanced by their shared Anglican faith, their practical work in the advice offices and their attention to the abuse of the human rights of people living in peri-urban and rural communities. They lived and worked in different provinces and Di was able to contribute to Sheena's understanding of the impact of apartheid in the Western and Eastern Cape and in KwaZulu-Natal during some of the worst years of repression. Personally and through their work, the two women also interacted regularly as leaders in the Black Sash, both serving at regional and national levels as well as on the Advice Office Trust.

Dot Cleminshaw
2 November 2011 and by correspondence
Dot was a committed civil rights and pro-choice campaigner in Cape Town and was more radical than Sheena in certain respects. Once Dot overcame her resistance to the fact that the Black Sash was a women-only, whites-only, non-party political organisation, she joined and became a respected and active Black Sash member and media monitor. She was also involved in the End Conscription Campaign (ECC). Dot and Sheena met only when Sheena spoke at or attended the Black Sash membership activities in Cape Town, but they worked well together and communicated frequently, particularly in the process of getting the Black Sash to adopt a pro-choice position on the abortion issue. Latterly, the two women were in regular e-mail contact and Dot shared her own tried and tested tips on pain management.

Emma Thandi Mashinini

25 January 2012

Emma and Sheena first got to know each other at the time when Desmond Tutu was the general secretary of the South African Council of Churches (SACC) and Khotso House was one of the only possibilities of accommodation for progressive and anti-apartheid organisations in Johannesburg. Sheena and Emma were both part of the tenant community — Sheena in the Black Sash and Emma first as union general secretary and subsequently in the Justice and Reconciliation division of the Church of the Province of South Africa. As well as their committed anti-apartheid activism, the two women shared a deep spiritual conviction and remained life-long colleagues and fond friends, providing mutual support in difficult times.

François Thomas Steenkamp

16 January 2011 (a short telephone conversation because François did not wish to be interviewed)

A younger generation policeman who had served the apartheid regime prior to 1994, François worked closely with Sheena over a period of several post-apartheid years on the Joint Investigation Team (JIT) appointed by Minister of Safety and Security, Sydney Mufamadi. In the course of their work, François and Sheena travelled long distances together by car. Despite their differences, they became friends for that period and shared many conversations, particularly about religion.

Frank Chikane

25 January 2012

Frank and Sheena first met — without knowing each other — when he interacted with the Black Sash advice office regarding challenges black young people had with the pass laws. Frank and Sheena subsequently worked closely together for many years, starting with his term as general secretary of the South African Council of Churches (SACC), when Sheena had herself just been elected for her first term as one of the vice presidents of the SACC and volunteered as his administrative assistant for several months. With the Black Sash office close by, Sheena was a more easily accessible SACC leadership backup to Frank than the two presidents of his time. Frank and Sheena conferred often and developed a supportive, mutually respectful relationship during a time when there were still debates and internal disagreements about the role the churches and the SACC should take to stop the system of apartheid. They developed immense respect for each other in the process. It was also a period during which Frank's wellbeing was seriously threatened by the apartheid regime and he had little support from his own church. As a founding leader of the United Democratic Front, Frank enriched Sheena's understanding of its objectives and, through her interaction with him, she also deepened her awareness of the spiritual needs of liberation movements, political prisoners and activists in exile.

Geoff Budlender

(Charlene Smith: 6 and 8 October 2010)

A younger generation human rights lawyer, Geoff was articled to Sheena's dear friend and legal mentor Raymond Tucker who himself generously gave legal support over many years to Sheena and other Black Sash members on matters related to the advice office work and the Advice Office Trust. Geoff was a founder of the Legal Resources Centre and he worked with Sheena regularly and rigorously on many legal issues, particularly around the pass laws and forced removals, for more than thirty years. They developed a mutually affectionate and respectful relationship.

gille de vlieg

19 June 2012

A younger more 'left' Black Sash member active in the same region, gille interacted with Sheena frequently, personally and in the course of their anti-apartheid work through their common interests and in the Johannesburg advice office. Gille also served on the regional leadership structures, regularly contributed to the *Sash* magazine, worked with the Transvaal Rural Action Committee (TRAC), co-ordinated the national Free the Children campaign for a year and took the lead in Black Sash voter education work across the regions in preparation for South Africa's first democratic elections in 1994. Like many of the older generation, Sheena exercised a motherly approach towards the younger members and gille felt confident that she could go to Sheena if she was in trouble, knowing that whatever was discussed would not go anywhere else. A talented photographer, who captured many historical moments in the struggle against apartheid, gille has generously given permission for a number of her photographs to be used in this book.

GLENDA GLOVER
5 March 2013
Glenda's relationship with the Black Sash started in the Johannesburg advice office where she first offered her time as a volunteer after her return to South Africa. She joined the Black Sash and, as a younger generation member in the same region, she came to interact frequently with Sheena, as a member, then as part of the leadership group on the regional council, through her work in the Johannesburg advice office and on rural and urban land issue groups. Glenda particularly appreciated Sheena's strategic thinking, her warmth, her intellect and her ability to keep the diverse and intelligent group of Black Sash women and their interests together, with each feeling that her own contribution was of value.

HILLARY MORRIS
29 March 2013
Hillary was not a Black Sash member but was appointed as the second professional national director of the Black Sash and in this capacity worked closely with Sheena and other trustees over a period of several years. She and Sheena spent many hours together and shared a jovial sense of humour.

HUGH FRASER
(Charlene Smith: 17 August 2010)
Hugh was a young architect and neighbour. He interacted frequently with the Duncan family on neighbourly issues and continued to visit Sheena from time to time after Neil's death.

ISHMAEL (ISH) MKHABELA
26 January 2012
Ishmael and Sheena knew each other for more than thirty years. They developed an affectionate and mutually respectful relationship that transcended their race, gender, age, language and other cultural and political differences, and that lasted until Sheena's death. Ishmael particularly admired her leadership style and Sheena was deeply impressed by the scope of this young Azapo leader's understanding of Black Consciousness. Most of the work they did together was through various programmes and projects of the South African Council of Churches (SACC), and at Wilgerspruit they were both involved in forming a structure called the Witwatersrand Network for the Homeless.

JACKLYN COCK
25 November 2012
An active, younger and more 'left' Black Sash member, Jacklyn shared with Sheena an incisive and well-informed intelligence, as well as similar views on controversial issues such as militarisation and a gun free society. They served together on various structures, including Gun Free South Africa and the campaign to abolish the death penalty. They had many disagreements too on, for example, feminism — not only as it relates to women's oppression but also in a wider more encompassing inclusiveness — and they differed in their understanding and practice of spirituality. Jacklyn was a frequent guest in Sheena's home when she settled in Johannesburg as a young academic. Their long-standing relationship was engaging, challenging to both and developed in a context of mutual affection and respect.

JANET CHERRY
24 February 2012
A younger generation member of the Black Sash in the Eastern Cape, Janet was an activist more to the 'left' of Sheena but, as a researcher, Janet engaged with several issues that were also priorities for Sheena — such as domestic worker rights and armed resistance — and they shared information. They interacted in the End Conscription Campaign and Sheena provided back-up to the group that supported Janet during her detention. The two women also worked together during the period in which Janet was employed by the Albany Black Sash.

JENNY DE TOLLY
12 July 2012
A younger generation active Black Sash member, Jenny served the organisation in the leadership structures of the Western Cape and nationally, including as Black Sash president, as well as on

the Advice Office Trust. Sheena and Jenny interacted frequently as they balanced the Black Sash's policies and sustained its values during difficult years of apartheid repression, during the period of the country's transition to democracy and then during the Black Sash's own transitions as an organisation. The two women differed in leadership style but shared an ethical perspective and enjoyed many hours of discussion within the organisation and when they stayed over in at each other's homes.

JILLIAN NICHOLSON
19 June 2012
Jill devoted many years as a volunteer and paralegal in the Black Sash advice office in Durban. As a younger generation Black Sash member and an anti-apartheid activist, she interacted frequently with Sheena, in person and through correspondence. This was possible because although Sheena was based in Johannesburg, she maintained close links through regular visits, not only to the regional membership and advice office but also to the Diakonia Council of Churches in Durban and its community-based resource centres. The provincial dynamics of the Black Sash, of the liberation struggle and of the period of transition towards democracy were unique, and Jill was one of Sheena's key sources of information. She was also able to act as a link between Sheena/the Black Sash and the independent trade unions.

JOAN KERCHHOFF
21 June 2012
Sheena met Joan through the Black Sash in Pietermaritzburg and at the Black Sash national conferences. They also knew each other through the Pietermaritzburg Agency for Christian and Social Awareness (PACSA), which was formed just a few years after the 1976 Soweto uprising. Joan, along with her late husband Peter, was also actively involved in opposing land dispossession, forced removals and other livelihood and security threats to township and rural communities in the area. Ideologically, Sheena herself understood the Kerchhoffs' commitment to trying to live more simply while working for justice and the elimination of the causes of poverty. Peter worked closely with the Black Sash, sharing information and publications on related issues, and Sheena frequently interacted with PACSA when she visited the province in the course of her responsibilities to the South African Council of Churches, Diakonia or the Black Sash.

JONATHAN WALTON
23 February 2012
Jonathan was employed as a paralegal caseworker in the Grahamstown advice office of the Black Sash for many years and interacted regularly with Sheena in this capacity, developing an immense respect for her integrity. He was also a community-based anti-apartheid activist with community organising skills and experience in labour-related matters and legislation. Jonathan subsequently included much advocacy in his approach to advice work and became involved with the national advocacy working group of the Black Sash. Both these areas of work were of particular interest to Sheena, and they were able to share experiences from different perspectives.

JUDITH HAWARDEN
22 January 2013 (also Charlene Smith: no date available)
A younger generation active Black Sash member in the same region, Judith became one of Sheena's closer friends. They interacted at regional leadership level as well as through shared human rights priorities such as, for example, education and land. Their only memorable disagreement was about whether Black Sash meetings should continue to be during the day (when many of the activists and Black Sash members who were in full-time employment could not easily attend) or in the evening, which did not suit some of the older members (including Sheena). Each woman in her own way experienced the grief of the death of a beloved child and, although Sheena did not speak of her own loss, Judith found strength and comfort in Sheena's compassion and understanding on this and other challenges. Judith holidayed in the bush with Sheena and her family and mutual friends, and they shared a sense of humour and enjoyment of the game of Bridge that provided temporary relief from the grim realities they faced in their anti-apartheid work.

Judy Bassingthwaighte

(Charlene Smith: no date available)

Judy had already met Sheena at the Central Methodist Mission working with homeless and destitute people and had known her for several years when Sheena contacted her personally to suggest that Judy come for an interview to take on the job of coordinator of Gun Free South Africa after Adèle Kirsten left. Judy, a generation younger, was initially uncomfortable with what she saw as Sheena's rather prescriptive approach but accepted the offer and ultimately found it a challenging and amazing time of working together. Judy also stayed in Sheena's home for an extended period while Judy was experiencing some personal challenges and, in the last years of Sheena's life, Judy reciprocated the care and was often part of the caregiving team, visiting Sheena almost daily.

Judy Chalmers

24 February 2012

Judy was an exceptionally active Black Sash member in the Port Elizabeth area and Molly Blackburn's sister. As well as providing strategic leadership to the membership, Judy was on the staff of the Black Sash as a fieldworker based in Port Elizabeth, serving rural communities in vast areas of the Eastern Cape. Judy and Sheena were firm friends and mutually respectful colleagues on many levels. Sheena frequently visited the area and mostly stayed over at Judy's home. After South Africa's first democratic elections, when Judy became an African National Congress member of parliament, she would phone Sheena regularly to ask her opinion about something that needed attention. The two women were also participants on an independent board of enquiry[1] set up after the apartheid government's attempt to poison Frank Chikane in the late eighties. Meetings used to be on Sheena's front stoep overlooking the garden — safe from security police bugs, which was a particularly relevant factor — with Sheena as chairperson.

June Crichton

24 February 2012

As a Black Sash member and senior employee in the Black Sash Port Elizabeth advice office, June interacted regularly with Sheena. The two women also worked together on several special interest social welfare and health issues, and it was with Sheena's encouragement that June pursued a dream of starting a haven for AIDS orphans.

Karin Chubb

3 July 2012

Although Karin was a member of the Black Sash in Cape Town, as a leader in the organisation both in the regional structures and nationally, she worked closely with Sheena on many matters. Together they were a crucial force in pressurising the apartheid government, through the Department of Home Affairs, to ensure that all South African citizens had an identity document that would enable them to register as voters for the 1994 democratic elections. Karin recalls how Sheena ensured a direct line to Piet Colyn[2] — and all Karin had to do was give her name and she would be put straight through to him! Karin especially valued the clarity of Sheena's vision and the fact that Sheena's commitment was not only an ethical and moral one, but was consistently based on an enormous amount of hard work and evidence. As one of the leading feminist thinkers in the organisation, Karin appreciated Sheena's willingness to tolerate all the various 'hobby horses' of individual members, not belittle them, but be able to slot them into where they were perhaps more important for the community and the Black Sash. Sheena, in turn, enormously respected Karin's keen intelligence, capacity for hard work and personal courage, and found herself enriched by Karin's commitment to feminism.

Kathy Satchwell

30 November 2011

Although Kathy followed in her mother's footsteps by joining the Black Sash at an early age

[1] An investigative body established in 1989 by the South African Council of Churches, it subsequently became the Independent Board of Inquiry into Informal Repression (IBIIR). Board members were Laurie Ackermann, Allan Boesak, Alex Boraine, Manas Buthelezi, Judy Chalmers, Frank Chikane, Max Coleman, Brian Currin, Sheena Duncan, Peter Harris, Eric Molobi, Jude Pieterse and Desmond Tutu. Some of its work is accessible at www.historicalpapers.wits.ac.za/inventories AG 2543. Bheki Mlangeni, one of the attorneys who worked with the Board, was killed by a bomb built into a tape recorder in 1991.

[2] Director General of the Department of Home Affairs.

and sometimes volunteering in the Grahamstown advice office while a student at Rhodes, her first direct interaction with Sheena was when she moved to Johannesburg as a law graduate. Kathy did her articles with Raymond Tucker, who had a close working relationship with Sheena and the Johannesburg Black Sash. Sheena welcomed her as a young newcomer to the city and Kathy became a frequent guest in Sheena's house and felt completely at home there. Even with a more radical outlook and young friends who considered the Black Sash too conservative for their political taste, and herself half the age of most of its members in the region, Kathy was drawn to the Black Sash's human rights work and to the gentler, less competitive nature of the organisation. Sheena and Kathy also worked closely together on the governance structure of the Human Awareness Programme (HAP). They remained friends until Sheena's death and, in the last few years, shared the cancer experience.

LAURA BEST
24 February 2012
A younger generation, more 'left' activist, Laura was part of a young group of Black Sash members in Pretoria when she first met Sheena. In that context she experienced and appreciated Sheena as someone who, despite a dislike of the Pretoria road and a fear of getting lost, understood the significance of having a Black Sash branch in the city which was the formal heart of the apartheid government. Sheena frequently drove to Pretoria to give special support, to encourage, provide an ethical and moral compass for their work and to motivate members to continue to strive for the ideals of the Black Sash, often using her wit to cajole and lead them forward in this quest. Laura was also guided in her work as a staff member by Sheena in both the Pretoria and Port Elizabeth advice offices over a period of many years and the two women shared a particular commitment to improving legislation, notably for domestic workers. They differed radically on issues of feminism and on the Black Sash's refusal to affiliate to the United Democratic Front. They shared a level of social defiance and enjoyed each other's company at the Black Sash and advice office conferences and workshops.

LAURA POLLECUTT
26 October 2011 (also Charlene Smith: no date available)
Laura was an active supporter of the (then) Progressive Party before joining the Black Sash and becoming involved in extra-parliamentary politics. Laura worked in the same region in which Sheena was based, and as a member of the regional council, she was active in its governance, including issues such as staff benefits, which were sometimes contentious. Laura's work with Sheena included times when Laura represented the Black Sash on campaigns and in protest action and her involvement in the Black Sash morning market, an annual fund-raising event. The two women also worked together in the campaign to abolish the death penalty and, because of Laura's work in black communities, they shared a common understanding of some of the challenges facing such communities. Their occasional disagreements were generally of a practical nature, for example whether Black Sash meetings should be held during the day or in the evening.

LAUREN NOTT
21 February 2012
As a younger generation Black Sash member and director of the Knysna Black Sash advice office for several years, Lauren was actively involved with several advocacy and rights issues that received encouragement and support from Sheena.

LAURIE NATHAN
11 February 2013 (telephone)
As a younger generation activist to the 'left' of Sheena, Laurie nevertheless appreciated the radical nature of her activism and one of the priorities they shared was a commitment to demilitarisation. They interacted on the End Conscription Campaign (ECC), although intermittently while Laurie was the national organiser because at that time he was frequently in hiding from the security forces. They held each other in high regard intellectually and Laurie particularly admired Sheena's forthrightness and courage and her exceptional sense of strategy.

Lindsay McTeague (Duncan)
20 November 2012
Sheena and Neil's elder daughter Lindsay has lived most of her adult life outside of South Africa after completing her graduate studies at the University of the Witwatersrand. Both daughters were close friends of Sheena and Neil and visited South Africa often. Neil and Sheena also visited Lindsay and her husband in their homes — first in the UK and then Switzerland. They corresponded regularly, mostly on a weekly basis.

Liz Lane
27 January 2012
Liz and Sheena were both Roedean girls and their husbands had also known each other as schoolboys. The two couples became good friends and often dined in each other's homes as well as taking some holiday time together. William was a lawyer and Liz a classics scholar so the conversation was always of a certain level and never banal, even if they sometimes disagreed.

Liz Mkame
20 June 2012
Sheena and Liz met at a Young Women's Christian Association (YWCA) conference in the early seventies and Liz was deeply impressed with Sheena's capacity to make law understandable. Some years later, when Archbishop Hurley wanted Diakonia to establish social action committees in KwaZulu-Natal, Liz started such a committee in her church and subsequently went to Johannesburg to train with Sheena — who she named Nolwazi[3] — at the Black Sash advice office. Her work there with Sheena enabled Liz to support other rural action committees and to know how to set up a resource centre. The two women worked together frequently over the course of the following thirty years and developed a fond and mutually respectful relationship.

Louise Colvin
18 June 2012
Louise is the daughter of the late Ann Colvin, one of Sheena's closest friends and political allies, although notably to the 'left' of Sheena. Louise has vivid memories of first meeting *this larger than life friend of Mum's of whom I had heard so much.* Sheena was part of a delegation meeting the ANC in exile in Lusaka and Louise, aka Angela Brown, was the convener of the meeting. But it was through her mother, with whom Sheena regularly stayed, that Louise feels *she got to know the person behind the persona.* As an activist in her own right — both in the anti-apartheid struggle and in the post-apartheid society — Louise shared many common interests and many hours of debate with Sheena.

Maggie Helass
(Charlene Smith: no date available)
Maggie and Sheena knew each other well as Anglicans active in the Church of the Province of Southern Africa. Maggie lived two doors down the road from the Duncans for many years and was a frequent visitor to their home in the evenings. After she moved to Australia, Maggie visited South Africa regularly and spent many hours interviewing Sheena personally, in preparation for possibilities of a memoir or biography.

Maggy Clarke
22 February 2012
As a Black Sash member and as Bob Clarke's wife, Maggy got to know Sheena when Bob and Sheena worked together through the Council of Churches' programmes in both the Natal Midlands and Albany regions, while living first in Pietermaritzburg and then Grahamstown. Maggy herself also experienced the level of support the smaller Black Sash regions received from Sheena, and Sheena would sometimes stay over at their home when she visited the regions. Maggy noted in her diary that she appreciated that *on two occasions when Sheena stayed with us, she did the washing up and she brought a bottle of brandy to make sure that she didn't drink all of ours — the ideal guest.*

Marcella Naidoo
15 March 2012
Although she worked for many years as the professional director of the Black Sash advice offices nationally, Marcella knew and interacted with Sheena for only a brief period before Sheena stepped down as chairperson of the Black Sash Advice Office Trust.

[3] Zulu name for a woman; meaning 'the one who has knowledge'.

Marian Nell and Janet Shapiro
24 January 2012
Marian was the director of the Human Awareness Programme (HAP) and Janet a senior employee before also serving as director for a short period, and both interacted regularly with Sheena who was chairperson of the HAP Board of Trustees for the first twelve years of the organisation's existence. Although they were not actually friends, Marian and Sheena spent many hours talking in Sheena's garden and when travelling to various places together to run a series of workshops on pensions. Janet worked closely with Sheena on several publications, including sets of fact sheets, which HAP tried to produce every second year. Sheena also attended some of the HAP workshops as a participant. Sheena consulted with Marian in the many instances where the Black Sash called on HAP for organisational development support, and Marian and Janet, working as Nell and Shapiro, were key facilitators in helping the Black Sash reach the decision to close the membership and retain only the advice offices and the Advice Office Trust.

Marj Brown
29 November 2011
A younger generation Black Sash member in the same region, Marj frequently worked with Sheena in the Black Sash and in the Transvaal Rural Action Committee (TRAC). They also worked closely in the South African Council of Churches (SACC) — particularly during the period when Frank Chikane was general secretary and Sheena was vice president. Because she admired her so, Marj made sure her own children got to know Sheena, too, and Marj and Sheena's relationship was close and mutually respectful. Marj was also employed as one of the Black Sash national staff members for several years. As a skilled researcher, she worked closely with Sheena on a regular basis and was invaluable in supporting the strategic thinking and advocacy work of the organisation and its leadership.

Mary-Louise Peires
22 February 2012
Mary-Louise was a member and, for some time, co-chairperson of the Grahamstown branch of the Black Sash and interacted with national leadership at that level. When her three children were old enough for her to work away from home, she volunteered at the advice office. She first met Sheena at a Black Sash meeting in Knysna and then regularly as Sheena visited to support and encourage the branch members and the advice office. Mary-Louise was impressed with Sheena's view that Black Sash members should value and use their respectability as mature, neatly dressed white women in apartheid South Africa, and this was particularly relevant when engaging with authorities in a 'university town'. Mary-Louise also interacted with Sheena in the End Conscription Campaign (ECC) and, although she was not involved in Gun Free, shared Sheena's views on guns. When her husband was offered a position at the University of the Transkei, they were uncertain about taking work in a 'homeland'. They contacted Sheena, who got a message through to the headquarters of the African National Congress (ANC) in Lusaka, and were told that it was quite OK to go because Bantu Holomisa was on the right side. Like other members in the branch, Mary-Louise made an important contribution to Sheena's understanding of the issues of the region — including in the so-called independent homelands of the Transkei and Ciskei.

Mary Burton
3 June 2013 (also Charlene Smith: no date available)
Mary and Sheena were friends and admired each other enormously. Their shared experience included leadership roles in the Black Sash where each served terms as president, as trustees on the Advice Office Trust and as members of the national executive. Their work in the church and various peace and reconciliation initiatives also overlapped and they were frequent guests in each other's homes, even though they lived in different cities.

Mary Jankowitz
3 November 2011 (telephone)
As an active organisational member of the Black Sash and parishioner at St George's Church, Parktown, Mary interacted with Sheena frequently and supportively. The two women held each other in high regard.

MARY KLEINENBERG
21 June 2012
As a Black Sash member, Mary was in the leadership and frontline activities of the Black Sash in the Natal Midlands. She is an advocate of women's issues, chair of the Pietermaritzburg advice office and also served with Sheena as a trustee of the Black Sash Trust. Mary and Sheena had an affectionate and mutually respectful relationship.

MEVAGH GLYN
(Charlene Smith: no date available)
Mevagh was Neil's cousin and, as an only child, he appreciated the closeness of the family relationship. The families and their children often spent time together, and a supportive space was offered in their home for Lindsay and Carey when Sheena needed to work during school holidays. Mevagh kept in touch with Sheena after Neil's death and visited her from time to time throughout Sheena's life.

MIKE EVANS
2 March 2013
A younger generation Cape Town based activist and lawyer, Mike knew Sheena mainly through the End Conscription Campaign (ECC) where, as well as her key role in initiating the campaign, she was also immensely useful in bringing together sons and parents when they did not fully appreciate each other's views on conscription into the apartheid military. Mike also appreciated Sheena's role in bridging some of the differences in the white community between the more radical extra-Parliamentary movement gravitating around the United Democratic Front (UDF) and the white opposition — including many Black Sash members — that gravitated around the Progressive Federal Party (PFP), now the Democratic Alliance (DA).

NANCY CHARTON
19 March 2012 (telephone)
Nancy was an active Black Sash member working closely with rural communities under threat in the Eastern Cape and one of the group of three who were the first women to be ordained as Anglican priests. She and Sheena interacted regularly and were able to enhance each other's understanding of many interests and values they had in common.

NOMALIZO LEAH TUTU
11 January 2012
Although they did not become close friends, as a sister Anglican and as Desmond Tutu's wife, Leah knew Sheena through the church and socially. Leah and Desmond had known Sheena's mother, Jean, and had dined at her home as well as with Sheena and Neil at theirs. The two women also interacted through the sustained work Leah did with domestic workers and in which Sheena provided regular support, serving on the board of the project but particularly in terms of rights education.

PADDY KEARNEY
18 June 2012
Sheena and Paddy became friends as they worked closely together in the South African Council of Churches (SACC) and she frequently interacted with the Diakonia community in Durban, which Paddy served for almost thirty years. They shared a deep and lifelong commitment to justice but also the love of a good laugh. Paddy experienced Sheena's presence in all church meetings they attended together as powerful and knowledgeable, but also respectful and friendly. They also met frequently at various conferences, and Paddy arranged for Liz Mkame to train with Sheena at the Johannesburg advice office before initiating community resource centres at churches in the Durban townships.

PADDY MESKIN
22 June 2012
Paddy worked closely with Sheena on inter-faith initiatives and in the World Conference of Religions for Peace (WCRP). As a friend, Paddy was further able to enrich Sheena's understanding of Judaism and of the diversity and range of responses to apartheid by Jews. Although they lived in different cities, the two women met quite regularly, at conferences and in each other's homes. Both personalities were characterised by incredible energy and wit, and they shared an unflinching capacity for hard work and a deep commitment to a faith-based perspective on justice and transformation. Paddy and Sheena developed a fond and trusting friendship.

PATRICK J. BANDA
22 January 2013
As a young activist on the run from the security forces, Patrick lived with the Duncan family

for more than a year before the apartheid police found and detained him when he was on a weekend visit to the township home of Daphne, his future wife. Patrick considered Sheena as a mentor and someone who taught him much about politics, spirituality, leadership and ethics. They maintained a fond and respectful friendship throughout Sheena's life and Patrick introduced her to Daphne and his children.

PETER STOREY

13 July 2012

When Peter asked Sheena to join Gun Free South Africa (GFSA), they already knew each other well from interactions in the South African Council of Churches (SACC). Sheena initially worked with Peter when he was chairperson and she patron of GFSA and then took over the chair when he left. They were both strong and sometimes dominant personalities, but although they had robust exchanges on how best to 'do the right thing', their commitment to demilitarisation and making the country gun free and peaceful was mutual. They forged a powerful bond of friendship, admiration and respect that endured until Sheena's death and offered a space for them to share thoughts, joys and sometimes deep disappointments about government actions and policies and the growing silence of the church in the post-Mandela period.

PRISCILLA HALL

22 February 2012

As a Black Sash member in the Albany region, Priscilla experienced the unstinting support and guidance Sheena offered to the smaller branches. Among other things, Sheena and Priscilla shared an interest in land rights issues and Sheena was particularly useful in meeting with Priscilla and community representatives, hearing what they wanted and then following up the legislative implications and potential loopholes. Priscilla found in Sheena a brilliant and capable thinker and researcher, and a person who made it her business to be a public profile — wherever and whenever it was asked of her — for the arguments and objections that had to be made. Through her interactions with local communities that she met through Priscilla, Sheena learned a lot about the complex realities of life in two of the so-called independent homelands — the Transkei and the Ciskei — and how the apartheid government manipulated the people in these areas. Priscilla enjoyed Sheena's warmly inclusive and consultative approach to organisational discussions and decisions and found her a wise guardian of the integrity of the Black Sash.

RICHARD STEELE

18 June 2012

Richard initially met Sheena through Anita Kromberg and his participation in the Justice and Reconciliation division of the South African Council of Churches (SACC). Richard, Anita and Sheena shared an understanding of pacifism that, although not dogmatic, did not support the 'just' war theory that was the dominant position in the church at the time. Richard found in Sheena an unusual and inspiring understanding of the radical nature of pacifism and all three found it refreshing to be able to discuss their views on violence and power without any need to defend their analysis. They also shared a sincere commitment to putting their ideals into practice. Richard experienced Sheena's ideas and solidarity over a period of many years in work with the International Fellowship of Reconciliation (IFOR), the conscientious objectors' support group (COSG) and the End Conscription Campaign (ECC), and they admired and respected each other greatly.

ROSEMARY (ROSIE) SMITH

21 February 2012

Rosie and Sheena interacted over many years and in many ways. Rosie was an active member and leader in the Grahamstown branch of the Black Sash, which she served as chairperson and co-chairperson. She also served the organisation nationally as trustee and as the director of its Grahamstown advice office. Rosie and Sheena shared many interests including a particular commitment to land rights, to securing justice for people caught in the minefield of 'independent' homeland legislation, and to securing equitable delivery of social grants to all South Africans. Rosie frequently hosted Sheena at her home when Sheena visited Grahamstown. They came to rely on each other for information and support and their relationship developed into an enduring and affectionate friendship

Rosie Meny-Gibert
13 July 2012
Rosie's association with Sheena was not only through her membership of the Black Sash, but included Rosie's many years of service as secretary to the national office, initially when appointed by Sheena in Johannesburg and then again in Cape Town when the national office moved. Rosie was in regular contact with Sheena, particularly during Sheena's years as president and vice president of the Black Sash and they had an affectionate and respectful relationship.

Sally Motlana
22 November 2012
Sally was the first woman to be elected as a vice president of the South African Council of Churches (SACC). Following in her footsteps, and continuing occasional interactions, Sheena admired and was influenced by Sally's outspoken attitude, and tried to build on her achievements within the council. When Sally was detained without trial in the mid-seventies, Sheena wrote to her to keep her up to date with matters in the church and as much about the politics of the day as would get past the prison censors. The two women also interacted through their work with the Black Housewives League.

Sean O'Leary and Cecile van Riet
(Charlene Smith: no date available.
Also correspondence with the author)
Sean was working in the Justice and Peace Department (J&P) of the Southern African Catholic Bishops' Conference (SACBC) in 1992. Political prisoners were released, exiles had returned, local comrades had abandoned their stone throwing and CODESA[4] was about to begin. At a meeting with Sheena — on the Duncan stoep — they agreed that there was a need to form a loose federation of like-minded organisations and the Independent Forum for Electoral Education (IFEE)[5] was born. Sheena and Sean, together with people like Barry Gilder who had been in exile, Smagaliso Mkhatshwa who had been in prison and Cecile van Riet from Lawyers for Human Rights (LHR), met frequently and got to know each other well over regular lunches, usually served by Neil after the meetings. Everyone had stories to tell, especially Sheena, and Sean delighted in *this strange company of fellows in the struggle*. He remembers that Sheena was already getting older and did not like to drive but that she would make an effort when they were meeting top officials like Frene Ginwala who became Speaker of the National Assembly from 1994 to 2004.

Shirley Moulder
24 November 2012
As an active Anglican and also a member of the Black Sash, Shirley worked closely with Sheena over many years — particularly on various church and South African Council of Churches (SACC) initiatives and projects, including the Justice and Peace/Reconciliation committee, the Victims of Apartheid programme and COACH,[6] as well as during a period when Shirley acted as interim director in the Johannesburg advice office of the Black Sash. The two women became firm friends despite their differences — notably around the relevance of a feminist analysis to guide transformation strategies. Sheena served, often as chairperson, on many committees of projects in which Shirley worked, and they also facilitated development and social justice workshops together from time to time, including with elements in the corporate sector seeking to move beyond stereotypical attitudes. Shirley particularly appreciated Sheena's capacity for work and her ability to create and hold a space in which people could trust her implicitly and *know that they would walk through fire for her, because they knew that she would walk through fire for them*. Shirley found that Sheena could *make magic* out of potentially disastrous situations and exercise great influence through a combination of gentleness and firmness. Sheena particularly appreciated Shirley's dedication to issues affecting disadvantaged children, conservation and land redistribution and Shirley's 'out of the box' thinking.

[4] Convention for a Democratic South Africa.
[5] IFEE comprised about forty church-based groupings and various non-governmental organisations, with regional offices and an elected executive of seven with a rotating chair.
[6] Three Anglican children's homes for orphaned and vulnerable children.

Steve McDonald

11 May 2012

Steve came to South Africa in 1976 as a young political officer in the American Embassy, covering black political affairs. When first he introduced himself to Sheena at the Black Sash offices as a thirty-one-year-old novice with an honest desire to learn what the apartheid system was and how it impacted people, she told him simply to sit in the offices and listen to the testimony and grievances of the people coming in for legal services and assistance. Steve believes that this was the best primer an outsider could possibly get and he returned to the Black Sash advice offices many times. In this way the two struck up a friendship and Sheena remained a close confidant over the next two decades. Steve also became a family friend and was entertained in the Duncan home often, formally and informally.

Sue Brittion

20 June 2012

One of the first women to be ordained as an Anglican priest, Sue knew Sheena well through regular interactions in workshops, retreats and conferences related to the church and the South African Council of Churches (SACC). Sue worked for 23 years at Diakonia, and met Sheena on her regular visits, including the year Sheena was the guest preacher at Diakonia's famous Good Friday dawn service and led the 3 000-strong procession through the streets of Durban. Sheena and Sue were among the founder members of World Conference on Religions for Peace (WCRP) and served together on the national committee of that inter-faith anti-apartheid movement. They shared a commitment to a non-violent faith-based struggle for justice and were also founder members of the End Conscription Campaign. Sheena learned much from Sue about the general attitudes that limited the scope of women's work in the church and appreciated her courage.

Sue van der Merwe

8 February 2013

An active, younger generation Black Sash member in Cape Town, Sue also worked as the coordinator of the Cape Town advice office for several years and in this capacity interacted with Sheena as the national advice office coordinator. Sheena enjoyed Sue's enthusiasm and energy, as well as her sustained interest in social development issues as these presented at the advice offices across the country. Sue was also an initiator of the Rural Advice Training (RAT) group of organisations and ensured that the Black Sash worked closely with other organisations to provide paralegal support, training and materials resources to rural communities under threat of apartheid in the provinces of the Cape. As with other Black Sash advice office/paralegal training, Sheena monitored this work closely and provided ongoing support — including ensuring, as a trustee, that the Black Sash raised adequate funds to sustain it.

Thisbe Clegg

10 July 2012

Thisbe was an active member of the Black Sash for many years. In addition to her involvement in protest, Thisbe served on the regional council in Cape Town and was employed as national financial manager of the Black Sash Trust and all the Black Sash advice offices. It was through the national work that the two women got to know and respect each other and found that they shared a great sense of humour. They often needed to consult on funding issues, and Thisbe was a frequent house-guest at Sheena's home when visiting Johannesburg.

Thudiso Virginia Gcabashe

25 June 2012 (telephone)

Thudiso Virginia and Sheena worked together closely in the South African Council of Churches (SACC) over a period of many years, most particularly while they both served two terms as vice president. Both were committed to strengthening the role of women in the church and communities in general as well as in the SACC.

Uli Albrecht and Dan Pretorius

25 November 2012

Uli and Dan were both younger generation workers in the Johannesburg Advice Office. Uli started as a foreign volunteer caseworker and eventually became the coordinator of the in-house paralegal training for community-based advice workers. Uli interacted closely with Sheena, who was the director of the advice office and who also helped Uli develop the training courses and facilitated several modules herself. Dan was employed to do research around the advice office case statistics and also became involved in some of the workers' employment issues. Because the Black Sash had functioned for a long time with unwaged volunteers[7] who were supported inside their own families by their husbands or by having an income of their own, dealing with people who needed to be paid for one reason or another, and paying them living wages, was a new thing for the Black Sash to deal with and sometimes led to some tensions.

Vivienne Walt

(Charlene Smith: 16 August 2010: Skype)

Daughter of the late Ethel Walt, who was one of Sheena's closest friends as well as a sister activist in the Black Sash leadership and governance structures, the advice office, and land and forced removal issues.

Wellington Ntamo

23 November 2012

Wellington first met and got to know Sheena when she was facilitating modules of the paralegal training project of the Johannesburg Black Sash advice office and he was a community-delegated participant. Sheena chose Wellington as the most suitable trainee to take his paralegal/advisory work to a more skilled level and she took him on as a volunteer in the advice office, where for several years he worked as caseworker — often alongside Sheena. He subsequently joined the staff in a salaried position in the same capacity, before becoming one of the senior paralegal advisors.

[7] The interpreters mostly received a stipend and had no employment benefits.

Additional Correspondence Resources

Sheena and Neil Duncan

With their daughters, with other family sometimes included: Sheena's first letter, dated 5 July 1987, is a handwritten air-letter; her final letter dated 26 January 2009 is a three-line e-mail.

Sheena to Anne Hughes

Anne first met Sheena through participating in Black Sash protest stands in the early nineteen seventies, a time when Anne was working with the Anglican Diocese of Johannesburg, particularly with the Mothers' Union. Anne was also a member of St Mary's Cathedral congregation and further interacted with Sheena when Anne worked as a staff member of the Dependants' Conference Division of the South African Council of Churches. Anne left South Africa in 1987 but remained a welcome guest in the Duncan home, often staying there for several weeks at a time on return visits to South Africa. The two women became firm friends and corresponded regularly over a period of several years.

WITH AUTHOR

Abderrahmane (Abdou) Haouach

Abdou was a fellow student of Sheena's daughter Carey at Cornell University and he and Sheena developed a fond and mutually respectful friendship after Carey and Abdou decided to marry. Abdou and Carey are the parents of Sheena and Neil's two grandchildren and Sheena's understanding of Islam was further enhanced through her personal interactions with Abdou and with his family in Morocco. Sheena enjoyed many discussions about the geopolitical state of the world with Abdou.

Albie Sachs

Although Albie did a lot of legal work with the Black Sash in Cape Town in the late 1950s, he and Sheena did not have much personal contact but each deeply respected and was influenced by the other's activism and thinking. Both played an early and significant part in identifying key aspects of South Africa's future constitution as well as in later stages of its development after the first democratic elections in 1994.

Corlett Letlojane

Corlett was a staff member of the Human Rights Institute of South Africa where Sheena served for many years as trustee on the governance structure. Sheena phoned Corlett almost daily when the institute was experiencing difficulties to provide support and encouragement.

Elizabeth (Liz) Reid (nee Sinclair)

Sheena's only sister, four years younger than Sheena. Although Liz moved to Scotland immediately after her marriage, she and Sheena kept in regular touch with letters and, latterly, by phone.

Gavin Evans

A younger generation more 'left' activist, Gavin interacted with Sheena through their commitment to the End Conscription Campaign (ECC) and on the Five Freedoms Forum.

Helen Zille

A younger generation Black Sash member, Helen participated in the leadership structures of the Western Cape region, and also interacted with Sheena through their common interest in education issues and *Sash* magazine.

Jeremy McTeague

Jeremy is the husband of Sheena and Neil's elder daughter Lindsay. He and Sheena developed an affectionate relationship and were able to argue with deep respect about issues on which their views differed.

Kenza Haouach

Sheena and Neil's granddaughter.

Liz Hagen

Even though they lived in different countries for most of their lives, the years Sheena and Liz shared as two young mothers while living in Zimbabwe developed into a lifelong friendship. The young couples used to play what they dubbed 'dirty bottoms bridge' which meant that they didn't have to tidy up too much after a day gardening and looking after children before meeting for an evening of bridge. Liz was one of the friends who supported Sheena and Neil through the period of grief immediately after the death of their son and she travelled to Johannesburg to spend time with Sheena a few months before Sheena's death.

Marian Shinn

A younger generation reporter on the anti-apartheid Johannesburg daily, the *Rand Daily Mail*, Marian met Sheena personally only a few times but the two women shared political convictions.

Patrick Lawlor

School friend to Neil, Patrick knew Neil and Sheena as a young couple from the time they were married. A few years later, Patrick married Rozel and the four young people lived in Zimbabwe over the same period. Although the Lawlors moved to the United Kingdom shortly after both couples left Zimbabwe, the deep bond of friendship between the two women was enriched by their common commitment to human rights and citizens' access to justice and it endured until Rozel's death — also of cancer — the same year as Sheena.

Robert Sinclair

Rob is Sheena's second brother, eight years younger. Although he lived much of his adult life outside South Africa, he was working on a contract not far from Johannesburg around the time of Neil's death and was a constant and loving support to Sheena over those months.

Stewart Ting Chong

Stewart and Sheena both interacted closely with Anglican and other spiritual leaders over several years of the anti-apartheid movement in South Africa and internationally. The bond that developed between them was enhanced by Stewart's technological skills and their shared commitment to introducing computer and communication technology to church structures and the organisations in which Sheena was active.

Bibliography

Ackermann, Denise M. *Liberating Praxis and The Black Sash: A Feminist Theological Perspective* (Thesis Doctor Theologiae, University of South Africa, 1990)

Allen, John (ed.) *The Rainbow People of God: Archbishop Desmond Tutu* (Doubleday, Transworld Publishers, London, 1994)

Austen, Jane. *Pride and Prejudice* (Penguin Classics, 1985)

Baer, Ulrich (ed. & translator). *The Poet's Guide to Life: The Wisdom of Rilke* (The Modern Library, New York, 2005)

Bizos, George. *Odyssey to Freedom* (Random House, Houghton, in association with Umuzi, Roggebaai, 2007)

Church of the Province of South Africa. *An Anglican Prayer Book* (Collins Liturgical Publications, London, and David Philip, Cape Town, 1989)

Church of England. *The Book of Common Prayer* (W.M. Collins Sons & Co, Glasgow, 1959, using 1662 version)

Clarke, Bob. *Anglicans Against Apartheid* (Cluster Publications, Pietermaritzburg, 2008)

Gasa, Nomboniso (ed.) *Women in South African History* (HSRC Press, Cape Town, 2007)

Harris, Peter. *In a Different Time* (Umuzi, Cape Town, 2008)

Joseph, Helen. *Side by Side* (Zed Books, London, 1986)

Kirsten, Adèle. *A Nation Without Guns? The Story of Gunfree South Africa* (University of KwaZulu-Natal Press, Scottsville, with funding from Open Society Foundation for South Africa, 2008)

Levine, Lou (ed.) *Hope Beyond Apartheid: The Peter Kerchhoff Years of PACSA* (Pietermaritzburg Agency for Christian Social Awareness, 2002)

Mashinini, Emma. *Strikes Have Followed Me All My Life* (The Women's Press, London, 1989)

Meek, Sarah and Stott, Noel. *Destroying Surplus Weapons: An assessment of experience in South Africa and Lesotho,* United Nations Institute for Disarmament Research, Geneva, Switzerland, and ISS Institute for Security Studies, Pretoria, South Africa (United Nations 2003)

Meer, Fatima. *Higher Than Hope: Rolihlahla We Love You* (Skotaville Press, Johannesburg, 1988)

Michelman, Cherry. *The Black Sash of South Africa* (Oxford University Press, London, 1975)

Mkhabela, Sibongile. *Open Earth and Black Roses* (Skotaville Press, Johannesburg 2001)

Olusoga, David and Erichsen, Casper W. *The Kaiser's Holocaust: Germany's Forgotten Genocide and the Colonial Roots of Nazism* (Faber & Faber, London, 2010)

Ramphele, Mamphela. *A Life* (David Philip, Cape Town, 1995)

Randall, Peter. *The Death Penalty and the Church of South Africa* (South African Council of Churches, Johannesburg, 1970)

Rogers, Mirabel. *The Black Sash* (Rotonews, Johannesburg, 1956)

Russell, Diana E.H. *Lives of Courage* (Virago Press, London 1989)

Sartre, Jean-Paul. *Anti-Semite and Jew: An Exploration of the Etiology of Hate* (Schocken Books, New York, 1965)

Villa-Vicencio, Charles. *Civil Disobedience and Beyond: Law, Resistance and Religion in South Africa* (David Philip, Cape Town, 1990)

Villa-Vicencio, Charles. *The Spirit of Freedom: South African Leaders on Religion and Politics* (Skotaville Press, Johannesburg, 1996)

Walker, Cherryl. *Women and Resistance in South Africa* (David Philip, Cape Town, 1982)

Wentzel, Jill. *The Liberal Slideaway* (South African Institute of Race Relations, Johannesburg, 1995)

Other Sources

Black Sash: Swart Serp/Sash Magazines (Mary Burton collection)
Gavshon, Harriet (director and producer). *Sheena Duncan, The Burden of Privilege* (Television News Productions by Free Film Makers, Johannesburg, 1995)
Jakobsen, Wilma. *The Witness Magazine*, A Globe of Witnesses website
www.thewitness.org/agw/jakobsen012303.html
Report no. 23, *The Abolition of Death Penalty in South Africa: SA CASE: S V MAKWANYANE*, Lindelöf, Agneta (Judge), with introductory remarks by Johann van der Westhuizen (Raoul Wallenberg Institute: Lunds Universitet Sweden, 1996)

From the personal papers of Marian Nell and Janet Shapiro
Militarisation Dossier: a joint publication of the Human Awareness Programme, SACC, SACBC: June 1986
Info '92: Facts and figures on South Africa for decision makers: compiled and published by the Human Awareness Programme
Info '87: A folder of facts and figures on South Africa: compiled and published by the Human Awareness Programme

Archive material: Cullen Library Historical Papers (University of the Witwatersrand)
Sheena Duncan personal papers: Collection number A3238
Black Sash: Collection number AE862
South African Council of Churches: Collection number AC623
Delmas Treason Trial Transcript: Collection number AK2117, reference no. 12.37 volumes 392,393 and 394, pages 22654-22917, (Pretoria, 1988)

Archive material: Special Collections (University of Cape Town)
Black Sash collections BC 668 and BC 1020

Archive material: Cory Library (Rhodes University)
Black Sash collection
Albany Council of Churches collection

Archive material
Roedean School, Johannesburg

With material from the archives it was not always possible to get full information about each source. Sometimes, age had worn a detail off a document; sometimes the material from Sheena's personal papers did not specify every detail; sometimes pages were missing. All source references, however, should give a reasonable amount of information to assist readers to explore further into a full text or to verify authenticity.

Index

In this index **bold** page references refer to major entries; <u>underlined</u> page references refer to photographs. Some entries found under Duncan, Sheena also have entries in their own right.

Milton Keynes UK
Ingram Content Group UK Ltd.
UKHW052039101223
434120UK00018BA/398